INTO THE SUNSET

INTO THE SUNSET

EMMETT DALTON AND THE END OF THE DALTON GANG

IAN W. SHAW

UNIVERSITY PRESS OF KANSAS

Published by the University Press of Kansas (Lawrence, Kansas 66045), which was organized by the Kansas Board of Regents and is operated and funded by Emporia State University, Fort Hays State University, Kansas State University, Pittsburg State University, the University of Kansas, and Wichita State University.

Library of Congress Cataloging-in-Publication Data

Names: Shaw, Ian W., author.
Title: Into the sunset : Emmett Dalton and the end of the Dalton Gang / Ian W. Shaw. Other titles: Emmett Dalton and the end of the Dalton Gang. Description: Lawrence, Kansas : University Press of Kansas, [2023] | Includes bibliographical references and index.
Identifiers: LCCN 2023008276 (print)
LCCN 2023008277 (ebook)
ISBN 9780700635498 (cloth)
ISBN 9780700635504 (paperback)
ISBN 9780700635511 (ebook)
Subjects: LCSH: Dalton, Emmett. | Dalton Gang. | Dalton family. | Outlaws—West (U.S.)—Biography. | Outlaws—Kansas—Coffeyville—History—19th century. | Coffeyville (Kan.)—History—19th century. | West (U.S.)—History—1890–1945. | West (U.S.)—Biography.
Classification: LCC F595.D15 S53 2023 (print) | LCC F595.D15 (ebook) |
DDC 978/.020922 [B]—dc23/eng/20230324
LC record available at https://lccn.loc.gov/2023008276.
LC ebook record available at https://lccn.loc.gov/2023008277.

British Library Cataloguing-in-Publication Data is available.

Printed in the United States of America

10 9 8 7 6 5 4 3 2 1

The paper used in this publication is acid free and meets the minimum requirements of the American National Standard for Permanence of Paper for Printed Library Materials Z39.48-1992.

CONTENTS

PROLOGUE: ANGELUS TEMPLE, LOS ANGELES, 1936

Emmett and Julia came regularly now to the circular and domed temple in Echo Park, sometimes for the Sunday services and sometimes for an hour or so of quiet contemplation during the week. It was a place that Emmett found very often fitted both his moods and his memories. The roof, the curve of the dome—on the outside just a mass of pale dun tiles, on the inside painted sky blue with groups of puffy white clouds in small patches across it. He knew it was supposed to represent the heaven above, and he had often seen people staring intently at it as if they expected God himself to appear from behind one of the groups of clouds. To Emmett, the curved sky of the dome reminded him of the western skies he had known so well and loved so much. The sometimes pale, sometimes bright blue skies of Missouri, Kansas, and Oklahoma, the skies that looked down on mining towns and cattle camps in New Mexico and the Indian Territory. The skies that presided over the graves of his brothers, mother, and father.

Below that enormous artificial sky inside the temple was a large stage, at the sides of which were equally impressive stained-glass windows and, at its rear, an enormous pipe organ, and in front an orchestra pit capable of holding a full orchestra. The rest of the temple was probably capable of holding the population of a small city, such as Kingfisher, Oklahoma, one of his old hometowns, certainly, and maybe even Coffeyville, the town that would always be associated with his name. Then again, he was not certain just how much Coffeyville had grown since he was last there. Even this vast cavern had barely enough space when Sister Aimee gave one of her illustrated sermons. At those times Aimee Semple McPherson became Sister Aimee or just "Sister" to the thousands inside the temple and the thousands outside who had not been able to beg, borrow, or sometimes steal a ticket to the biggest show in town. Over and above all those numbers were, of course, the millions listening to the show on the temple's own radio station, broadcasting from one side of the country to the other, to Canada and maybe even Mexico and other places Emmett had once dreamed of visiting.

Emmett and Julia had been to one or two of those Sunday-night "illustrated sermons," but he was not totally comfortable, physically or psychologically, crowded together with thousands of people all watching what was basically a morality play. Often, he found that the crowd's faith and enthusiasm far exceeded his own. His health was also increasingly an issue—he was sixty-five, and his body had absorbed a lot of punishment in those years. He had some concerns about what might be coming next, in both this life and whatever would follow it. There was an attraction of sorts, however, to the theater of what Sister Aimee was regularly able to produce. Emmett himself had dabbled, in fact, more than dabbled, in Hollywood productions and knew just how much was required for success. But, unfortunately, not everything she touched had been successful.

He and Julia had not been there, but they had heard gleeful critics laughing about the first night Sister Aimee had introduced the "Traffic Lights" illustrated sermon. As was usual on such occasions, the temple was packed, and the stage was a mass of flowers that included a tree made entirely from rhododendrons. At one side of the stage was a motor car and a large traffic light, twice the normal size; above both was a sign saying "Traffic Lights" picked out by spotlights. Three young girls—one in bright red, one in bright yellow, and one in bright green—led out a choir of forty-five women and twenty men, all wearing long white smocks with a large red crucifix on the chest. As they entered, the orchestra, on this night the Los Angeles Police Band, played an overture.

The service continued with more music; two hymns sung by the choir now supported by the temple's pipe organ and police band. The notes of a third hymn, this one sung by a young female soloist, were just fading away when Sister Aimee strode briskly onto the stage, her corn-gold hair reaching almost to her waist, wearing a long white satin dress, a cape across her shoulders, and a large rhinestone cross hanging from a chain around her neck. Every time she moved, the facets on the rhinestones shot little flashes of light across the stage and the audience. Sister looked around the stage and, speaking into a microphone, admired the flowers and the arrangements, and she thanked Broadway Florists for sending such beautiful blooms to the temple.

Sister Aimee then turned to the three little girls in their traffic light dresses. Each stepped up to the microphone to sing a song, and then all three sang together, songs about how in life, as on the roads of America, you could stay out of trouble if you were always on the right side. Sister then climbed into the car, but when she tried to start it, nothing happened. When the troublesome engine did start, the car's steering also proved problematic, the car going offline and scattering some chairs and choristers before stopping near the rear of the stage. Sister Aimee was able to turn that into a homily, too, about how the devil was always looking to interfere with the work of the Lord and those who did that work.

The evening was not over. The choir and orchestra performed one final hymn, and then Sister Aimee offered a prayer and a wish that, as her robed assistants moved among them, the people in the temple would find it in their hearts to contribute to the work of the temple with a $5 bill or perhaps even $10. As the last notes of the orchestra died away, Sister Aimee offered up a final prayer that concluded with a call to God to bless all policemen. As people began to file out of the temple, Sister Aimee climbed down from the stage and moved across to a special area where a crowd of people with ailments waited, some of them in wheelchairs and with assistants; it was not unusual to see a number on stretchers too. Sister walked among them, talking to all, and laying hands on some. Without any fanfare, she finished and disappeared, and the giant temple was soon once again very silent and very empty.

Emmett and Julia had seen it all, and more than once, but Emmett and Aimee Semple McPherson also had a more personal relationship. Emmett had been baptized into Sister Aimee's Four-Square Gospel Church and considered himself a born-again Christian and as near to God as he was ever likely to be in this life. He was also well enough known (some would say notorious enough) to be allowed to meet privately with Aimee McPherson, just as Charlie Chaplin was doing on a regular basis. With Aimee, Emmett had shared some of his hopes and just a few of his fears.

Emmett had come to terms with the fact that he was approaching the end of his life; he was diabetic, had hypertension, and had recently suffered a minor stroke. Parts of his body had not worked properly since that day forty-five years ago, and he carried the scars inflicted by the bullets and buckshot pellets in and on his body. He could share his guilt at being present during so much dying and so much killing and the fact that he had once lived so far beyond the law. What he wanted was reassurance that his sins would be expiated in the next life, that he would be reunited with his family, mother and father, brothers and sisters, and, most particularly, his brother Bob to whom he owed so much. Sister Aimee had said that he would enter God's kingdom, but then he also understood that the devil sometimes interfered and that the car wouldn't start or couldn't steer.

And that was perhaps where the devil had dwelt during Emmett's entire life, just out of sight, over there in the shadows.

1 BLOODLINES

For Lewis Dalton, the main reference point in his life, the time that delineated the time before and the time after, was what happened during the Battle of Buena Vista, February 22–23, 1847, where he was tried and tested, but could never be certain if he passed the test. If he did not pass, at least he survived, and that was all that mattered in the long run.

By nineteenth-century standards, it was not a very big battle, but then, by these same standards, it was not really a very big war. It was, however, a war that was a long time in the making, a decade at least and probably a lot longer. It could be traced back to the events at the Alamo outside San Antonio and the massacre of the Texan forces there by a Mexican army under General Antonio Lopez Santa Ana. Even that had its antecedents in the seemingly inevitable march of the *norteamericanos* from the original thirteen states that had formed the United States of America. Those thirteen states had grown to twenty-seven with the admission of Florida in 1845, another state taken from what had once been extensive Spanish Empire holdings in the Americas.

That Spanish Empire had broken apart, and one of its successor states was the Republic of Mexico, which, once again, found itself under pressure from the seemingly insatiable hunger for land that characterized its northern neighbor. The Mexican state of Tejas had become the Republic of Texas when the Americans who had settled there organized their own army, an army sufficiently strong—thanks to the United States—to wrest control of Tejas away from the Mexican government. And now that illegitimate Texan republic had been admitted to the United States as the twenty-eighth state.

For Mexico, her state of Tejas had always been part of the body politic of Mexico itself, and no declaration of independence or annexation by a foreign power could change that immutable truth. The Americans annexed Texas in the last week of 1845; clashes along what was now an international border began during the first week of 1846. The small and isolated clash slowly grew into something approximating armed conflict and culminated in an attack by a Mexican cavalry unit on a force of US soldiers under the command of General Zachary Taylor, killing more than ten before following up by laying siege to a US military installation on the Rio Grande.

Aided by reinforcements, Taylor went after the Mexican troops, winning two small battles at Palo Alto and Resaca de la Palma. On May 13, the US Congress declared war on Mexico; Mexico never formally declared war on the United States.

US forces had follow-up victories as they pushed farther and farther into Mexico and Taylor's troops drove deep into the Mexican state of Monterrey. There they were confronted by a superior force of Mexican troops under the command of General Santa Ana, recalled from exile in Cuba and determined to save his homeland. Rushing north, he met the advancing Americans as they built defensive lines at a narrow gap between the mountains in northern Monterrey. The gap was known as the Angostura Pass, and the fighting there would be known as the Battle of Buena Vista.

War with Mexico was not universally welcomed in the United States; it was most popular in the West and the South where the movement of the frontier toward both Mexico and the Pacific was seen as partially fulfilling the United States' destiny of occupying the continent rather than just the lands to the east of the Mississippi River. There were new lands to occupy, and those lands would be occupied in the main by people who supported slavery. For precisely the same reason, the war was less popular in the north of the country.

Congress allotted quotas for recruitment to each state in the union. The western state of Kentucky, for instance, was authorized to raise a force of 2,500 men, a fraction of the 13,000 who volunteered as soon as recruitment began. One of those who volunteered was a thirty-year-old farmer from western Kentucky named Lewis James Dalton, a man who had not been especially successful in anything in his life so far but who could proudly trace his lineage back to French immigrants who had arrived in America the previous century and who spelled their name with an apostrophe, D'Alton.

Dalton was young enough and fit enough to be one of the 2,500 successful volunteers and was drafted into Company I of the Second Regiment of Kentucky Foot Volunteers; he was given a rifle and a fife. Both were important to Dalton the soldier, but the fife would be critical to Company I at Buena Vista.

Company I and the Second Regiment were part of an army of 7,000 men that General Taylor had led successfully down into the heart of northern Mexico, brushing aside the light opposition they had so far faced. Aware that Santa Ana, with an army estimated to number at least 15,000, had made a forced march across semiarid wastes to now confront him at Angostura, Taylor sought to fight a defensive battle on ground of his choosing. That ground was not especially favorable to either side. The right of Taylor's line was anchored on broken ground unsuitable for any fighting, a series of small ravines and gullies where men quickly disappeared from sight and just as quickly became lost. The left wing was anchored by a long plateau sloping down toward Taylor's center, itself anchored on the Buena Vista road.

Battle was joined on February 23, but it was a desultory battle. Brief charges and counter attacks, artillery exchanges and cavalry scouting for weak points. The main battle commenced the following morning when Santa Ana's men crashed up onto the plateau and proceeded to push US infantry and artillery back down the plateau toward the road, threatening to roll up and over Taylor's center. Especially effective for Santa Ana were the San Patricios, the St. Patrick's artillery brigade composed primarily of German and Irish Americans fighting for the cause of their coreligionists.

By the middle of the day, the battle was in the balance, and Taylor called for his reserve to come forward. Part of that reserve was the Second Regiment of Kentucky Foot Volunteers, sitting back and watching the battle from their position behind the broken ground on the right.

When Taylor's order arrived, the regiment's commander, Colonel William McKee, and his second-in-command, Lieutenant Colonel Henry Clay Jr., quickly organized their men into battle order and led them to the center via the most direct route, through the broken ground at their front.

From his vantage point Taylor watched the Kentuckians advancing, their heads and hats bobbing up and down as they crossed the ravines and gullies, now exposed to enemy fire and now in cover, but moving inexorably toward the center, now crowded with the forward elements of the Mexican army. They arrived just in time to prevent the center from being overrun and continued forward, pushing the Mexicans back onto the plateau where they came under withering fire from reinforced US batteries.

Lewis Dalton survived, but more than seventy of his unit did not, killed in the gullies and in the open. Among the dead were McKee and Clay and many men from Company I. Dalton had done well, though. Marching at the right end of his company's line, Dalton's fife, ordering changes of direction and closing the ranks up to cover the losses, had been heard clearly above the cacophony of battle—as it was supposed to do—and Company I was part of the reason the center held, and, because it held, forced Santa Ana to leave the field to Taylor. The Second Regiment won both glory and a battle cry, "Hold 'em Kentuckians!" that Wednesday, but it came at a high cost. Lewis Dalton was alongside men who were cut down by bullet and shrapnel, saw men calling out for their mothers as their life's blood flowed through hands covering hideous wounds, and felt the fear that imminent and shocking death brings.

In the years to come, Lewis Dalton would tell his children that he had seen enough violence to last a lifetime and wanted no further part of it. Those children would want to know more. There were many children, and there were many, many questions.

When his twelve months of military service ended, Lewis Dalton returned to Kentucky and to his itinerant work as a farm laborer and horse trader. By 1850, he had been successful enough to retain his interest in the buying and selling of horseflesh while also running a small saloon in the village of Westport, a settlement that would eventually become

Kansas City. It was there that he met and, on March 12, 1851, married Adeline Lee Younger; he was thirty-six years old, and Adeline sixteen.

Adeline was part of a family that, in many ways, represented the complexities of frontier life on the western edges of the United States at that time. Her father, Charles Younger, had been born in Virginia in 1779, and around 1821 had moved west to the new state of Missouri, admitted to the union in 1821. For a time, Younger operated a ferry crossing the Missouri River from Clay County to Westport. However, he quickly moved on from that and became a land speculator and then a man of substance with properties in the counties of Clay, Jackson, Cass, and St. Clair.

In addition to those considerable land holdings, Younger acquired the honorific "Colonel" and at least twenty slaves to go with his eight legitimate children born to his two wives, the first of whom died in middle age. Younger would also father a number of children with his slaves, one of whom became his particular favorite. Falling pregnant at just fifteen, Elizabeth Simpson bore two of Younger's children in just three years. Charles Younger was sixty-eight and seventy-one years old when the children were born.

Then scandal struck. Younger moved once more, this time to the small settlement of Osceola in St. Clair County in western Missouri. He took Elizabeth Simpson and their two small children with him, leaving his legitimate family behind in Cass County. Both families were spared further embarrassment when Charles Younger died in 1854.

Younger's family, especially Adeline and her children, would tell a different narrative about the life and death of Charles Younger. In that narrative, he became a southern abolitionist who freed his slaves and paid for this act with his life, ambushed and murdered by Jayhawkers, Kansas Unionists who believed that what he did was all some kind of trick. One of his grandchildren, born more than fifteen years after Younger's death, wrote of the man he had never known: "Colonel Younger was a man of firm convictions, high moral conviction and independent spirit; a zealot for any cause he espoused. As a Whig—the forerunner of the Republican Party—he had come to believe that the holding of slaves was wrong. Hence, even before the war, he freed all his blacks, an act that was not at all popular in Missouri at that time. Good blood, stern courage, fiber; he transmitted these qualities to his children."

Usually just answering to the name Lewis, Dalton was a genial man, and at more than six feet tall and 200 pounds, bigger than most but with a gentle, accommodating manner. He had lots of goodwill and, if you listened to Lewis, he had lots of good ideas too. Early on, he had been a man of some passion, but what the Mexican War hadn't taken away he more than willingly gave up for marriage. Lewis had always been a drinker, a man who loved his whiskey, but young Adeline had a detestation of the stuff, and one of the conditions she placed on her much older husband was that he would not take hard liquor around her or bring it into the house. She was a teetotaler, and when the children came into their lives, she did not want them exposed to liquor.

What he did when he was away from the family was his own business, and, if it involved liquor, so be it. But it would not happen at home.

Lewis took the advice to heart, and his children would always remember him to be an abstemious man. They had no way of knowing what he did when he was not at home, and Lewis Dalton was a man who would spend a lot of time, perhaps the majority of the time, away from home, because of another passion, one he just could not walk away from. Dalton was a horseman and believed himself to be an outstanding judge of horseflesh, whether it was in the buying or selling or in backing one particular specimen to run a set distance faster than the several others. It was a passion he continually tried to turn into a business, and a business that continually failed.

Lewis Dalton was away from home for weeks and sometimes months at a time because he followed horses, bought and sold horses, and, if he had money, put it on horses in races in larger towns and smaller settlements. And when those horses failed to win—and far too many of them did—he would stay away from home, working small jobs to make enough money to once more invest in his passion. It would cost Adeline and the children who were yet to be born more than one of the properties they would call home, and, ultimately, it would cost Lewis his marriage.

Charles Younger gave his daughter Adeline a number of gifts he considered appropriate to mark her wedding to Lewis Dalton. One was the grand piano that Adeline had always loved to play, a second was one of his servants, a former slave that everyone in the family knew as "Aunt Jenny," and the third was a decent-size parcel of land, probably in St. Clair County, with a small house on it that the newlyweds could call home. It would become evident quite early that the house would not be large enough for what would be a rapidly growing family.

The Daltons' firstborn, a son they named Charles Benjamin Dalton, was born on February 24, 1852. The boy would always be called "Ben" by his family and would grow into a tall and strong child, but one who would also be regarded by that family as being a little "slow." Ben was more than capable of looking after himself and would prove to be a great help on their various farms, but he usually needed to be told what to do and seemed to struggle with complex decision-making. Ben never married and always lived at home with his mother and his younger siblings.

The Daltons' second child, another son, was born on November 26, 1853, and christened Henry Coleman Dalton; like his older brother, he would grow up being called something else, in his case, "Cole." Then, on the first day of the new year of 1855, Adeline gave birth to her third son, Lewis Kossuth Dalton. Young Lewis did not survive childhood, dying at seven years of age in January 1862 at the family home in western Missouri.

On October 2, 1857, the Daltons welcomed their fourth son, Litt—Littleton Lee Dalton—followed by Frank (Franklin) in May 1859 and Grattan Hanley "Grat" Dalton in March 1861. With six young sons, Adeline would have been run off her feet, but it was four years before she had another child. Perhaps not coincidentally, those four years covered the US Civil War and some of the most vicious episodes of that war took place in the Kansas/Missouri borderlands where the Daltons were living. The family was touched both directly and indirectly by what happened there.

For the first two years of the Civil War, hostilities ebbed and flowed around those western border regions, with regular clashes of arms. Occasionally, those clashes would involve regular soldiers in regular uniforms, the blue of the Union against the butternut grey of the Confederacy. More often, though, the clashes involved men wearing bits and pieces of uniforms taken from those they had captured or killed, fighting small unit actions from ambush rather than large-scale set battles. It was the theater of the guerrilla and the bushwhacker where personal debts were canceled in the name of a greater good and where grudges became matters of military expediency.

Lawrence, Kansas, where Grat had been born shortly before hostilities started, was almost completely destroyed because of its citizens' zeal for the abolition of slavery and for the Union cause in the Civil War. Most of the town was burnt and more than 300 of its residents were killed by one of the largest guerrilla bands. Among the guerrillas, led by "Colonel" William Quantrill, was a young man named Cole Younger, Adeline's nephew. Riding alongside Younger in Quantrill's band were Frank and Jesse James, two men who would also play a role in the story of Lewis and Adeline's children.

It is possible to speculate that Adeline's somewhat tenuous link to the largest guerrilla band in western Missouri kept her and Lewis and their family safe during the Civil War, but that is all it would be—speculation. The interesting fact remains that ten years of marriage produced six children, but the four years of war produced none.

The family continued to grow as peace returned to the newly reunited states. Shortly after the cessation of hostilities, on June 1, 1865, Adeline gave birth to her seventh son, William Marion "Bill" Dalton. And then, at last, the Daltons had a daughter, Eva May Dalton, born on June 25, 1867, as the two-year cycle of births was resumed. Next was Robert Rennie "Bob" Dalton, born on May 13, 1869, and, almost precisely two years later, Emmett Dalton, born May 3, 1871. Three years later, on July 17, 1874, another girl, Leona Randolph Dalton, was born, but was born with a cleft palate, and she would have speech difficulties throughout her life. She never married and remained living in the family farm until old age forced her to look elsewhere.

Another daughter, Nannie—Nancy May Dalton—was born in 1876, and the last children, twins they named Hannah and Simon Noel, were born on July 6, 1878. Unfortunately, Hannah died during childbirth or shortly afterward.

Twenty-six years separated the youngest and the oldest Dalton child. The world the oldest—those born before the Civil War—knew would be very different to that experienced by the youngest. Several of the older boys had left home and moved halfway across the continent before their younger brothers and sisters were born, and the siblings would barely know one another. All would remain very conscious that they were Daltons and would support family above all else. And all would remember the times spent on the family farm near Benton in Cass County, Missouri, as being one of the special times in their lives.

The property gifted to the newlyweds by Adeline's father was long gone, sold in part to repay Lewis's debts, and shortly after the end of the Civil War, the Daltons moved onto a 640-acre farm in Cass County, a property that was home to Adeline and the children for more than fifteen years and a sometime abode for Lewis. Emmett would remember it well, his memories perhaps tinged with nostalgia:

> From the high hills one could catch the beckoning glint of the muddy Missouri, rolling down from strange, far lands and occasionally saw the smoke plume which hung over Kansas City, the sprawling, boisterous Westport of old. Closer to home ran the Little Blue River where in wooded hollows my dog made stirring music on the trail of possum and fox; where we swam our horses; where we fished and, swinging in wild gyrations from the vines, plunged to our Saturday afternoon bath on summer days, shrill with the cry of locusts.

Adeline was a good mother; she had to be because so much of the child-rearing was left up to her. She would let Lewis, when he was home, teach the boys about horses and farms and firearms, but she would ensure that they all—boys and girls together—had as rounded an education as they could be given at that place and time. All her children would be sent to school until they finished the eighth grade, the boys later joking about the three Rs: "reading, 'riting and 'rithmatic." An accomplished pianist and sometime singer herself who would often take time out from other tasks to play the piano and sing hymns, Adeline encouraged all her children to learn to play a musical instrument. Among the boys, she was most successful with Bill, who learned to play well and had a beautiful singing voice. Emmett tried hard but had to content himself with a reasonable mastery of the mouth organ.

Adeline was also reasonably successful, and at least a lot more successful than her husband, in teaching the children how to run both a farm and a household. In fact, some of Lewis's contributions to his family's upbringing came on the back of his wife's bloodlines. There is family lore that, when Emmett was eight years old, his father gave him a fine bay horse named Katie. There was some history attached to Katie: not only had she once belonged to Jesse James, the best-known outlaw in the United States, but she had also been ridden by him on one of his raids. Another story concerned Lewis telling the children to stay inside while he went out to speak to two men on horseback who had come to the Dalton homestead one day. Only later did Lewis reveal that the two horsemen were Jesse James and Cole Younger.

It wasn't Lewis's familiarity with outlaws that brought about the next big change in the Daltons' lives but rather his unfamiliarity with successful business practices. A series of deals involving the purchase and sale of cattle fell through, and, unfortunately, he had used the Cass County farm as collateral—the family would have to find somewhere else to live. The family moved to a farm near Vinita in the Indian Territory, where Lewis had leased the property from the Cherokee who owned it. The farm was quite close to Vinita, then just a little village about 200 miles southwest of Cass County and about 100 miles east of Guthrie, then capital of the Indian Territory. They made the move in a small wagon train, and again Emmett would later recall the excitement that a young boy could experience during such an adventure: "I helped drive the stock. It took us several weeks. . . . The long marches beside the creaking wagons, the lilt of the cattle bells, the evening camp fires, the beckoning horizon of the unknown toward which we bore—this was sheer delight to my eleven year-old mind."

It was a destination Emmett thought worth the journey: "a vast expanse of wild grass, relieved by timbered hills and sweetwater creeks. Settlements were few." It was a new home for the Daltons, but not all the Daltons would live there.

The first of the children to leave home was Cole Dalton, who made his way to California in the early 1870s and who eventually became a farmer in that state's Central Valley region. Soon afterward, Cole was followed by a nineteen-year-old Litt Dalton, who settled in the same area, at Broderick in Yolo County, just across the river from Sacramento. One of the reasons Litt would later give for moving away from his family was the increasingly rambunctious behavior of his brothers. It was no surprise, then, that he would spend most of his working life as a mule-driver and a shepherd; he did not mind the solitude, and somehow found it easier to work with animals than with people.

It seems that the Daltons lived on the property outside Vinita for only a couple of years, and the reasons for their moving from it can only be guessed at. But they did move, and this time to an established farm just a few miles to the west of Coffeyville in southeastern Kansas, not too far from the Indian Territory. It was at Coffeyville that young Emmett finished his formal education, and it was at Coffeyville that his younger siblings continued theirs. They would all look back fondly at those years on the Coffeyville farm. But the family continued to splinter as the older sons matured and eventually left home.

Cole and Litt had moved well away from home in part because employment options for young men in Cass County, Vinita, and Coffeyville were limited. For those who had grown up on farms, the opportunities were more limited than they were for others because, unless they were on an enormous property that could be subdivided, it would usually pass on to the eldest son at the owner's death. Other sons, if there were any, could be left with little more than memories. The general procedure for those other sons was to work as a farm laborer or cowboy on one of the larger ranches—which would sometimes mean moving well away from home—working up through the ranks until reaching a level where the rewards allowed saving up for a property of one's own. Or, perhaps, working as a hired hand until something better came along.

This latter path was the one that both Frank and Grat Dalton took when they reached adulthood. Frank went one step further when, in 1878, at twenty-five he married Nancy Kestesson when they both lived in Missouri. The new Mrs. Dalton died the following year. The following year, Frank and Grat both became officers of the law. In the Indian Territory, in the Cherokee Nation, the tribal leadership had authorized the establishment of a special Indian Territory police force to be formed at the same time as other nations were doing the same thing. The Cherokee police force was formed under the leadership of John Jordan, and two of Jordan's first hires were Frank and Grat Dalton. In doing so, he employed an exemplary law enforcement official, and what may have been a ticking time bomb.

At first glance, Frank and Grat were typical Dalton males; tall, good-looking with slightly protruding ears, blue eyes, and that kind of dirty-blond hair that grows darker with age. Both were excellent horsemen and excellent judges of horseflesh, traits inherited directly from their father, and both were excellent shots with both rifles and six-shooters, traits characteristic of young men in the West at that time. But where Frank was both considered and balanced, Grat was a street fighter by choice, a man who expected to be challenged in most human interactions and who responded accordingly.

One of Grat's issues may have been that he grew up quickly, very quickly. At sixteen he was almost fully grown, a man among boys who even then was developing a taste for hard liquor. Grat was fiery and quick to anger; comments that others may have let pass could provoke a violent and physical response from Grat. He walked through the world with a chip on his shoulder but with no clear path to follow. Emmett remembered his older brother as being "aimless, discontented, troubled. Peculiarly alone even though he was by nature decidedly social." The rub of it all was that Grat was very much a Dalton and would rarely challenge the authority of his more "accomplished" brothers, Frank, Bill, and Bob. He did have a softer side, though, and it appears that he may have married a woman named Mary Hughes in 1880. This cannot be confirmed, and, if true, his wife learned quickly that marriage to a Dalton inevitably led to long periods of separation.

Service with the US Indian Police was a challenge. Members of the service were entitled to enforce the law anywhere throughout the Indian Territory and not just in the nation that employed them. The police occasionally assisted in the enforcement of tribal laws, but their remit was much wider than that. They could, and did, arrest criminals whom they would hand over to deputy US marshals, and they spent a lot of their time removing illegal squatters and intruders from tribal land. The first priority for the police was always to interdict the supply of liquor into the Indian Territory. For doing so, the Indian Police officers would be paid a salary of between five and fifteen dollars a month by the US government on top of whatever they were being paid by their Indian Nation.

Frank soon won a reputation as an effective, open, and honest law enforcement officer, so professional in his attitude to his job that he was offered a position as a deputy US marshal, an offer he accepted in 1884. Frank would now be working out of Judge Isaac Parker's federal court in Fort Smith, Arkansas. Parker's jurisdiction covered the Western District of Arkansas plus the Indian Territory, an area that covered about 70,000 square miles. To police that vast area, there would never be more than 200 deputy US marshals, and 65 of those lost their lives in that service.

The prestige attached to his new job may have been higher and the work a lot more variable, but Frank was never going to grow rich on what he earned as a deputy US marshal. His basic pay would include $2 for each prisoner he brought to court and a 6 cents per mile allowance when doing so. However, monies earned would be slow and intermittent in their arrival. Some payments had to be approved not only by the local marshal at Fort Smith but also by jurisdictional courts and even departmental bureaucrats in Washington, DC. And then, when the payment finally arrived, 25 percent of it had to be paid to the chief marshal of Isaac Parker's court.

Being a deputy US marshal had one notable advantage over being a US Indian policeman—the deputy marshal could appoint his own posseman, a kind of paid junior assistant who could escort prisoners, serve on posses, and the like. For his posseman, Frank Dalton chose his younger brother Bob. There is no record of Grat having been offered the position, and, if he was, he must have turned it down. Instead, he chose to head to California to look at the lay of a land that Litt and Cole found so attractive. He was not and never would be a farmer, but he sensed that there would be other opportunities for him somewhere in the golden West. Besides, another of his brothers, young Bill, had indicated that he was about to head west also, first to the goldfields of Montana and, if that didn't work out, down to California to have a look at prospects there. At the last moment, Emmett, just fourteen and fresh out of school, asked if he could go to California, too. Adeline had no successful objections to that, so another cohort of Daltons headed west.

If you distilled all the physical qualities of the Dalton brothers into one archetypical figure, that figure would be Robert Rennick Dalton. Tall, blond, and blue-eyed, from his early teens Bob displayed both character and balance, qualities not always associated with the Dalton boys. He possessed a native intelligence and—despite what his brother Bill might claim—was probably the smartest of all of them. Bill, though, viewed life through the prism of monumental self-interest, always considering which course of action would result in the best outcome for him. Bob differed from this, looking at life and the boundless prospects it offered through a viewfinder that he would use to calculate which of the many possible outcomes of an action was most likely to succeed.

Bob could match Grat for aggression if he believed aggression was more rather than less likely to be successful. But, equally, he could use reason and moral suasion when he considered it either appropriate or necessary. For a young man on the borderlands of the American West in the closing years of the nineteenth century, he possessed a set of skills that were always desirable and occasionally essential; Bob Dalton could ride and fight better than most and could certainly outshoot all of his contemporaries, especially when it mattered most, under pressure.

Before he joined Frank as a posseman, Bob had completed a Western apprenticeship. He had helped out on his own family farm, had gone on a cattle drive, and had worked at or with cowboys from two of the region's largest ranches, the Double H and the Bar X Bar, where he had also made a lot of contacts with like-minded young men. He had honed his skills, too, paying boys to throw targets in the air when he practiced his shooting. Finally, he had become the role model for his younger brother Emmett. Just two years separated them, but to Emmett Bob was half a lifetime ahead. All Emmett could do was listen to and emulate his brother and hope that sometime, in some place, they might be regarded as almost equals.

It was about as routine as anything the deputy US marshals working out of Fort Smith, Arkansas, ever did. An outlaw named Dave Smith, wanted for horse theft and smuggling whiskey into the Indian Territory, had been spotted in a camp along the Arkansas River bottoms in Sebastian County, and it was likely that he would still be there. The spot was just a few hours' ride from Fort Smith, so during the morning of November 27, 1887, deputies Frank Dalton and James Cole loaded up their horses and rode out to where they believed Smith was camped.

Finding Dave Smith turned out to be easier than they thought. The information they had been given about Smith's probable campsite had been accurate, and after checking that they were not riding into an ambush, the two deputies tied their horses and approached the camp, a couple of tents and a cooking area, with a temporary holding yard for several horses. As they moved into the open area of the camp, a man emerged from one of the tents holding a Winchester rifle, which he fired several times. One of the shots hit Frank Dalton in the middle of the chest, and he went down hard. James Cole was also hit, but his was not a fatal injury and, firing back, he edged his way into some cover and back to where he had left his horse. Mounting it, he rode back fast to Fort Smith to report on the action and the death of his companion.

A posse was quickly formed and equally quickly set out for the Sebastian County campsite. It was still light, and when they arrived there, they learned two things. Frank Dalton had not been dead when Cole escaped but whoever had shot him had finished him off with two further shots to the head. They also learned that Smith and his companions had left. The posse caught them some days later, however, and another shoot-out occurred. In this one, Dave Smith and another outlaw, Will Towerley—the man who had shot Frank Dalton—were killed, as were one of the deputies in the posse and a woman named Jennie Dixon, caught in the crossfire.

By then, Frank Dalton's body had been returned to Coffeyville, where Adeline and the other Daltons scraped together enough money to pay for a funeral and an impressive headstone over his grave in the town's Elmswood Cemetery. All the Daltons who could attended the funeral, and from California Grat let his family know that he was on the way home, too. Frank's death while upholding the law was a tragedy and badly affected the brothers closest to him—Grat, Bob, and Emmett. Their response was to shape the history of the family.

PART I

THE SONS OF LEWIS DALTON

2 ALONG THE OUTLAW TRAIL

I

Frank Dalton's death had several knock-on effects for the Dalton family. Grat and Emmett Dalton had traveled to California almost two years earlier, followed by Bill Dalton a short while later. Emmett had lasted weeks rather than months before returning to Coffeyville and opting to become a cowboy down in the Indian Territory. Bill remained in California with Cole and Litt Dalton, but Grat came straight back to Coffeyville when he learned of his brother's death. For Grat, action was always a more appropriate response than reflection.

That action began almost immediately, with Grat appointed a deputy US marshal, reporting to Isaac Parker's federal court. Bob was now also a deputy marshal, and the two brothers often rode together, on occasion joined by Emmett, sometimes as a posseman and sometimes as an unpaid assistant. By all accounts, the Dalton brothers were regarded as good law officers—brave, polite, and, most of all, effective. Both made several important arrests, but during one of the arrests, Grat was shot through the arm.

The brothers soon faced a major issue that had plagued the US Marshals Service since its inception: the irregularity of the pay. If their money arrived on a monthly or bimonthly basis, or even with a predictable regularity, there would have been few complaints from the deputies, but this was hardly ever the case.

As they worked and waited for their wages—in some cases for up to eight months—their own expenses continued to pile up. They had to eat, as did their horses, and they had to have a roof over their head when they were not out on the trail. There were little annoyances on top of this. For instance, they were required to pay for the burial of any man they killed if the victim had no known relatives, and that was often the case. Relatives of the "Buckshot Kid" and the many John Smiths and William Browns that became wanted men were generally hard to find.

The irregularity of the wages was probably not as significant for Grat as it was for Bob. Grat was a gambler, a card player, and a very good one. He could always find a game at Fort Smith or any of the larger centers they passed through, and sometimes even when out on the trail. If he had genuinely married earlier, that marriage was now over, and Grat never was one for long-term planning anyway. Bob was different. There was always something down the road for Bob, something bigger, better, and more stable than what he had. In 1888, in Missouri, he had married Lucy Ann Johnson, a marriage unaccompanied by any of the usual fanfare. A photograph of the couple, dated May 9, 1889, shows them dressed formally and looking somewhat somber, but they would have been happy at that time. Lucy was pregnant, and she gave birth to a daughter they named Jennie May Dalton in November that year.

Looking for some extra income, in 1888, Bob applied for and was appointed to the position of the first police chief of the Osage Nation. More mature than his years would suggest, Bob was still only nineteen years of age. The Osage chiefs, sick of squatters and a seemingly endless trail of whiskey-peddlers, applied for assistance to the US federal court in Wichita, Kansas, and were given permission to raise their own police force. Bob was offered the police chief's position partly on the basis of the work he had done with his brother Frank and partly on the basis of the reputation he was forging for himself. Bob was the youngest police chief ever appointed in the Indian Nations.

Bob Dalton's Osage Police Force was responsible for most of the northwestern section of the Indian Territory and, like the deputy US marshals who also worked the area, was under the jurisdiction of federal authorities in Wichita. Bob was also authorized to raise a force of up to twenty police officers, and in a short while he had recruited twelve Osages he considered suitable. He was also authorized to choose his own posseman, and he was again able to find and appoint a suitable candidate almost immediately. It was his seventeen-year-old brother, Emmett.

When Emmett returned from his brief sojourn to California, his stay at the family home outside Coffeyville was equally brief. After catching up with family and friends, he was soon on his way again, this time riding southwest into the Indian Territory and to the Bar X Bar Ranch, one of the largest properties in the north of the territory. For a Dalton, becoming a cowboy had become something of a rite of passage, and Emmett was following a trail forged by Frank, Grat, and Bob. He would soon be riding, bunking down, and rubbing elbows with cowboys who had ridden with one or more of his brothers. In the freemasonry of the saddle in the Indian Territory, the name "Dalton" was a recognized password.

The Bar X Bar was one of three well-known ranches that had been established in the northwestern corner of the Indian Territory. Founded on land that straddled the Seminole and Cherokee Nations by a businessman from Kansas named George Rollins Davis, the ranch changed hands when Davis decided to move to Texas. When Emmett began work there in 1887, it was owned by Ed Hewins and Milt Bennett. The ranch was located in what was known as the Triangle Country, land bounded on the north and east by the Arkansas River, on the south and east by the Cimarron River, and with the Pawnee Nation abutting it to the west. Its 105,546 acres carried 10,000 head of Texas longhorn cattle.

The other ranches in that part of the territory, home to more cowboys, were the Turkey Track Ranch directly to the south of the Bar X Bar and located in the Sac and Fox Nation, and the Halsell brothers' expansive Double H Ranch, further to the south again. One of the larger-than-life characters who would take Emmett under his wing for a time was a product of the Double H Ranch: Bill Doolin.

Doolin had been even younger than Emmett—perhaps fourteen, no more—when he rode into the Double H Ranch from his native Arkansas a decade earlier, asking to speak to whoever was in charge about a job as a cowboy. The person in charge was Oscar Halsell and, over time, he saw something in Doolin that he didn't see in many cowboys. In the following years, he would teach the young cowboy to read and write and how to look after his own finances. As Doolin grew into adulthood, tall, red-headed, and sometimes impulsive, Halsell gave him more responsibility for the running of the ranch. Then it all suddenly changed.

It was never brought into the open, but there were suggestions of a run-in with the law, harsh words, and accusations. Whatever the reason, Doolin left the Double H and was working at the Bar X Bar when Emmett also began working there. For Emmett, there was an immediate comparison with his brother Bob; both were big, competent, and confident. In Doolin, though, Emmett found that the qualities were pushed a little too hard, with confidence becoming brashness and competence becoming foolhardiness. They never tipped over like that in Bob. Despite some misgivings, Emmett grew close to Doolin and to a small group of cowboys from the Bar X Bar and Turkey Track ranches, friendships that grew over time.

Emmett learned that all the cowboys had a backstory, a set of circumstances in their past that had brought them to this work in this part of the country. He also learned that many had used more than one name in their journey or answered to a nickname and that there was usually a story behind that.

One of the cowboys Emmett grew close to was the enigma that was Bill Powers. At the time the two met, Powers was in his mid-twenties, a big, brawny man whose most distinctive feature was a thick, black handlebar moustache. Powers admitted that he had in the past used the aliases Bill Power and Tom Evans, and Emmett subsequently learned that Powers could speak fluent Spanish and was a more than competent violin player. He learned, too, that Powers cherished the idea of one day purchasing a hacienda somewhere in northern Mexico and ranching there with cattle and horses.

There were stories about Bill Powers just as there were stories about all the other cowboys. The most persistent story charted a good start in life, somewhere in Texas, where he later became a wagon boss on long cattle drives to railheads in Kansas and Missouri. After one of these cattle drives, Powers was returning to Texas via the Indian Territory when he was offered work at the Double H Ranch by Oscar Halsell. After working there for a while, Powers moved on to the Bar X Bar where he became friends with Emmett and another young cowboy named Dick Broadwell. Apart from those sketchy details, all his companions knew about Powers was that he was an experienced cowboy, a good shot and a good rider, and a man who could put up with hardships. That, plus the fact that he was a bit of a dandy; so was his friend Broadwell.

Richard "Dick" Broadwell was in his early twenties when he met Emmett. Tall and slender, smooth-shaven, and with what some would describe as classic features to go with his fair skin and dark hair, Broadwell freely admitted to using the aliases Tom Moore and Texas Jack in his travels. He also had an interesting backstory to go with those aliases, but it was a story that he would only share with people he knew and trusted, because it was a story of a broken heart and betrayal.

Broadwell was born into a respected and well-to-do family from Hutchinson, Kansas. As a young man he decided to try his luck on the land when a section of what was known as "Old Oklahoma" was opened up for settlement. He claimed what he considered a good parcel of land and soon learned that a young woman had taken up an adjoining claim. The young couple met, and over a relatively short period of time, Broadwell fell in love with her. When discussing a possible future together, the young woman revealed that she had taken up the land on speculation, hoping to make money on reselling the property rather than working it. In the months since she had moved there, the property's value had increased significantly.

The young woman also revealed that she had developed "feelings" for Broadwell. In discussions about what to do next, the young woman suggested they could both sell their properties, pool their resources, and travel to Fort Worth, Texas, to start a new life together. And that was pretty much how it went. The properties were sold for a reasonable profit, and the young lovers traveled to Fort Worth with a substantial amount of money. The morning after they arrived, Broadwell woke up alone in a fancy hotel room. The woman of his dreams and all the money he had in the world had gone, and search as he might, he never saw either again. Rather than return to Hutchinson, he took to the road, became a cowboy, and eventually made his way to the Bar X Bar Ranch.

Proximity and common interchanges out on the range meant that the cowboys from the Bar X Bar and Turkey Track ranches spent a lot of time together, sometimes working and sometimes socializing. Cattle foraging on the plains and river bottoms ignored notional boundaries, as did the cowboys. The contacts allowed Emmett to meet three of Bob's and

Grat's old riding partners, the two Charlies—Bryant and Pierce—and one of the real characters among the cowboys, George Newcomb.

Charlie Bryant was hard to miss. He had a large black powder burn tattooed on his left cheek, and he was known throughout the territory as "Black Face" Charlie Bryant. When asked, and you had to be either a close friend or very brave to ask, Bryant would tell you that he received the distinctive mark when a black powder weapon was fired at him from close range. That explained the mark but did not explain where either the bullet it propelled or the man who fired it had finished up.

Bryant was not as physically impressive as some of the other cowboys. He was of medium height with a slight build, and there was a reason for this, too. Somewhere in his travels across the US South, Bryant had contracted at least one disease, which, from the reported symptoms, may well have been malaria. He may have also picked up a second disease, syphilis, in those travels; at times his symptoms and behavior were what could have been expected from such a sufferer. Bryant was believed by some to be a Texan of good birth, a man who had made a couple of bad choices and was now paying for them. For others, he was just a bad man, a person of violence who was bound to come to a violent end.

To his friends, however, and he counted the Dalton brothers among them, Bryant was a good cowboy and a reliable back-up in a tight spot. They enjoyed his twisted grin and laughed at his sardonic jokes. There were rumors, too, that Bob Dalton was sweet on Charlie's sister Daisy, who was living on a family property in the Indian Territory.

The second Charlie, Charlie Pierce, also had a nickname, "Cockeye," because he had a small cast in one eye, but he apparently let it be known that he did not appreciate the use of that nickname. Like so many of the others, Pierce came from a respectable family, his parents living on a property near the Blue River in Missouri. Unlike the others, though, he seemed to have chosen a life of crime over the other possibilities. After devouring stories of the James brothers and the Youngers as an adolescent, he followed them into a life of crime, and at sixteen his family suggested that he leave Missouri immediately because there were warrants out for his arrest. He took their advice and moved to the Indian Territory, where he was almost immediately in trouble, spending time in the Fort Smith jail on more than one occasion.

Despite his criminality and his prison record, Pierce was an engaging character. His family had valued education, and at some time Pierce himself had been a good student—he could use words and concepts that were just a little too high-brow for many of his fellow cowboys; at times, he would blush bright red when he realized that the person he was talking to had absolutely no idea what he was talking about. Before arriving at the Turkey Track Ranch, Pierce had been rustling cattle and occasionally stealing horses. At the ranch he was just one of the cowboys, a good cowboy, too, tough, but with an unfailing good nature and positive outlook.

George Newcomb, the final member of the little group that coalesced around the Daltons, quite enjoyed his nickname of "Bitter Creek." It was a name taken from Newcomb's habit, when he had had more than a few drinks, of singing out loud one of the songs popular on the frontier at that time. The relevant line from the song's chorus was "I'm a she-wolf from Bitter Creek, and it's my night to howl!" "Bitter Creek" was the nickname others had given him. When he first became a cowboy, he went by a different moniker, "the Slaughter Kid," and there was a story in that, too.

Newcomb, now in his early thirties, had been born into a prominent family in Fort Scott, Kansas, but at an early stage—some say he was just twelve years of age—he ran away from home to join one of those cattle drives that occasionally went past his hometown. The one he chose was from Texan John Slaughter's ranch, and young George returned to Texas with the cowboys and was offered work by Slaughter himself. In honor of that early experience, Newcomb took to calling himself "the Slaughter Kid," an appellation he carried during his subsequent work life at Halsell's Double H and the Turkey Track.

It was almost impossible not to like Newcomb. Compared to some of the other big, brawny men, George was a bantam, barely five and a half feet tall and weighing in at perhaps 130 pounds. He was overarchingly proud of his moustache and little goatee beard and seemed to find humor in everything around him. He did have one habit that sometimes spooked the others. He would often wake up at odd hours during the night and, unable to go back to sleep, would wander around the bunkhouse or campsite, and sometimes even go for long walks in the surrounding brush. On those nocturnal walks he would often make plans about his land claim near what was the first capital of Oklahoma, the little village of Guthrie.

Somewhere along the cowboy trail, Newcomb and Pierce became firm friends. Their personalities and outlooks were complementary. They were both eternal optimists and were both generous to a fault. Either or both would offer money if one of their companions seemed to be down on their luck and would just as easily offer the loan of a horse or a saddle, a Winchester, or a six-shooter. Emmett thought, in fact, that the two might just be a little too generous, because their generosity sometimes bordered on gullibility. George and Charlie were soft touches; their willingness to help whenever they could led them to sometimes misjudge character and motives, and they could become targets for some who looked to take advantage of them. Within the confines of the bunkhouse and the work camp, it was a minor issue. Elsewhere, it could have disastrous consequences.

Emmett and the other cowboys had all this companionship and more for thirty dollars a month, plus board. For everyone but Emmett, still filled with his childhood dreams, being a cowboy was a way station on the road to something better, a farm outside Guthrie, perhaps, or a hacienda in northern Mexico. For most of those cowboys, the issue was primarily how to move further, and more quickly, down that road.

Emmett, though, loved every minute of the cowboy life, viewing it—accurately as it turned out—as his initiation into life as an adult. Many years later, he recalled those days through the rose-colored lens of nostalgia: "We rode line together, this sextet of able, rowdy punchers and myself, the kid of the outfit. Branded the calves, wrangled the horses and tested our shooting eye in matches. Charged across the hills in sudden spurts of sheer animal spirits, shared our bacon and our ponchos, and slept under the stars together. Braided all those gutsy, careless days and common experiences into a reata of firm friendship." More ominously, he also recalled, "Among those boys I learned to speak the language of the forty-five with considerable accuracy."

II

Bob Dalton lasted fewer than twelve months as chief of the Osage Police, with low pay and isolation being the most likely reasons for his resignation. He stayed in law enforcement, and simply transferred back into the US Marshals Service as a deputy marshal, again working out of Fort Smith and again riding alongside his brother Grat, with Emmett sometimes joining them as a posseman. The Dalton brothers had always enjoyed reputations as tough, efficient law enforcement officers, reputations handed down from Frank. Now their reputations began to include less effusive character assessments, which all seem to have begun with the shooting of Charlie Montgomery near Coffeyville in August 1888.

Montgomery was a wanted man, with outstanding warrants for horse theft, impersonating a law officer, and several lesser offences. Bob Dalton was part of a three-man posse sent out to arrest Montgomery, who opened fire on the posse as soon as he spotted them. He fired off two shots before being killed by a single shot from Bob Dalton's Winchester rifle. The posse took Montgomery's body back to Coffeyville for identification and burial, and that was when the rumors started. The first was that Montgomery had been bushwhacked by Bob, who killed him with a single shot to the back of the neck. The second was that Bob had killed Montgomery because he was a love rival, presumably in pursuit of Lucy Johnson, now in a personal relationship with Bob. Both rumors were demonstrably false, and both only emerged after other, darker things had come to pass.

The other rumors that began to circulate were based around the same problems that had prompted Bob to transfer to the Osage Police in the first instance: the low rates of pay and the even slower remittance of monies owed to the law officers. Pay rates for arrests and per diems for traveling had not changed in the slightest in the year that Bob had been away, and just a few months after resigning as a deputy US marshal, Bob found himself broke despite being owed hundreds of dollars by the US government. Grat was in almost as bad a position. Worse for both was that the crisis came at a time when their larger family needed all the support they could muster.

Lewis and Adeline's marriage had been a procreative one, but it had never been a meeting of the spirits or a meeting of the minds. Lewis was by nature a drifter, a chaser of dreams usually involving quality horses at a racetrack or a stock saleyard, and life had proved him more successful at the latter than the former. Adeline, having grown up on the land, wanted the stability that a property offered. The two lifestyles were increasingly incompatible, and by 1888 Lewis and Adeline were moving in opposite directions. Divorce proceedings were initiated and, with the assistance of a Coffeyville lawyer and newspaper editor named David Stewart Elliott, concluded amicably.

There was no major division of property and assets because as the Daltons' marriage was coming to an end, a new opportunity was opening up not all that far away from Coffeyville to the southeast. In 1889, part of the original Indian Territory was formed into the Oklahoma Territory and opened for settlement. The Daltons joined in the rush and claimed land around the small settlement of Kingfisher. Adeline claimed 160 acres of good river bottom land six miles northeast of Kingfisher, and Ben Dalton claimed a similar block to the northwest of the village. He would live with Adeline and his siblings on his mother's claim, working his own farm during the day.

There were suggestions that Adeline's property was actually claimed in Lewis's name, but that is unlikely because they were divorced by then, and there is nothing to suggest that Lewis ever set foot on either of the Kingfisher properties. Instead, the Coffeyville farm was sold, and all that Adeline and her remaining children would need was packed into a covered wagon for the journey to the southeast. Adeline was accompanied by her daughters Leona and Nannie and sons Ben and Simon. Another daughter, Eva, had recently married a businessman named John Whipple across the state in the town of Meade, Kansas.

Lewis Dalton chose to remain close to Coffeyville, making his plans to buy and sell quality horses and picking up occasional work on local farms. He did not long survive the loss of his family, passing away at Dearing, near Coffeyville on July 16, 1890. He was buried in that town's Robbins Cemetery.

The folks around Kingfisher thought highly of the Dalton boys, especially the deputy US marshals, Bob and Grat, and their posseman brother, Emmett. The two older brothers knew how to look after themselves in a scrape; Bob's reputation as a crack shot had preceded him. On the whole they were just the kind of men the new territory needed. That was not the set of opinions held by many in the Western District of the Arkansas federal court, the area they were employed to protect. Many of those who had settled in that part of the southwest had begun to seriously question which side of the law the Daltons were actually on.

The step over the line was a short one. Although that step was not documented, it probably took place when the Dalton brothers were owed hundreds of dollars in back pay and had their own bills piling up. It was probably somewhere in the Osage Nation, land all three brothers had come to know well, and it most likely involved a couple of ne'er-do-wells and a substantial amount of whiskey they were smuggling in for sale to the local residents. Caught in the act, the whiskey-runners offered the peace officers a considerable amount of money to pretend the encounter had never taken place, and for both parties to go their own ways secure in the knowledge that no one else would ever know what had occurred—there would be no real losers in the transaction. In the end, it was an easy decision to make.

What had been an exception soon became the norm. They continued to "enforce" the law, especially in the Osage Nation, making up their wages with the fines they first imposed on and then collected from the whiskey-runners who crossed their path. There were also persistent rumors that the brothers were not above planting whiskey in the wagons they stopped, then finding that whiskey and imposing a level of fine they thought their victims would pay. On more than one occasion they also sold the whiskey they had confiscated. The rumors about them were both frequent and specific enough to force authorities to act.

On March 21, 1890, Bob and Emmett were arrested at Fort Smith and charged with "introducing intoxicating liquor into the Osage Nation on 25 December 1889." After a brief hearing, Emmett was acquitted because all witnesses agreed he had stayed on the road some distance away from where the alleged illegal transaction had taken place. Bob, however, was committed to stand trial for the offense on September 1,1890; he was then released on bail.

The brothers may have officially remained on the right side of the law for a while longer; some accounts have Bob and Emmett working for a time with the Cherokee Nation Police and Grat remaining a deputy US marshal until he allegedly placed an apple on a boy's head and then shot it off to demonstrate his marksmanship. The fact remained that their primary legal source of income had dried up and the brothers needed something to replace it; fortunately, an alternative was close at hand. When Lewis Dalton died, he left his family little beyond several horses and a good knowledge of horseflesh. The horses were most likely sold to provide some working capital, and the knowledge was put to work to increase that capital.

The brothers had not been above claiming any unbranded horses they came across, but, with the money running out and little chance of gainful employment, in June 1890 they became professional horse thieves. That month, they found and stole three small bands of horses, seventeen in all, in the Indian Territory, and herded them deep into Kansas, to Baxter Springs, where they claimed to be the legal owners of the horses and where they sold them for what was reportedly a tidy sum. Fifteen minutes after they left Baxter Springs, a posse that had been trailing them from the Indian Territory rode into own.

A second foray into rustling, again stealing horses in the Indian Territory and overlanding them for sale in Kansas, albeit at a different town, was as successful as the first, but the brothers' luck ran out on their third attempt. This time they were spotted by a posse that had been searching for them. A chase ensued, with the brothers using every trick they had learned as law enforcement officers. To some extent they were successful; both Bob and Emmett escaped. Grat was not so lucky; captured by the posse, he was taken to Fort Smith and lodged in jail there to await trial. At least he was in familiar surroundings. While he was being held, warrants were issued for the arrests of Bob and Emmett.

The brothers went to ground, most likely at a predetermined spot in the Gloss Mountains, a spur of the larger Ozark Mountains. It was a spot they both knew from their days as cowboys, and it was also a base to which they invited a small group of acquaintances they had met at the Double H, the Turkey Track, and the Bar X Bar ranches. Those who accepted the invitation to be part of the first iteration of the Dalton Gang were George Newcomb and Charlie Bryant plus a new friend of theirs, a young cowboy from Arkansas named Bill McElhanie. To Bob, it was obvious that their next move in the outlaw business, whether or not that business involved the theft and sale of quality horses, should be well away from southeastern Kansas and the Indian and Oklahoma Territories where there were extant warrants for Emmett and himself. A more appropriate base might be the boom town of Silver City, New Mexico, where the sheriff—Ben Canty—was an old family friend of the Daltons.

By the time the gang visited Silver City, its days as a wild frontier mining town were over, but wild it had been. In the 1870s and 1880s, gunfights and daylight robberies were as common as reports of isolated miners and prospectors being killed and scalped as they pushed even farther into what were traditional Apache lands. By 1890, the little town in the southwestern corner of the state had settled into a more traditional role as a center for not only silver mining but for the extraction of both gold and copper from mines in the nearby mountains. The gang was not looking for long-term employment, however, but for quick and easy windfalls, and in the search they quickly found a valuable ally.

Her name was Florence Quick: that was the name she had been given at birth, but it was not necessarily the name she would always use. When she wanted to appear as a demure young woman, she was Eugenia Moore, quiet, well educated, and respectful. She could also become Tom King, a hard-riding, hard-drinking cowboy, and just about anything in between. History, and historians, have endowed Florence with almost superhuman qualities; she could outride and outshoot most men, was an expert telegraphist, and could wheedle secret information out of men using a combination of skills and charms that left all men wanting more. To Bob, she was an attractive woman, and to Florence, he was an attractive man. They were soon in a deep and passionate relationship.

It was probably Florence who convinced Bob that conducting any sort of robbery in Silver City would not be a good idea. It was an isolated, well-armed community; any robbery would attract a vigorous response, and unless you knew the country as well as the locals, you would either be caught, and caught quickly, or perish in the inhospitable mountains and deserts that surrounded the town. Instead, a suggested site was Santa Rosa, another small town on the Pecos River near the geographical center of New Mexico. There, all four directions offered escape routes, with Oklahoma just a couple of days' ride to the east. Best of all, there were a couple of saloons in the Mexican part of town that hosted big card games. It was not unusual for thousands of dollars to change hands on some nights. So Santa Rosa it was.

The target turned out to be more of a shanty than an upmarket saloon, but the actual robbery went smoothly. With one of their number, possibly Bill McElhanie, remaining outside with their horses, the other four gang members entered the saloon and, after circulating through the main room, took up the positions they had been assigned by Bob. At his signal, guns were drawn and waved in the faces of the gamblers. Threats and abuse commingled, and money was snatched from hands and tables and placed in a chaff bag that one of the gang had carried inside. Any form of resistance was met with a curse and a gun in the face. Then, quite quickly, it was over. The gang backed out, guns still raised, and mounted their horses under the watchful eye and rifle of McElhanie.

Not far behind them, a posse had formed and set off after the bandits. The gang had scouted their escape route and were prepared. At a spot chosen by Bob, they dismounted and ambushed their pursuers, and a short, sharp gunfight ensued. The Daltons did not have it all their own way in the exchange. Their packhorse wandered over to near Emmett's firing position, attracting some fire from the posse. One bullet struck a frying pan in the animal's pack and ricocheted, striking Emmett in the right arm. The wound healed, but it left a scar that Emmett carried for the rest of his life. Bob's return fire was particularly accurate and, taking their wounded, the posse returned to Santa Rosa to plan their next move.

The next day, after some hard riding and direction changes, the gang stopped to divide up the takings from the robbery and plan for their next moves. The robbery was apparently successful, yielding several thousand dollars, enough to enable them all to lay low for several months. Bob thought that the Oklahoma and Indian Territories were now becoming a little too hot for him, and he didn't want to spend too much more time in New Mexico either. Florence made her own way to Oklahoma to look out for suitable home sites, hideouts, and business opportunities for them, and Bob thought he might head west, to California, to have a look around and catch up with his three brothers there. He had agreed to take young McElhanie with him.

Pierce and Newcomb were both also keen to return to the territories where they had farms and/or families. Emmett said he would ride with them because he, too, wanted to see his mother and siblings and get a better feel for life as an adult in that part of the world. He also promised to get word to Grat about where they all were and what they were all doing. Somewhere out on the high plains of eastern New Mexico, the gang parted ways, promising to come together again in the new year of 1891 to see how the land lay and perhaps plan some more moves.

Emmett was as good as his word. Shortly after making his way back to the Indian Territory, he was able to get a message through to Grat in the Fort Smith jail. Within a few days, Grat was released without charge, the reason for his release given as insufficient evidence to proceed with the horse theft charges. He, too, called in to see his mother and siblings in Kingfisher, telling them that he was also continuing on to California to spend time with his brothers. It promised to be some sort of reunion.

3 WEST

The rest of the family had always thought that Bill was going to be the one, that if any Dalton was going to achieve significant fame or success or make a name for himself in something out of the ordinary, it would be William Marion Dalton. Among themselves they joked that Bill was born to be the shortest of the Dalton men but that what he lacked in height he certainly made up for with big words, and lots of them. Bill could talk himself into an argument and then talk his way straight back out again. At times, even Bill would admit that he could sound a bit too glib. Fortunately, he was also blessed with an abundance of tact, causing his family to further suggest that they all thought he would make a great politician. At twenty years old, he announced that he was leaving home to make his own way in the world. Some of his siblings, and certainly his mother, were certain that he was ready for the world; they just weren't as certain that the world was ready for him.

The first part of Bill's plan when he left home in 1884 was to travel to Montana, to set himself up on the goldfields there to see if he could strike it rich. He couldn't, or at least not in the short time he spent actually digging for gold, and continued on to the Central Valley of California where he caught up with his brothers. Litt and Cole welcomed their younger brother, as they had earlier welcomed Grat, and organized some short-term work for him at the Turlock Hotel in the town of the same name. Through that work, he learned of job opportunities on farms and worked briefly on two before being employed by the Bliven family, who owned two substantial farms in central California, one near Estrella and one near Livingston. The head of the family was Cyrus Bliven, who also had a daughter named Jane, and the two young people met, fell in love, and were married.

Jane's preferred name was Jennie, and on her wedding day of June 15, 1885, she was already pregnant with the couple's first child, a son they named Charles Coleman Dalton when he was born exactly six months later. Charles was followed in almost three years' time by a daughter they named Grace, a delightful child who would be partly crippled in a childhood fall. Despite the circumstances of the courtship and marriage, which could have strained the relationship between Bill and his in-laws, Bill was accepted warmly into the family, and no doubt Cyrus Bliven helped Bill purchase a wheat farm near Cholame and Paso Rubles on the Salinas River, to the north of San Luis Obispo in Tulare County.

As his family would have predicted, Bill was an immediate hit in his local community. He knew how to turn on the charm, sure, and in a way that his Irish antecedents may have called blarney. But he was also a genuinely charming young man who really did enjoy being the life of the party. He could play the piano, soon learned the guitar, had a good singing voice, and was a natural raconteur. Among the stories he loved to tell was one about the time he had just arrived in California and was working odd jobs while his brother Grat was working in a saloon in Livingston. Bill found a dead cat, which he put in a shoe box and hid in the hotel's storeroom. When the smell grew too much, he helped Grat track down and bury its source, wondering aloud who would do such a thing.

Bill was also quite open about his political ambitions. In this, he was in the right place at the right time. Californian politics was fairly evenly poised between Democrats and Republicans, and the area where Bill had settled in Tulare County had been populated by Democratic Party–leaning Southerners in the years following the Civil War. They had a natural enemy in the area, too, the Southern Pacific Railroad, which was referred to as "the Octopus," whose tentacles extended everywhere. In the mid-1880s, it was exercising its right of way in California's Central Valley. There had already been clashes over this, and people had died, and Bill Dalton saw it as a possible route to the California legislature. By 1889, he was active on the Democratic

Central Committees in San Benito and Merced Counties. These plans were soon put on hold.

Bob Dalton and Bill McElhanie made no effort to hide the fact that they were in California after they arrived, nor did Grat when he arrived several weeks later. Bob and McElhanie originally stayed at the home of a cousin of the Daltons named Sam Oldham on his wheat farm a mile east of Kingsbury in Fresno County. However, local opinion turned against them when the three men appeared at a local dance wearing their six-shooters, a terrible social faux pas in that part of the world. They were also regarded as uncouth cowboys, with one local rumor having the two Westerners lying on their backs in a barn, practicing their marksmanship by shooting patterns in the barn's roof. Following the incident at the dance, Bob and McElhanie relocated to Bill Dalton's farm where they were soon joined by Grat, who divided his California time between Bill's farm and the saloons in Fresno.

The Oklahoma Daltons chose an untimely moment to arrive in central California. A later compendium of local Tulare County history records how "the southern part of the county had been sorely afflicted in the past by train robbers. These bandits have not been citizens of the county but have made the rather isolated region from Goshen to Alila their range, seeming to give the highwaymen better opportunity to secure their plunder and escape to the mountains before any organized pursuit could be made." To be fair, there hadn't been a rolling crime wave in the county, and the fact that the target of the highwaymen was the Southern Pacific Railroad dissipated some of the sympathy for the robbery victims that might have otherwise been felt. However, there had been the beginning of what could be a disturbing trend.

The first robbery had occurred early in the evening of February 22, 1889, at the small town of Pixley. As Southern Pacific Train No. 17 pulled away from the station, two masked men jumped aboard and ordered the engineer to stop the train. When it was stationary, they ordered the engineer back to the express car where they detonated a small bomb under the door. This was followed by a loud demand for the door to be opened accompanied by a threat that the engineer and fireman would both be killed on the spot if it wasn't. As this was happening, two of the train's passengers, one a policeman from Modesto and the other a teenager, wandered down to see why the train had stopped. Both were cut down by a shotgun blast, the policeman killed instantly.

After looting the express car, the bandits ordered the engineer to get the train moving and, when it was underway, they disappeared to the east. Details of the amount stolen varied widely, from $400 to $3,000, but this was not unusual because both railroads and insurance companies had their own reasons for downplaying the losses. An extensive search of the area was undertaken, but no arrests were made. The prime suspects were two local bad men, Chris Evans and John Sontag. All the authorities really had to go on was a description of the bandits as "a large man and a small man."

A second train robbery took place near Goshen during the evening of January 21, 1890. The pattern of the robbery was almost identical to the Pixley holdup. Two masked men climbed over the train's coal tender and at gunpoint forced the engineer to stop the train. The engineer and fireman were marched back to the express car, where the messenger was ordered to open the door. Again, curious passengers who exited the train were warned off with a "Damn you!" and a shot fired over their heads. A tramp who had been traveling on a brake bar between carriages was not so lucky. When he appeared unexpectedly, one of the bandits shot him in the face; he later died. The messenger was given ten seconds to open the door, or the engineer would be shot. The door was opened, the express car was ransacked, and the two bandits disappeared toward the east. This time, the take was estimated to be between $6,000 and $25,000.

There was a third train robbery, during the evening of February 6, 1891. The target was again the Southern Pacific Railroad's Train No. 17, but this service—running on a Friday night between San Francisco and Los Angeles, was called the Atlantic Express. On this particular night, its passenger car was full, many of those passengers en route to health resorts in and around Los Angeles. Around 9:00 P.M., the train pulled into a right-of-way at the tiny station of Alila near Tulare in the San Joaquin Valley. As it came to a halt alongside the water tank, three men jumped onto the coal tender and went forward to the engine.

All three men were masked, and two of them took engineer Charles Harwell and fireman George Radliff back to the express car where they demanded that the messenger open the door. He did, but only wide enough to open fire with a rifle at the bandits. In the short, sharp gunfight, twenty-six-year-old Radliff was shot in the abdomen—he died the following day—while the bandits fled into the night. This attempted robbery differed to the previous two holdups: this attempt was unsuccessful, and this time three bandits were involved.

The morning after the attempted holdup, Tulare County sheriff Eugene W. Kaye examined the scene of the robbery and found horse tracks leading toward the Coast Range Mountains, but little else. By the time he returned to his office, the rumor mill had spat out the first list of suspects for him. Unlike the earlier Pixley and Goshen train holdups, the botched attempt at Alila had been undertaken by three outlaws. The three Dalton brothers already resident in central California were known to be law-abiding, but three more Dalton brothers—Bob, Grat, and Emmett—had arrived from Oklahoma recently, and some of their behavior was thought to be questionable. Plus, all three appeared to be cowboys.

Six days after the holdup, on February 12, a Southern Pacific Railroad detective named Hickey made the first arrest in the case when he detained Grat at a hotel in Fresno. Hickey was very close-mouthed about the arrest, but the Southern Pacific was not backward in letting it be known that Grat, when arrested, had been in possession of several $2 notes that could be traced back to the earlier train robbery at Goshen. Reporters were quick to point out that the Goshen robbery had been undertaken by two bandits, believed to be the desperadoes John Sontag and Chris Evans. At Alila, there had been three bandits; the reporters left their readers to draw their own conclusions.

Grat was not without his own supporters and was able to offer a clear rebuttal to the charges and allegations that had been leveled against him. On the evening of the attempted train robbery at Alila, he had been 100 miles away, in Fresno, where he had spent most of the evening playing cards. If necessary, he could call at least twenty witnesses to support that claim. He could also explain the suspect $2 notes. He knew Chris Evans, Grat said, not well, but both men had worked together as cowboys at the Granger Union. Just a couple of weeks earlier he had bumped into Evans and had subsequently sold him a horse. Evans had paid for that horse with the $2 notes.

Within hours of his arrest, Grat was released without charge, but he was followed closely.

With no obvious developments in the case, Grat was rearrested during the last week of February while visiting Bob at his farm. Eugene Kaye, who made the arrest, subsequently announced that there was now more than enough evidence to justify the grand jury returning an indictment against Grat and other, unspecified persons. Kaye must have been prescient because that was exactly what happened. Shortly after that initial announcement, Kaye again spoke to local reporters to inform them that the Tulare County grand jury had indicted Grattan and William Dalton on two charges each, one of robbery and one of murder. Sheriff Kaye indicated that Robert and Emmett Dalton were also being sought as accessories to the act.

More was to come. Kaye later let it be known that the grand jury had indicted four of the Dalton brothers—Bill, Bob, Grat, and Emmett—for additional offences relating to the attempted holdup at Alila. Elsewhere, the Southern Pacific Railroad and Wells Fargo announced that, after both companies had offered rewards of $5,000 for the capture of those involved in the attempted robbery, they would pay an additional $1,800 for the capture of anyone associated with the robbery who was still at large.

Then, on March 2, 1891, Cole Dalton and one of his employees, a man named Jack Parker, were both detained at Kaye's direction. Parker was pressured to reveal everything he knew about the Dalton brothers, which was not actually a lot, and Cole was required to appear before the grand jury, where he was quizzed about his brothers, especially their movements and activities during their time in California. Cole told the grand jury most of what he knew and most of what he believed, that none of his brothers had anything to do with any of the train robberies that had occurred in Tulane County; he also gained the distinct impression that very little of what he said was actually believed. He and Parker were released without charge. One of the first things Cole then did was advise his brothers to skedaddle.

Two men took that advice. Bob Dalton and Bill McElhanie had been lying low ever since the Daltons had first been named as suspects in the attempted robbery at Alila, probably at the ranch of one of their brother Bill's supporters. As soon as they heard Cole Dalton's warning, they prepared to escape the county, the state, and the entire region. Bob knew he would be charged, and for McElhanie, still believed to be Emmett Dalton, the idea of being shot down through mistaken identity was both real and unattractive. The young men evaded the posses that were still searching Tulare County for bandits and rode east, being last spotted at San Luis Obispo. On March 8, they left their horses at a railroad station 100 miles east of Mojave and boarded the train that would take them even closer their homes in the new Oklahoma Territory.

In early April, the two men were spotted in Oklahoma, not far from Kingfisher, presumably because Bob was visiting family there. After that, the two fugitives disappeared, Bob into the Indian Territory where Florence, his friends, and some relatives, and a hideout, awaited. McElhanie may also have stopped over there before riding back to Arkansas and off the pages of history.

Bill was rearrested during the first week of March, joining Grat in the county jail at Visalia. Both were then charged with being accessories after the fact in relation to the attempted train robbery. Bail for Bill, set at $4,000, was easily raised by several of his friends, but Grat had no such luck and remained in jail until their trial, scheduled for May 18 in the Tulare Superior Court. That court also appointed lawyers to conduct the brothers' defense, attorneys Ahrens of Bakersfield and Larkins of Visalia. While waiting for the trial to begin, Eugene Kaye traveled all the way to Oklahoma seeking Bob and Emmett Dalton. Not unsurprisingly, he returned to California empty-handed.

Legal authorities in Tulare County decided to try the Dalton brothers separately, with Grat scheduled to appear in the Tulare Superior Court in Visalia in mid-June 1891. Legally, it would prove to be an extremely difficult case for the prosecution to argue. To begin with, they had to present compelling evidence that Grat was indeed one of those three masked men who had attempted to hold up the train at Alila. The best they could do was to have several witnesses describe the bandits who were directly involved in the robbery attempt. One of those men was described as being tall and straight, the second short and heavy-set. Bob Dalton was known to be tall, and the prosecution suggested that the second man could well have been Grat, who was solid, but not nearly heavy-set, and at six feet could hardly be described as short. The suggestion that this second robber could be Bill Dalton was closer to the mark but still very tenuous; some would describe Bill as "short and stout," but at five feet and nine inches tall, he was still above average in height.

The circumstantial evidence was on a par with that of the identification of the perpetrators. The men who had attempted the train robbery had ridden west after the action, belatedly pursued by a hastily put-together posse. That posse followed the trail as far as Cholame, where it was lost. And Bill's farm was not far from where the trail ended. Sheriff O'Neal of San Luis Obispo and Will Smith, a Wells Fargo detective, told the court how they, literally, went over all possible trails associated with the crime, interviewed all possible witnesses, and made two arrests, which may or may not have been germane to the actual crime.

Other evidence introduced by the prosecution into the case included two pairs of spurs found at a campsite that had allegedly been used by the Dalton brothers in the hours after the robbery, a pair of worn-out horses, and a pair of tin cutters that fugitives could use to cut barbed wire fences as they tried to escape their pursuers. There does not appear to have been any clear forensic focus to link these items to either the Dalton brothers or the train robbery they were alleged to have attempted.

To be fair, those responsible for Grat's defense against the charges left something to be desired. Grat had provided his attorney a list of at least a dozen citizens of Fresno who were prepared to swear under oath that on the night of the attempted train robbery, Grat had been 100 miles from the scene, playing faro and poker in the Grand Central Hotel in Fresno. A number of those prepared to appear were solid, reliable citizens, too, not the riff-raff usually associated with gambling dens. His attorney assured Grat that it would not be necessary to call those witnesses; the state's case was so flimsy, his primary method of defense would be to highlight the inadequacies in their case and call for all charges to be dropped and for a mistrial to be declared. If that failed, he would immediately appeal to the state's supreme court.

The trial had meandered rather than proceeded and, after two and a half weeks of inconclusive evidence and posturing rather than proofs, the judge was able to somehow conclude that Grat was indeed guilty of involvement in the attempt to rob Southern Pacific Railroad Train No. 17 at Alila. The judge then announced that sentencing would be postponed for three weeks while the court sought additional information about the defendant. When Grat's attorney indicated that he would follow through on his earlier commitment and appeal the conviction to the California Supreme Court, the judge said he would further postpone Grat's sentencing for an additional two months.

Before Grat could be sentenced and before Bill's trial had commenced, another Southern Pacific Railroad train was held up, this time at a small stop named Ceres, located 200 miles from Visalia. A number of newspapers, whose editors should have known better, postulated that perhaps known or unknown Dalton brothers may have somehow been involved in the robbery. Stimulated by that speculation and by Grat's pending appeal to the California Supreme Court, authorities in Tulare County realized that there could be difficulties prosecuting and convicting Bill Dalton, especially given his political connections and the reputation of the railroad. The charges against him were quietly dropped, and his bail money returned to those who had put it up.

All that remained now was the outcome of Grat's appeal to higher authorities, a process that was taking an inordinate amount of time, and the disposition of his case on the basis of the outcome of the appeal.

That process would never be completed if, indeed, it had ever been started. In mid-September 1891, three days before the date provisionally set for his sentencing hearing, Grat escaped from jail. Like so much else surrounding the story of the Daltons, the tales concerning Grat's escape from imprisonment have evolved from the likely to the implausible, and then some. One of the most widespread of these tales has Grat being transferred between two towns, usually without any reason for that transfer. The identity of the two towns and the timing of the trip are also both a little fluid.

In one telling, Grat was handcuffed to a detective in a railway carriage on what was an extremely hot day in central California. So hot, in fact, that the detective attached to Grat drifted off to sleep, and other passengers had opened every window in the carriage in an attempt to cool down. Grat himself had his eyes closed, also apparently fast asleep. But when he struck, it was with the speed and accuracy of a rattlesnake. In one blindingly quick movement, Grat snatched the key from the pocket of the detective sleeping next to him and undid the cuffs. In almost the same instant, he leapt headfirst through the open window on the other side of the detective.

Grat's timing was impeccable. He exited the carriage window just as the train passed across a bridge over the San Luis Obispo River. Grat not only cleared the window frame, he cleared the bridge and its railings and dived down into the river's deepest channel where he swam hard underwater as far as he could. By the time the startled detectives aboard the train realized what had happened and ordered the conductor to stop the train, Grat was just a bobbing head in a surging river, too far away for them to catch. All they could do was stop at the next station and use the telegraph there to let authorities know that their prisoner had escaped. It was all very dramatic, but simply not true.

The truth was less prosaic and almost mundane. Just days before facing the sentencing hearing, Grat and two other prisoners escaped from the Visalia jail. There were stories of smuggled hacksaw blades, cell bars cut through and replaced with blackened broom handles, ladders, horses, and hidden Winchesters, but the most likely method of escape was through bribing one or more jailers with a mixture of demonstrated promises and implicit threats. There probably was a horse secreted somewhere for Grat, and it is also probable that Grat separated almost immediately from his fellow escapees, both of whom were caught within a few days.

Grat was not, and obviously went to ground somewhere. It was not at any properties directly associated with his brothers in California; Cole, Litt, and especially Bill were being closely watched at the time. It was unlikely to have been at cousin Sam Oldham's farm either, and Grat most probably lived out at a friend of a friend's initially before moving to a safer location as the search for him lost some of its earlier impetus. That location is now known as Dalton Mountain, and there his small camp was strategically sited and regularly supplied by another wanted man named Riley Dean. Dean may have been careless with his talk or in his movements, because Grat's presence on the mountain became known to law enforcement.

Sheriff Kaye and Fresno County sheriff Hemsley, with a posse of six men, prepared to raid Grat's hideout and capture Grat and Riley Dean, dead or alive. They set off from the ranch of Judson Elwood at the foot of the mountain in freezing rain and inched their way up the initial slopes. In one version of this story, Grat spotted them from a distance; in another, a stray dog he had taken in barked a warning. In any case, there was a brief exchange of gunfire, after which the outlaws fled. Dean was captured within a couple of days, but Grat again escaped the net closing around him. He made his way down the mountain to the Elwood ranch, where he stole a horse—which he would subsequently arranged to have returned—and once more rode off into the distance.

Again, Grat lay low while Tulare County was crisscrossed by posses looking for him. For two weeks, he was hidden at the ranch of one of his brothers' confidantes. At the end of that period, he was given a good horse and a goodbye. Grat rode east, skirting deserts and mountains when he could and carefully picking his way across them when he couldn't. Mostly he rode alone; he was now—again—a wanted man, an outlaw with a price on his head. He begged for food if he thought that was necessary, stole for himself and his horse when he found it prudent. One hundred and three days after leaving Tulare County in California, in December 1891, Grat Dalton hitched his horse to a rail behind his mother's house in Kingfisher, Oklahoma, both of them lean and worn from the journey. Then he settled down to learn what had happened while he had been away.

There was a lot to learn, too. After Grat's escape, authorities in California, legal and otherwise, had maintained a close eye on all three of his brothers resident there. Bill was something of a focus for them, and he soon felt that his future in California had been compromised beyond redemption. For this, he partly blamed the Octopus, the Southern Pacific Railroad, the root of so many evils he had pledged to fight. Any political future in California was now but a distant dream for Bill, so he had upped and left, arriving in Oklahoma in November 1891, several weeks ahead of Grat. He was communicating with his wife, Jennie, using a number of synonyms and a number of addresses. Jennie planned to bring young Charles and Grace out to Oklahoma when Bill was able to organize a new job and a new home.

Then, there was the other family news. Ben and Simon, Leona and

Nannie were all doing well, and the two farms the family owned near Kingfisher were also starting to take shape. Eva and her husband, John Whipple, had built themselves a fine new house over in Meade, Kansas, but both hoped that John's emporium business would pick up a little. There was not a lot that could or would be said about Bob and Emmett. Upon his return from California, Bob had called in briefly at Kingfisher, but had then continued on into the Indian Territory where he had caught up with Emmett.

He caught up with a few others too, rumor would have it: cowboys, mainly, from the old Bar X Bar and Turkey Track ranches. People were already talking about "the Dalton Gang," and law enforcement officers were beginning to appear in some numbers around Kingfisher. There was a lot of muttering, too, about a train robbery at a place called Wharton in the Indian Territory and just what the Dalton Gang might have had to do with that.

4 CATHCHING THE KATY

I

When Bob Dalton and young Bill McElhanie headed to California in the wake of the holdup at Santa Rosa, New Mexico, Bob's expectation was that he would remain in the far West until the situations in New Mexico and the Oklahoma and Indian Territories were more conducive to his return. He probably expected to be in California for anything up to a year, but events related to the Alila train incident reduced that by half. Bob was back in his old haunts by the end of March 1891, a wanted man and, though not quite penniless, he was now a man of limited resources. Bob had asked the other members of the embryonic gang to separate, set themselves up somewhere, and wait there for his return. That return was a bit sooner than he had expected, but Bob was always someone who played the cards he was dealt. He would see how the others had fared.

Bob and Florence Quick had agreed that she would find somewhere for them to live when they could not live anywhere else, and he suggested that she look at a place he had previously used when working on both sides of the law in the Indian Territory. Located in a valley in the Gloss Mountains, the cabin was on a ranch owned by Jim Riley, a man both Frank and Bob Dalton had known for some time and someone who was both discrete and trustworthy. The cabin was nothing to look at but could be made comfortable, which was what Florence set out to do with the money Bob had given her. It would be their home, but it would always be a temporary home, somewhere to live while they planned for something better.

Emmett had escorted Florence to Jim Riley's ranch and then on to the little cabin, but he didn't stay on there after he had determined that Florence knew how to look after herself. He promised to also call in regularly to make sure that she was coping, but most of his time was spent with Charlie Bryant. Bryant had originally retired to a hideout he had made for himself near Kingfisher, but he subsequently agreed to help Emmett build something more permanent in the Indian Territory. A site was chosen near the Triangle, in an inconspicuous valley near the South Canadian River. A solid, double log cabin was constructed, part bunkhouse and part fortress.

Set on a small rise toward one side of the valley, the solid building commanded all its approaches and offered good fields of fire. It was built to absorb a lot of punishment from small arms. Nearby was a concealed horse pen that could hold around fifteen horses; there were always several quality mounts there. Water was available from several creeks nearby, and six people could live there comfortably. Bryant took to dividing his time between the cabin and his own hideout. Dick Broadwell was also a regular visitor. Even George Newcomb would ride down from his farm near Guthrie, and both Bill Powers and Charlie Pierce were aware of its location. It was probably also where Bob called the gang members to meet after he returned from California.

That meeting, or series of meetings, was for them to look ahead, to discuss at least a short-term plan to bring in money to replace the almost-depleted takings from Santa Rosa. Lawful work was now out of the question because all of them were wanted men, sought by authorities in at least two jurisdictions, if not for the actual commission of crimes, then for being an accessory before or after those crimes. Bob recognized that before any of the plans they made could be fully realized they would probably need a stake, seed money that would allow them to buy the weapons and supplies they would need later.

What the men knew best, and what had proved to be an easy way to raise cash quickly, was stealing horses in the Indian Territory and overlanding them for sale in Kansas, and that was what they did. The thefts began almost immediately, a few good horses here, a few more there.

The operation was not without problems, though, and two of the horse thieves were spotted by a rancher named Thompson, and he quickly notified federal law enforcement officials. A posse was formed, led by a deputy US marshal named William Starmer, and guided by Thompson.

At some stage, Bob became aware that his little reunited band and its herd of stolen horses was being followed by a posse. With those extra horses, he understood that it would be difficult to lose the posse, so he chose another tactic instead. Rather than continuing northwest toward Kansas, Bob turned south, retreating farther into the Indian Territory where, on May 2, 1891, he selected an ambush site near Twin Mounds in what is now Oklahoma. After hiding the horses in a small gulch and leaving one of their number to guard them, Bob assigned everyone firing positions, and they all sat back to wait.

They only had a couple of hours to wait. The outlaws heard the posse's horses first and then both horses and riders appeared. Seemingly completely unaware of what they were riding toward, the posse headed straight into the ambush, into a volley of rifle fire that saw Thompson hit and unhorsed as the others scattered for cover.

William Starmer was the first to recover, leaping from his horse, running across to the wounded Thompson and dragging him to safety back in the brush. He then called out to the others, in cover nearby, to say that he and Thompson were safe, but Thompson was badly wounded. He also told them to stay where they were while he went forward to scout out what they were facing. Starmer moved away quietly into the dense brush, and soon after he disappeared, three shots rang out in quick succession.

Soon afterward, the rest of the posse heard the sounds of a number of horses galloping away from somewhere behind the ambush site. They waited a few minutes and then moved forward cautiously. Ten yards into the brush they found the dead body of Starmer, with three bullet wounds in the middle of his chest so closely grouped that they could be covered by the palm of a single hand. Legend has it that one of the members of the posse said that the only man he knew who could shoot like that was Bob Dalton.

After Twin Mounds, two things became obvious to Bob. The first was that for the next few weeks, that part of the Indian Territory would be combed over by posses looking for horse thieves and cop killers. Almost immediately, the gang split up, its individual members heading back to their individual boltholes while the stolen horses were simply turned loose. The second realization was that horse theft was becoming a high-risk/low-reward occupation. If the Dalton Gang and its members were to make enough money to retire to a more sedentary life, they would have to choose easier and more lucrative targets. Bob had a plan he had been working on for a while; now might be the time to execute it.

Whether through direct experiences in his own life, or through the vicarious experiences of others, Bob knew quite a lot about railroads and their operations. He knew, for example, that the way the trains were put together for their normal runs varied little from company to company and from route to route. The locomotive was at the front with its coal tender immediately behind. The express car usually followed the coal tender; sleeper cars toward the rear, well back from the noisy and smelly engine; the saloon and smoking cars in the middle of the train.

From his time as a deputy US marshal and chief of the Osage Police, Bob also knew that each year the railroads also carried significant amounts of money. Sometimes their express carriages would carry tens of thousands of dollars in annuities to the various tribes in the Indian Territory, the monies promised them by the US government for giving up their ancestral lands. At other times, those tens of thousands of dollars would be generated by the sales of the annual cotton crop or of the vast herds of cattle overlanded to the stockyards of the western and midwestern metropolises.

Bob was also familiar with the arrangements the railroads made for the carriage of those monies. Almost every express car in service carried two safes that were the responsibility of the express messenger; one was known as the "through" safe and the other as the "way" safe. The through safe carried money. Large and heavy, it was not supposed to be opened at all during the journey. The way safe was there to carry only those things needed to be delivered at stations along the train's routes and could be opened by the messenger to remove what they contained at the appropriate stop.

The through safe was locked at the train's departure point, and its combination then sent, by telegraph and in code, to the train's terminal station. The railroads also let it be known that the only people who knew the combination to the through safe were individuals at the start and end of the train's route. In most cases, this was simply not true.

For a long time afterward, there were stories about Florence Quick and her almost supernatural ability to gain information on what each train was carrying in its express car. She was an expert telegraphist, it was said, able to tap into telegraph lines to read what was being transmitted and sending and receiving her own messages. In her role as Eugenia Moore, she used her female wiles to loosen men's tongues, and, if necessary, Tom King would appear to muscle the information out of recalcitrant railroad employees.

Again, the truth was relatively mundane. Dick Broadwell had a brother named Frank, who had a small business in Seward, a flyspot settlement around seven miles south of Guthrie in the Oklahoma Territory. That business primarily involved selling timber to the railroads for use in various construction projects. Frank Broadwell was also an experienced telegraphist and, moreover, occasionally filled in for the regular railroad telegraphist at Seward. The Daltons had their own circle of informants and contacts, thanks to their days as law enforcement officers and cowboys, and through their own family connections. Frank Broadwell fitted nicely into that circle. They therefore had no need for the intelligence-gathering activities later attributed to Florence, regardless of which guise she may have used to collect that intelligence. Anything that Florence actually uncovered was the icing on the cake.

It was that intelligence network that let Bob know that on Saturday May 9, 1891, an Atchison, Topeka and Santa Fe service known as the Texas Express would be carrying a large amount of money destined for a bank in Guthrie. He also learned that at 10:30 P.M. on the evening of that day the Texas Express was scheduled to make a brief stop at the small settlement of Wharton, sixty miles south of the Kansas border in the heart of the Cherokee Nation. A quick reconnaissance of Wharton revealed a village built around half a dozen businesses—a dry goods store, hotel, and the like—plus a few houses. The Santa Fe Railroad's facilities were located a short distance from the center of Wharton and consisted of a rudimentary platform, a depot office, and some associated outbuildings.

During the afternoon of May 9, Bob and Emmett Dalton, accompanied by Charlie Bryant and George Newcomb, rode to the outskirts of Wharton. There, they found a quiet, secluded area in the neighboring brush and light timber where they carefully went over, and over again, what each of them would be responsible for later that evening. Shortly after 10:00 P.M., Bob and George Newcomb briefly joined the small group of people waiting in and around the depot news. Their presence was not unusual because each train that stopped attracted prospective passengers, greeters, and others with genuine business to conduct. Satisfied that they would not be walking into any form of setup, the two men returned to the darkness on the other side of the tracks where Emmett and Charlie Bryant, and their horses, were waiting for them.

The Texas Express was on time that night, and as it slowed to a stop at Wharton, the four bandits fired a volley of shots over the front of the train. Hearing those shots, the depot clerk doused all the lights in the depot while the bystanders scattered in all directions. Appearing from the darkness, a masked Bob Dalton and George Newcomb jumped up onto the locomotive and, when the train stopped, led the engineer and fireman back to the express car where Emmett and Charlie Bryant, also wearing masks, took over guarding the prisoners.

The messenger in the express car had closed and locked the car's door as soon as he realized what was happening. Standing outside the door, Bob called out to the messenger, telling him to open the goddamn door and then open the goddamn safe. The messenger called back that he didn't have the combination to the safe, but soon afterward he swung the carriage door open. Faced by two masked men carrying Winchester rifles, the messenger realized that he did indeed have the combination to the through safe, which he then proceeded to open. Inside were two packages, one large and one small, which were both dropped into a burlap bag Newcomb was carrying.

While this was happening inside the express car, outside Emmett and Bryant loosed off occasional shots over the depot office and passenger carriage to encourage those inside not to venture outside. The robbery complete, the four bandits came together and marched the engineer and fireman back to the locomotive where, at the point of their guns, they ordered the men to get the train moving again. When it did, the men retreated into the darkness to where they had left their horses tied up, and then rode off into the night.

They may have rested somewhere for a few hours that night, but the next day the four men rode hard, deeper into the Indian Territory, to put as much distance between themselves and the inevitable pursuit that would start in Wharton. At some stage, too, the men stopped, spread a blanket on the ground and looked at what their efforts had brought them. The larger of the two packages would prove to be a disappointment. All it contained was an extensive collection of receipts, waybills, and other assorted paperwork customarily associated with the operation of a railroad, none of which was of any value to the gang. The smaller package provided at least some compensation for their efforts. It was found to contain banknotes in various denominations adding up to $1,745. What the gang would never know, though, was that the quick-witted express messenger, as soon as he realized what was going on, had opened the through safe, removed a large package of banknotes, and then shut the safe again. He hid the package in an unused stove in the carriage.

En route to their hideouts in the south, the gang stopped for several days at a ranch owned by Al Yountis, a man they all knew and trusted. The break there gave them a chance to recharge their batteries after a hectic few days and before they all went their separate ways. Newcomb said that he planned to return to his farm near Guthrie and Bryant to his hideout near Kingfisher. Bob and Emmett would proceed farther into the Indian Territory, each to the isolated cabin that was waiting for them. Before they separated, they would have a brief look back at the Wharton holdup to assess what worked and what didn't, and how they could work it better in future.

Next time—and all assumed there would be a next time—they could use some extra bodies. There would certainly have been trouble at Wharton if the train's crew and passengers and the locals had combined to act against them. They would have been in equal trouble if their horses had either strayed or been found during the robbery, and it would help if someone could be assigned to look after them next time. Bob rode away confident that the next job would be better, better and bigger.

Within twenty-four hours of the holdup, a posse was on the trail of the bandits. The warrants they carried were "John Doe" warrants, issued for generic perpetrators rather than specified individuals, but early newspaper reports were far less circumspect and identified "the notorious Dalton Gang." Bob had used all the tricks he had learned to throw off pursuers; he led the others up and down watercourses and through herds of grazing cattle to puzzle those who would follow. The tactics, including the final separation of the gang members, worked, and the posse did not get anywhere near the fugitives, the "John Does" they sought.

For law enforcement officers, suspicion had settled, quickly and correctly, on the Daltons, and they were known to have long-standing connections within the Indian Territory. Federal authorities in that territory let it be known that they were looking for the Dalton brothers and those who had ridden with them, and that there was an attractive reward. The results were surprising, but they should not really have been.

In the Seminole Nation, a group of young braves killed three men and took their bodies to the Sac and Fox Agency, saying they believed that all three were Daltons. None of the three was either a Dalton or someone who had ever been associated with them. But all three were wanted men—"outlaws and whiskey peddlers"—who had fled to the Seminole Nation to evade arrest elsewhere. Six days after this incident, three more itinerant whites were killed by Yuchi Indians and their bodies taken to an agency for identification. Again, none of the dead men had any previous involvement with the Daltons or their associates. The two incidents prompted an inquest and a stern warning to the Indian Nations not to take the law into their own hands.

Elsewhere, an intermittent stakeout started of Adeline Dalton's farm outside Kingfisher and of Eva and John Whipple's home in Meade, Kansas.

The Wharton holdup honed some of the skills Bob and the others had been developing since they all crossed from one side of the law to the other. Threats of physical violence, brandishing firearms, and using those firearms to intimidate both participants and bystanders, and above all else being seen to control the situation would become part of the Dalton Gang's modus operandi. Wharton was not a watershed moment for the gang or for any of the four men responsible for the robbery. There had already been many of those in each of their lives. It was, however, an incident, an occurrence that allowed Bob to develop and refine a template for success in train robberies.

All that followed was based on that template, one that Bob would continue to refine as he searched for the formula for the perfect robbery, the one holdup that would be so successful that they would never have to undertake another. The Dalton Gang continued to evolve, too, as Bob thought more closely about what they could do. Some of the coming changes were brought about through Bob's assessment and planning. Others were brought about by the kind of natural selection that went hand in hand with life in the American West.

II

More than once, in those moments that generally occurred while they were all sitting around a campfire late at night, especially after the whiskey had been passed around, Charlie Bryant would return to a theme. He was sick, he knew, and sometimes he was very sick, but he always came back from that, and he was determined that no sickness, no ailment, no malady, would ever put him in the ground. No, if Charlie was going out, it would be with a gun in his hand and his face to his enemies. That was said right up until the time he was struck down by fevers and pains in August 1891.

Bryant had been lying low at his hideout near Kingfisher, but when the fever and the aches and pains came this time, they were bad, and he knew he would need medical assistance to pull through. He was too well known in and around Kingfisher and chose to ride to Hennessey, twenty miles to the north, to seek medical assistance. Once there, he checked into a hotel to wait until a doctor could be summoned.

Unknown to Bryant or any of the others, a hard-driving deputy US marshal named Ed Short had been assigned to follow up leads on the

Wharton robbery a few weeks earlier. Short suspected Bryant of involvement in the holdup and also knew that the Daltons had family and friends scattered throughout the northeast of the Oklahoma Territory. Bryant himself was believed to have a brother living somewhere near Kingfisher. As luck would have it, Short chose to base himself in Hennessey, and routine detective work revealed that a very sick man, with a description that matched Bryant's, had checked into a local hotel the previous day, August 1.

Short wasted no time, arresting Bryant at gunpoint as the outlaw lay shivering in his bed in his hotel room. Hennessey had no lockup facilities, and, fearing that Bryant's colleagues might try to rescue him, Short sat up guarding Bryant throughout the night, with the sick man handcuffed to his bed. The marshal and his prisoner boarded the first train out of Hennessey the following morning, heading north to the federal detention facilities in Wichita, Kansas. They traveled in the express carriage, Bryant seated and handcuffed, Short sitting opposite, rifle across his lap, six-shooter in a holster at his side.

As they approached the first stop since their departure, Short told the express messenger that he would exit the train at that stop. It was just an isolated waystation, and though he didn't expect anyone to be there, he would stand guard outside the carriage while they were stationary. He instructed the messenger to guard Bryant while he was absent, to not take his eyes off the outlaw, and gave the man his six-shooter, telling him to use it if necessary. When the train stopped, Short took up a position on the platform looking for anything out of the ordinary; there was nothing. When the fireman signaled that they were about to get underway, Short returned to the express platform.

Circumstances inside the carriage had changed dramatically during the brief stop. After Short left, the messenger had continued with his normal routine, now with a pistol in his hand and half an eye on Bryant. At one point, he put the pistol on a shelf because he needed both hands to shift something. That was all the opportunity Bryant needed. In a flash he was out of the chair and across the carriage, the six-shooter now in his manacled hands and pointed at the messenger's head. Ordering the messenger to stay silent and to move to the rear of the carriage, Bryant moved to the carriage door just as Short approached it from the opposite direction.

The two men spotted each other at the same time, and Bryant was marginally faster to react. He fired first, the pistol bullet striking Short in the chest. As he staggered back from the impact, Short still managed to raise his rifle and fire a single shot, which struck Bryant in the heart and killed him instantly. By the time the messenger made it from one end of the carriage to the other, both men were dead, their bodies just a few feet apart. "Black-face" Charlie Bryant had exited life in the manner he had always wanted.

This time the gang came together at Bob and Florence's hideaway in the Gloss Mountains. They all knew of Bryant's demise, and were saddened by it because he had been a good companion, but they equally accepted that violent death was part and parcel of who they were and what they did. Bob had thought they had been a little undermanned at Wharton, and Bryant's death had created another shortage, which Bob had addressed. Joining Bob, Emmett, and George Newcomb at the remote hideout were Bill Doolin, Dick Broadwell, Charlie Pierce, and Bill Powers.

Their target this time would be a service operated by the Missouri, Kansas and Texas Railroad, known almost universally as the "Katy." As Bob explained it, on the 15th of each month, the Katy carried the wages for the workers at the coal companies operating at Lehigh in the Choctaw Nation. He believed that those wages would be in excess of $25,000. Plus, Bob believed that the train would be carrying some of the proceeds from that year's cotton sales back to the cotton growers in Texas. They would hold up the Katy service at Leliaetta, a tiny flag stop station in the eastern Oklahoma Territory. Leliaetta itself, he said, was little more than a general store and a few houses. Its main purpose was as a water and cattle-loading stop, with extensive cattle yards north and west of the town and the station. The service they were targeting would normally stop at Leliaetta only if there were passengers to pick up. It was a four- to five-day ride to Leliaetta, depending on their starting point, and Bob said they would all meet at a spot near Wagoner, a small town that was within easy riding distance of Leliaetta. They should travel to that rendezvous point singly or in pairs to avoid attracting attention.

After the others left, Bob confided to Emmett that if this robbery paid off as it might, he thought that he and Florence might move away, perhaps to Mexico. If Emmett and Julia Johnson, Lucy's sister, whom Emmett had been courting, were interested, perhaps they could join them, and even Grat, if he could ever get out of that trouble in California.

The gang members made their own ways to the rendezvous outside Wagoner, Bill Doolin stopping en route to have his photograph taken for his current paramour. Not far from the rendezvous point, and still early in the afternoon, they found a suitable campsite where they watered and fed their horses and then themselves. Bob went back over what they were to do that evening and then asked Emmett to spread a blanket on the ground and bring out his deck of cards. There, in an isolated glade, as the men sat around a campfire smoking and cleaning their weapons, Bob introduced a new ritual.

As the men squatted around the blanket, Bob explained the rules. Each man would be dealt a card, face up, and that card would determine his role in the robbery. The high card would take the most dangerous job, that of forcing the express carriage open; whoever drew the low card would mind the horses during that robbery. Because forcing the express car was the most dangerous job, whoever drew the high card would be able to nominate an assistant of his choice. Emmett dealt the cards, decisions were made, and the men settled down with their own thoughts as they prepared for the evening.

After dusk, the men slowly rode the four miles to Leliaetta, reining their horses in at a small patch of timber that was relatively close to the station but that also offered concealment. As the scheduled time for the train's arrival approached, the men went to their assigned positions. Bill Powers and George Newcomb went to one side of the tracks, in shadows but not far from the depot. Charlie Pierce and Dick Broadwell took up their positions, opposite the first two and on the other side of the tracks. Bob had somehow engineered that he would be paired with Doolin—he was well aware of Doolin's impetuosity and quick temper. Those two now lurked in the shadows beneath the water tank. Emmett, who had drawn the low card, had stayed behind guarding the horses.

Right on time, the Texas Express appeared out of the dark, headlight glowing. As it approached Leliaetta, the train slowed down, signaling a request to the depot, asking if the track was clear. The depot clerk signaled back that the track was indeed clear, but before the engineer once more opened the throttle, a masked Bob and Doolin leapt into the cabin of the locomotive. Rifles raised, they ordered the engineer to bring the train to a halt. As it continued to slow, Powers jumped up onto the platform of the express carriage, covered by Newcomb, who remained on the ground alongside the train, rifle at the ready.

When the train stopped, Bob and Doolin directed the engineer and fireman back to the express carriage, where Powers, frustrated that the messenger had refused to open the door, called out that he had dynamite and was prepared to blow the goddamn door open. Elsewhere on the train, the unscheduled stop at Leliaetta had prompted several passengers to leave their carriage to see what was happening. Sensing that his control of the situation might be slipping away, Bob called on the others to fire a volley over the roof of the passenger carriage. At the sound of gunfire, most of the passengers either took cover or scurried back onto the train, but the depot agent simply ran off into the night.

Powers's threats and the sound of gunfire had also convinced the express messenger to open the door, only a little at first. It was enough for Bob, who jumped up, pushed the door wide open, and strode into the express carriage where he peremptorily ordered the messenger to put all the money in the car into a sack he offered him. When the messenger had done that, he was to place the sack on the platform alongside where they had stopped. There, the sack joined the engineer and fireman and several of the bandits in a scene being observed by several of the braver passengers who had once again ventured down from their carriage.

The sight of those passengers infuriated Doolin, who strode up and down the platform, yelling abuse at anyone he saw and firing occasional shots into the air. The tactic certainly worked, the errant passengers hurrying back to their seats and anyone else who was out disappearing into the darkness. Doolin's actions also allowed Bob to call the gang together to check that everything was still going according to plan; it was. The engineer and fireman were then escorted back to the locomotive and ordered to get the train moving. When it had pulled away, Bob gave Doolin the money sack and the men headed back to where Emmett was waiting with the horses. They still had a hard ride ahead of them that night.

They did ride hard the next day also, stopping around mid-afternoon to rest and to check on how much they had taken from the express carriage at Leliaetta. Again, the totals claimed varied widely. The railroad initially conceded it had lost $3,000, but Emmett later claimed that the gang rode away with $19,000. Included in that amount was a large consignment of silver dollars, perhaps $3,000 worth, which had made their loot sack heavy and hard to carry. There was one surprise when the money was divided up among the gang members. Bob announced that he and Emmett would be taking larger shares than the others because they had done all the work, and incurred all the expenses, in setting up the robbery.

There was another surprise after the takings had been divided up. Bob simply announced that he was through with being a bandit and living the life they were all living. After a stunned silence, Powers spoke up, saying Bob's decision seemed wrong because they had only just got started. The others joined in with similar comments, but Bob would not be shaken. They all had their money and could do with it whatever they chose. For himself, he would now be looking around at other things. With that, the men split up and went their own ways.

The holdup at Leliaetta attracted national headlines, including in California where Bill was trying to clear himself of allegations that he had been involved in a similar event at Alila. The success of his brothers in the Indian Territory may—or may not—have had something to do with his decision to soon shake off the railroad detectives who had been following him and make his way across country to Oklahoma. There he would set himself up in business as a land trader in Bartlesville, in the next county to Kingfisher and not all that far from Coffeyville in neighboring Kansas. He would be close to family and old friends, but he would also be close to the Osage Hills where the Dalton Gang were rumored to have a number of hideouts.

Three days after Leliaetta, Grat Dalton broke out of jail at Visalia and, after some further adventures in California, began his long, lonely ride back to Oklahoma. The jailbreak and Leliaetta were not dependent on each other and had nothing beyond a temporal relationship, but the implications of Leliaetta were certainly a kind of magnet for Grat. And in Meade, Kansas, Eva and John Whipple were also affected by the events in the Indian Territory. Now, whenever something was stolen in Meade or in the surrounding settlements, the Daltons were blamed and fingers were pointed at anyone associated with the family. Under this pressure, Eva, John, and little Maude Whipple decided to sell their new house and relocate. The town they chose to relocate to was Kingfisher, Oklahoma.

The younger members of the Dalton family—girl and boys—were all coming home again just as their name was on everyone's lips.

III

A new iteration of the Dalton Gang was formed in the months following the Leliaetta robbery. Bob's authority and his direction of their activities were never challenged by other members of the gang, who recognized not only his leadership qualities when they were all in action, but also his ability to recognize and seize opportunities when they presented themselves. Plus, physically, he was probably the toughest of them all. Bob was down in spirit as he rode away from Leliaetta, but the months that followed gave him the time and space he needed to work through his own priorities and to think about where and how he could achieve the things that were becoming increasingly important to him.

With some of his share of the takings from Leliaetta, Bob set up an alternative home for himself and Florence in Greer County, originally part of Texas but now claimed by Oklahoma. There they lived a quiet and respectable life, and there they received visitors, including Tom Evans and Texas Jack, the names used in those parts by Bill Powers and Dick Broadwell. Also visiting there were his brother Emmett and Julia Johnson. There is even a suggestion that the two couples traveled across Texas to Galveston, partly on holiday and partly to investigate the possibilities of moving across to Mexico or sailing all the way down to South America and starting anew in one of the countries there, maybe Argentina, maybe somewhere else.

Bob and Florence spent the winter of 1891/92 at their new home in Greer County. When spring came, Bob had renewed energy, renewed plans, and a conviction that 1892 would offer opportunities far more lucrative than he had seen in 1891.

The new year also promised to be a big one for two of Bob's brothers. Bill Dalton found success in Bartlesville. He was a canny businessman, and as a land dealer had the skill to buy properties when the local market was down and sell them when the market was high. Bill was also keen to assist in community activities, and most of Bartlesville accepted that; like his older brothers in California and Ben and young Simon over in Kingfisher, he was one of the good Daltons; the bad Daltons were presumably somewhere down in Mexico by now. It was only partially accurate as an assessment. The persona Bill showed in public was that of a good and responsible Dalton, making his way in the Oklahoma Territory as well as he could, building up a business and saving money until he could bring Jennie and the children out to Bartlesville to help grow the town.

There was another side that Bill kept well hidden. He remained in close contact with his "bad" brothers, Bob and Emmett, and he may even have tried to bend Bob to his will. This was never going to happen, and on more than one occasion Emmett had to act as a peacemaker between the two. The two did reach an agreed modus operandi whereby Bill would have some input into the gang's plans but Bob would retain control over the action on those plans. For his part, Bill was to remain the gang's main conduit to the wider Oklahoma community. He would keep his ear to the ground, listening for details of potential targets while also monitoring the activities of local law enforcement officers. If necessary, he would pay for information, something that was becoming a steady drain on the gang's finances.

Early in the new year they all received a boost when Grat arrived after his epic cross-country ride and then a few clandestine days with family in Kingfisher. He spoke of his experiences in his short, hard-bitten manner, and it was a story that still moved Emmett forty years later: "To ride fifteen weeks, as Grat did, with a constant eye for pursuit or ambush; to march with only one phantom shadow day by day across interminable plains and heedless hills. To dwell aloof night by night beside tiny chip fires, with saddle for pillow and rifle for bedfellow. To look askance at every chance wayfarer—all this compels a man's mind inward to take profound stock of himself."

His brothers found that his experiences had also changed Grat, not a lot but enough to be noticeable. His bitterness, never far from the surface, had grown to include grudges against railroads, courts, lawyers, and practically the whole of the state of California. Paradoxically, Grat had also developed a self-deprecating sense of humor, an attitude that saw everything as part of a grand cosmic conspiracy against him. When things didn't work out as he wanted them to, he laughed, because this confirmed his suspicions about his role in life. If they went his way, he laughed even more because he had just put one over on whoever it was pulling the strings. Mostly, he just seemed happy. He was back with the brothers he loved, back with the brothers who loved him.

Bob and Bill Dalton's various contacts and sources came up with an interesting possibility. One of the Katy's services was expected to be carrying around $70,000 on one of its scheduled runs. The money was the annuity for the Sac and Fox Nations and was sent to their agency in the Indian Territory. Bob believed the best place to stage a holdup of that particular train would be at Red Rock, a small stop forty miles south of Arkansas City in the Indian Territory. He knew Red Rock; the place consisted of a depot and a trader's store, some cattle pens, and a few Indian shanties.

The train carrying the Sac and Fox annuities was scheduled to pass through Red Rock late in the evening of June 1, 1892. After some general discussions and sounding the others out, the men who had been at Leliaetta, plus Grat, had several meetings at a number of venues in May. It was agreed that they would all meet at a designated point not far from Red Rock early in the afternoon of Wednesday June 1. It was also agreed that they would travel to the rendezvous point singly or in pairs to avoid arousing suspicion. The gang and its members were known and wanted; all eyes were looking for them, all arms were raised against them.

The gang met as planned at a quiet and secluded spot within easy riding distance of Red Rock during the early afternoon of June 1, all positive they had not been spotted or followed. Again, weapons were checked and rechecked, and roles determined by the turn of a card. Later, when it was dark, they rode to Red Rock where they left their horses in the charge of George Newcomb, who had drawn the low card, and were all in position before the train's expected arrival time of 10:40 P.M.

The train pulled in right on time, but, looking at it, Bob realized that something was not right. The rest of the train had all its traveling and interior lights on, but the smoking car—usually brightly lit and containing groups of men smoking, reading, and the like—was dark, and it was impossible to see what was within. He called to the others to stay where they were and to not make a sound. Bob was correct to do this. The train was a special rather than a regular service and was carrying $70,000 for the Sac and Fox annuities, but authorities had received reports of "suspicious characters" hanging around Red Rock. The darkened smoking carriage contained a large group of heavily armed men under the command of Wells Fargo detective Fred Dodge and Deputy US Marshal Heck Thomas. Had the gang attempted to hold up the train, there would have been a bloodbath. So, they sat back in the darkness and waited while the train pulled in, stopped, and pulled out a few minutes later.

While they were waiting for Red Rock to settle down after the departure of the special train, one of the gang spotted the headlight of another train approaching Red Rock from the same direction as the special train. It was the regularly scheduled service, and Bob thought they might have a look at what it carried. As it approached the station, the men all returned to their original positions. That train always stopped at Red Rock, and as it slowed to a stop this time, the gang went into action.

Charlie Pierce and George Newcomb, released from his shepherding duties, jumped up into the cabin of the locomotive, surprising an armed guard who had been sitting on a pile of wood at the front of the tender, eating a sandwich. The guard stumbled as he attempted to stand up and was quickly confronted and disarmed by Newcomb. The guard, the engineer—a man named Carl Mack—and fireman Frank Rogers were ordered down from the locomotive and at gunpoint marched back to the express carriage. There, they found the rest of the gang standing back and staring at the express carriage door. A standoff had quickly developed.

There were two men inside the express carriage; the messenger, a man named Elston Whitlesey, and a guard named John Riehl. When they saw shadowy figures outside as the train pulled into Red Rock, the men extinguished the lights in the carriage and locked the door. They also agreed not to open the door to anyone. When rough voices from outside demanded that the men open the door, they called back a refusal, something that prompted a fusillade of bullets through the door. Whitlesey and Riehl responded in kind, firing their own volley through the door and scattering the bandits outside. Even someone shooting up at them from underneath the carriage did not force the issue with the locked door.

Finally, Bob told two of the others to take Frank Rogers back to the tender to collect his coal pick and bring it back to the express car. There, Bob ordered Rogers to smash a way through the door. Carl Mack, realizing that his fireman would probably be killed by those on the inside if he attempted to break down the door and by those on the outside if he didn't, pleaded with Whitlesey and Riehl to stop shooting. They did, and within just a minute or two Rogers had smashed a hole in the door large enough for a man to crawl through.

Bob then ordered Rogers to climb through the hole he had made and unlock the door from the inside. Once in the carriage, Riehl told Rogers to go to the rear of the car and lie on the floor. The guard then called out to the bandits, saying he would shoot the first person to appear in the hole in the door. The response to that was quick and brutal—the gang poured bullets into the carriage for ten seconds; later estimates were that sixty bullets were fired in that time. At the end of the fusillade, Bob once again called on those in the express carriage to surrender, promising them that no one would be harmed.

After a hurried conference in the carriage, the three men surrendered and opened the shattered door. First into the car were Bill Doolin and Grat Dalton, armed with a sledgehammer, cold chisel, and their firearms. Whitlesey repeated the mantra that he did not have the combination to the through safe, but it did not matter this time. The outlaws simply smashed both safes open and emptied their contents into a grain sack they had brought with them for that purpose. As they were doing this, other gang members were going through the consignment boxes in the carriage, removing a number of women's dresses.

The holdup had taken a lot longer than Bob was comfortable with—

probably more than twenty minutes—and he was keen to see it over. In a last check of the express car, Doolin and Grat took all the firearms they could find and, as a final insult, took Riehl's gold watch. Mack and Rogers were escorted back to the locomotive and ordered to take the train away to its next stop. Guns still in hand, the gang waited until the train had pulled away from the station before collecting all the loot they had taken from the express carriage and carried it back to their horses, loaded up, and again disappeared into the darkness.

The gang followed the procedures Bob had insisted upon after previous robberies. They rode hard that night and into the next day, aiming for their various hideaways deep in the Indian Territory. At times they doubled back and at other times they separated into pairs for several hours. Where there were trails that others had used, they used them, and sometimes they just rode hard and straight.

When he believed the time was right, Bob called a halt to examine and divide up what they had taken from the train. The money from the safes in the express carriage was a disappointment. Emmett later claimed that the take was $11,000 but, again, he wildly overstated the amount the gang actually stole. It was more likely to have been around $6,000; the railroad claimed only $3,000.

There was more loot this time. Several firearms, Riehl's gold watch, and other valuables from the safe added up to a sizable sum; a dozen or so dresses in the latest styles would soon brighten the lives of certain young ladies in and around Kingfisher and Greer County. It wasn't enough to contemplate moving to South America, and it certainly wasn't the $70,000 in annuities they were after. It was enough to keep them all out of trouble until next time, and that just might be the big one they were looking for. Somewhere on the trail they split up and went their own ways, looking back at the recent past and contemplating the immediate future.

IV

Once again, a posse was sent out after the holdup at Red Rock, and once again the bandits got clean away. No one could accuse the authorities of not trying, however. In the hours after the robbery, the county sheriff put together a posse of more than twenty-five men, and in the days to come more than a hundred law enforcement officers would be involved in either investigating the crime or searching for those who carried it out. None of them were in any doubt over who had robbed the train, and the wanted posters that were printed once more carried the Dalton name in large print.

Catching them proved to be another matter. Bob's expertise at avoiding those sent after him was becoming legendary. The sheriffs and deputies and possemen knew all the tricks he would try, but still couldn't find where he had led the gang. This time, too, they had an additional factor in their favor. The Dalton Gang was becoming increasingly unpopular in the former sanctuary, the Indian Territory. Their activities were drawing unwanted numbers of law enforcement officers to the territory, something that was disturbing for many of its residents. They were no longer prepared to cover for the Daltons or give them the support they once enjoyed. They were not prepared to turn them in, though; they might dislike the Daltons, but they disliked law enforcement officers even more.

Two weeks after they were sent out, all the posses were recalled to their starting points, where they were disbanded.

The take from Red Rock had disappointed Bob, and his dreams of taking Florence far, far away were as distant as ever. Another opportunity offered itself almost immediately. Through his usual sources, Bob learned that another Katy service, officially known as Train No. 2 and running between Denison, Texas, and Kansas City, Missouri, would be carrying a substantial amount of money on its regular run on July 14, 1892. There was not a lot of time to plan and prepare, but he and the gang needed to strike and get away before they ran out of time and country. This time, they came together quickly at a spot they had already scouted, a large cave within easy riding distance of Tulsa. Once more, Bob walked the others through the target and how it could be held up. They would stage the robbery at a small stopping point at Pryor Creek, twenty miles north of Leliaetta in the Cherokee Nation.

Pryor Creek had come into existence only twenty years earlier as a camp for construction workers pushing the Katy through from Kansas to Texas. It was still a scheduled stop for regular services, but it was such a small settlement that Bob doubted that there would be more than a handful of people there. The No. 2 train was due to stop at Pryor Creek at 10 P.M. on Thursday, July 14. It would be carrying a substantial amount of money in its express carriage; the gang wanted that money.

The Daltons did not have the privilege of taking their time in preparing for the next robbery, of returning to old haunts and relaxing because northeastern Oklahoma and the Indian Territory were becoming infested with law enforcement officers and their informants as the reward for their capture, dead or alive, continued to grow. The eight men who had been together at Red Rock came together again at a quiet spot a short distance from Pryor Creek. A blanket was laid on the ground, Emmett produced his deck of cards, and the familiar ritual began, this time with Grat dealing.

Bill Powers was dealt first and drew the ace of diamonds. That meant he would be the point man when forcing a way into the express carriage. Now entitled to select one other to assist in the riskiest of the holdup roles, without hesitation, he chose Bob. Bill Doolin drew a jack, meaning he would be responsible for guarding the train's passengers and crew once the holdup was underway. He was allowed to pick two men to assist him in this and nominated Dick Broadwell and George Newcomb. Grat dealt himself the second-highest card, the king of spades, which meant the second hardest job, that of taking over the locomotive. He, too, was entitled to an assistant and selected his brother Emmett. With a two, Charlie Pierce was got horse guard.

They had just finished that part of their preparation and were talking about what the evening might bring when disaster struck. A local farmer, an Indian, rode into their camp and spoke to the men. A number of his pigs had broken out of their pen and he was trying to round them up. Had the men seen any of them? Bob answered that they had not but would certainly keep an eye out for them. The farmer thanked the men and rode away.

Their accidental discovery put the gang in a quandary, especially as they knew there were many men out there looking for them. They would have to abandon their campsite, but Bob was adamant that doing so did not mean they would have to give up their plans for the train. Rather, they would relocate the site for the holdup to the next stop after Pryor

Creek. That stop, an additional nine miles to the north, was Adair, and Bob knew a bit about it. He told the others that Adair was larger than Pryor Creek, but that he did not think that would affect what they were going to do. It was also farther away from where they were, and so, after cleaning and checking their campsite, the men rode north, avoiding all habitations on the way.

Bob had once lived near Adair and knew its layout, and as they rode, he outlined it to the others. The station there was a raised platform about 100 yards long with the depot office at its northern end and a coal shed on the other side of the tracks and down a bit toward the other end. The platform ran parallel to Adair's main street. Because Adair was a larger settlement than any other in the immediate region, Bob suspected that there might be people on hand to meet the train. They could not afford to have those people wandering at large as they attempted to rob the train. Therefore, before the train arrived, they planned to round up everyone on the platform and hold them in the depot office until they were ready to depart.

Just at dusk, the men rode through Adair, singly or in pairs and at staggered intervals, so that they could all have a look at the town and its station. They came together in light brush a distance beyond the station. Shortly before 9 P.M., they then rode to a small gully where they left the horses in the care of Charlie Pierce. From that spot, it was a short walk to the station, where they immediately rounded up the few people who were on or near the platform and took them to the depot office. There, the depot clerk was also bailed up and forced to open the small office safe and hand over everything of value. Then, twenty minutes before the scheduled arrival of the train, Newcomb was left in charge of the prisoners while the others moved outside to take up their assigned positions.

Katy's No. 2 train arrived at Adair's station at 9:42 P.M. It rolled to a halt with its locomotive a few yards past the end of the platform and with its smoking carriage fair and square in the middle of the platform. That it slightly overshot the platform was perhaps understandable because the last thirty seconds of the trip were undertaken with the engineer and the fireman very aware of the two masked bandits standing behind them and of the rifles they held being aimed at their heads. Told to stay quiet or their brains would be blown out, the fireman was told to grab his coal pick, and the two men were then directed back to the express carriage where three more masked bandits waited. Grat and Emmett had carried out their roles perfectly.

Elsewhere, the conductor and porter stepped down from the last carriage to be confronted by a masked bandit, Powers, who threatened them with death if they did not follow his orders. At gunpoint, Powers escorted them to the depot office where they joined the other prisoners still being guarded by Newcomb. His work done at that end of the train, Powers joined Bob and Broadwell at the express carriage. At the front of the train, Doolin was also keeping a lookout just as Powers had been doing at the rear. Neither man noticed four figures exit the smoking carriage and, ducking low, scramble across the few yards to an open-fronted shed, the coal shed almost opposite the depot office, and disappear into its dark interior.

The four figures were all law enforcement officers, part of a heavily armed squad of nine who had boarded the train at Denison and intended to ride it all the way to Kansas City. They were not all ordinary law enforcement officers either. Senior, by dint of circumstances, was John J. Kinney, "Captain Jack," head of the railroad's team of detectives. He was joined in the coal shed by Charlie La Flore, in charge of the US Indian Police; US Marshal Sid Johnson; and a Katy railroad detective named Ward. All four were armed with rifles and six-shooters.

At the express car, Bob and Broadwell, also both masked, had called out to the express messenger to open the carriage door. The messenger, George Williams, called back that the door was locked and bolted, and that he was certainly not going to open it. Bob then called that he was not there to argue; he had dynamite he would place under the carriage and blow the damned thing open. At that point, the two at the express car were joined by several others. Powers had walked up from the rear of the train, and Grat and Emmett, with the engineer and fireman, arrived from the locomotive, the fireman with coal pick in hand.

The sight of the five outlaws in the open, clearly visible in the moonlight and the ambient light from the train, was too much of a temptation for the lawmen in the coal shed. Telling the others to aim carefully to avoid the train's crew, Kinney opened fire, with the others immediately joining in. Unfortunately, the lawmen's ambition exceeded their capacity, and all they did was succeed in stirring up a hornet's nest. Bob yelled at the fireman and engineer to get down—they were already in the dirt—and led the return fire, shooting several times in several seconds as the others opened fire, too, from hastily chosen firing positions.

The gunfight lasted less than a minute, but passengers on the train estimated that up to 200 bullets were fired in that time. For those caught up in the action, it was an intense, almost surreal experience, even though they had all been in gunfights before. For Emmett, "the whole thing had been like a jumbled kaleidoscopic picture; flashes of fire, shoutings, running figures, bullets booming like bullbats in my ears; the haunting sense that my own weapon had perhaps taken some kind of toll in the darkness." It may have been Bob, both fast and accurate, who quickly suppressed the firing from the coal shed. Or it might have been Doolin, almost as good a shot, and now dropping to the ground to fire underneath the tender at the gun flashes in the dark.

In the coal shed, there was chaos. Unlike the outlaws in the open, the lawmen in the shed did not have the option of moving around or seeking cover. Plus, the volume of fire pouring into the shed meant that sooner or later someone would be hit. They were, and suddenly John Kinney went down after a bullet passed straight through his shoulder. Almost simultaneously another bullet struck Sid Johnson's watch, embedding the timepiece in his arm, while the stock of Charlie La Flore's rifle was shattered by another bullet, with the splinters being driven into his arm. With Detective Ward now required to assist his wounded colleagues, all firing from the coal shed ceased.

Elsewhere, chaos gave way to mayhem. The other five lawmen on the train, shamed into action, left the smoking carriage to confront the outlaws. A couple of their shots prompted many more in return, and that was enough for the lawmen. One ran off in the dark toward Adair, and the others returned to the smoking carriage where at least one divested himself of his weapons, which he then hid under a seat. Stray bullets just added to the confusion. One of them ricocheted off into the night from an engine drive wheel with an angry singing noise; another knocked a coal scoop off its rack in the tender.

The real damage was done in Adair. On warm summer evenings, many of the town's residents would sit outside on porches, especially if the train was due—you never knew who might be getting off in Adair.

This night, among those sitting outside were two medical men, Dr. Goff and Dr. Youngblood, the town's old and new physicians. Earlier in the year, Goff had relocated to Fredericktown in Missouri, but had made a return visit to Adair to catch up with old friends and discuss cases with his replacement, Youngblood. Which was what they were doing that evening, sitting in front of the pharmacy in the Skinner Building, looking across at the station just sixty-five yards away.

When the gunfight commenced, the lawmen in the coal shed opened fire at the outlaws, and behind them was the train; behind that was the town. In the short gunfight, a number of bullets flew wide of their mark. The Daltons were firing at the coal shed, with a couple of shots at the deputies who came down off the train. Some of the bullets fired deliberately or accidentally missed all targets and finished up in Adair. Goff and Youngblood were both hit by those stray bullets where they sat.

The gunfight ended all opposition to the robbery of the train. Now back on their feet and back at the express car door, the bandits once more ordered George Williams to open the carriage. Now he was told that if he did not do so, the door would be smashed to pieces and, to emphasize that they were serious, several bullets were fired through it. This time, Williams didn't hesitate, and the door was soon opened. Doolin and Grat smashed the safes open and within two minutes the carriage had been stripped of everything of value.

A spring wagon pulled by a single horse had been brought from where it was hitched behind the depot office, and all they had taken from the express carriage was piled into it. At just the right moment, Pierce arrived leading a string of horses. They left Adair the way they had arrived, riding through the town, spread out and moving quietly and not causing any sort of disturbance. Somewhere out there in the darkness, all the loot that had been thrown into the back of the wagon was sorted and divided among the riders. It might also have been at that point, but more probably when they were riding south the next day, the cash from the express carriage was shared among them. Emmett later said that it was $17,000, but it was probably much less than that, around $10,000. Whatever the amount, it was well short of the substantial payday they had all been hoping for.

Behind them, in Adair, they had left a scene of considerable confusion. "Captain Jack"—John Kinney—believed that he had just faced the full strength of the Dalton Gang and that there had been up to a dozen men, and perhaps more, in the gang. Forming a posse to chase them was just not feasible; he and the next two senior officers had all suffered wounds that required treatment, but that treatment couldn't be given at Adair. The two doctors' cries for help had been heard, and their injuries were serious enough to require urgent medical attention. Given what he had seen and heard at the Adair station that night, Kinney was also uncertain about the reliability of some of the men who would be in the posse. He chose the safe option, instructing that all men wounded be placed aboard train No. 2 and taken to the next station, Vinita, where he had organized medical assistance for them all.

At Vinita, the wounded were treated by the town's doctor. Kinney's was the worst of the lawmen's wounds; the other two were largely superficial, fixed with a cleaning out and a stitching up. Kinney also insisted on stitches and bandages on the grounds that he still had work to do. The doctors' wounds were found to be even more serious than they had first appeared. Goff's was quite a horrific wound; his knee had been completely shattered by a bullet but, more significantly, several major blood vessels had been severed, and he had lost a lot of blood. He died on the operating table. Youngblood's foot wound was also serious, with dozens of small bones so badly broken that the doctor had no choice but to remove part of his foot; a permanent limp would be his memento from the raid.

Perhaps feeling crestfallen and maybe feeling a little embarrassed, Sid Johnson and Charlie La Flore joined Kinney on the next train south to Muskogee, where the lawmen hoped to organize a large and well-armed posse to chase the Dalton Gang. They would not take the deputies from the train (they had proved unreliable), but Kinney believed that with suitable men he could take on the gang again, and this time wipe them out.

Bob was generally a positive person, a man who saw opportunities where others saw problems, someone whose optimism and enthusiasm had the capacity to both inspire and drive others. If he was ever to become pessimistic, to share with his brother Grat the view that the cosmos was always plotting to upset him, it would have been on the ride away from Adair. Whereas the others would have laughed and ribbed each other over what each had or had not done as the robbery unfolded, Bob would have replayed the action over and over again in his mind. It had been a close-run thing, for sure. If the lawmen had been better organized, had shown more heart, or had been better shots, not all of them would now be riding away.

Bob suspected that things would now grow harder than they had been to date. Every train carrying a substantial amount of money would also be carrying a substantial number of armed guards. Even the regularly scheduled trains, like the one they had taken at Red Rock, would be carrying an armed guard in the locomotive, another in the express carriage, and who knew what else. They had been lucky so far, but it would be foolhardiness to try to push that luck. He had also heard Grat say earlier that the train had been expecting trouble at Pryor Creek. If that was true, it meant that somewhere in the gang or among their contacts was someone who did not know how to keep their mouth shut.

Among the discussions Bob had never held with the others was that of exactly how much money a man would need to take his woman to a new country and a new life. Bob suspected it would be a minimum of $10,000, but $20,000 or even $30,000 would be preferable. Given that was an amount for each of them, a successful robbery would need to net the gang tens of thousands of dollars, and that was a minimum. Any trains carrying that amount of money would now be so well guarded as to be impregnable.

The only realistic alternative was now a bank, and a bank in a large enough town to have a requirement to carry that amount of cash. Bob knew of such a bank and he knew of such a town, and it was a place that he and his brothers knew well because they had grown up nearby. It was in Kansas and its name was Coffeyville.

PART II

COFFEYVILLE

5 THE PEOPLE OF THE MIDDLE WATERS

On the fertile plains of southeastern Kansas, along the banks of the Verdigris River, the idea of a town named Coffeyville, and of farmers and buildings and bankers, was very much a nineteenth-century concept, because before that century in the beautiful wilderness there was only the annual changing of the seasons, the vast herds of buffalo whose movements followed those seasons, and the Native Americans whose lives were intertwined with those of the buffalo. And even then, those Native Americans, the Osage, were relative newcomers to the area. The Osage—the People of the Middle Waters—had been pushed south and west to that part of the plains by stronger tribes, such as the Iroquois, who moved into the Osage's traditional hunting territory in the Ohio River valley. They arrived at the end of their migration, the verdant plains that would eventually form part of Kansas, in the early seventeenth century, around the same time as Spanish explorers from Mexico were pushing northward into the area. The Osage stayed; the Spanish did not.

As they lived their lives, the Osage were unaware of what was happening far away to the east until increasing pressure from other displaced Native American tribes and the arrival of white, European faces changed their way of life forever. They were not aware, for instance, that up until the year those white men called 1803, their range had been considered part of the French Empire (if they were even aware that such a thing existed), or that in the year of 1803 their lands had been sold to a new country called the United States of America. In the coming years, however, the changes would be more noticeable, more frequent, and almost completely irreversible. In 1827, some distance to the north, a US Army colonel named Henry Leavenworth established a fort he named after himself. Ironically, one of the reasons Fort Leavenworth was established was to provide a place to settle disputes among Native American tribes on what was regarded as the western frontier of the United States. The irony was that many of those disputes were actually caused by US encroachments into tribal areas.

The same year that Fort Leavenworth was established, the first white American farmer prepared land for cropping in what would become the Territory of Kansas. His name was Daniel Morgan Boone, and his father was one of the most famous of all American frontiersmen. Increasing numbers of white travelers were also crossing Osage lands on what they called the Santa Fe Trail, but it was the politicians in faraway Washington who would now determine the future of the region. One of the first imperatives those politicians addressed was their citizens' apparently insatiable appetite for land in the south and west. To feed that appetite, Native American tribes were cajoled, bribed, or simply forced to cede their land to the United States and then relocate to a vast reserve given the somewhat disingenuous title of the Indian Territory, rich country to the northeast of Texas. There, the Cherokee Nation would sit alongside the Choctaw and Pawnee Nations, the Sac and Fox and Seminole Nations, and, ultimately, the Osage Nation.

A second imperative was balancing the power between slave and free states, and Kansas became part of the political maneuvering that would ultimately end in the Civil War. In the rush to balance the ledger between the competing interests, in 1854 Kansas was declared an official territory of the United States and opened up to closer settlement. That original Kansas Territory included all of present-day Kansas but extended west to the peaks of the Rocky Mountains. While settlers streamed into the new territory from pro-slavery areas in Missouri and Texas, abolitionist emigrant companies, primarily in New York and New England, also sent armed pioneers, guaranteeing there would be bloody clashes in the territory in the run-up to its statehood.

That statehood was enacted on January 29, 1861, when Kansas was admitted to the union as the thirty-fourth state. It was not without disappointment, because the western third of the territory was excised to become part of the new Colorado Territory. Just a few months later, the

Civil War broke out, convulsing the country for four years. In the wake of that conflict, the western frontier of the newly reunited states would undergo a remarkable transformation, driven in part by veterans from both sides in the war. Coffeyville, and its story, is broadly typical of that transformation.

In southeastern Kansas, the transformation was driven by steel and, in particular, the steel rails that carried the rolling stock of the various railroad companies vying to open up the great plains for exploitation. One of the first in that race was the Atchison, Topeka and Santa Fe Railroad, first chartered in 1859 but inactive during the Civil War. It began track construction in 1868, laying track south from Topeka to Emporia in central Kansas, its expansion across the state being matched by that of the rival Kansas Pacific Railroad. At key points along the tracks, and sometimes ahead of the advancing work, small settlements sprang up to either support construction or to tap into the opportunities that the railroad offered. Across Kansas, and across the Great Plains, the steel rails brought a new civilization into an ancient landscape. The 1870s and 80s saw 300,000 people move from somewhere else into the newly opened areas of Kansas.

There were several attempts made to establish a settlement on the rich plains of southeastern Kansas. The first was in 1869 at a small spot a band of entrepreneurs named Clymore after the chief of a local band of Osage Indians. It contained a single trading post and soon failed. The following year, a second attempt was made at a site just a mile south of Clymore, given the name Westralia, before it, too, simply disappeared. That same year a third, and ultimately successful attempt was made on the west bank of the Verdigris at a point halfway between two Osage villages. Two miles to the north was Clymore's home village and two miles to the south was the village of a band headed by a warrior named Black Dog. The new site was chosen by two men, a businessman and an entrepreneur; the businessman was Napoleon Bonaparte Blanton and the entrepreneur James Asbury Coffey.

Both Blanton and Coffey had already been integral to the history of

Kansas. James Coffey was a native of Illinois, born in the south of that state in 1827, the third of twelve children. Coffey grew up on a farm, and at twenty-one brought his own farm and got married. Not long into his career as a farmer, Coffey found that he did not really enjoy the work, so he sold his farm and moved his young family to Harrisburg, Illinois, where he became a storekeeper. When Kansas became an US territory and large parts of it were opened for settlement, Coffey again prepared to move his family. He learned that the area around Lawrence, in the territory's northeast, had been settled by emigrants from New England. Coffey decided that would be the place for them; there would be churches, good schools, and appropriate values.

Coffey was an abolitionist and soon became involved in the rough and tumble of Kansas politics, and in doing so became acquainted with leading figures in the struggle for a free state. He knew Jim Lane, a leading abolitionist firebrand, and he knew John Brown and fought alongside him at the Battle of Potawatomie Creek. Coffey also acted as a commissary agent for the abolitionist forces, and family lore has it that he was twice captured by pro-slavery forces, but was also released without harm on both occasions. His politics brought him into contact with Blanton. Both men served with Union forces during the Civil War, Blanton becoming a substantive captain and Coffey earning the honorific "Colonel."

The two men maintained their friendship after the war, and that friendship also developed a commercial side. It was probably Coffey who spotted the opportunity that existed on the banks of the Verdigris River, but the planning of a new settlement during 1868 was certainly a joint venture. The men saw the opportunity to establish a trading post that would serve in part as a way station for goods, services, and people entering the Osage and Cherokee Nations in the Indian Territory just more than a mile away. (Coffey was so impressed with the possibilities that he learned both languages.) The site they selected was also close to several cattle trails and somewhere in the general area of a proposed railroad line. Having chosen their site, Coffey built and stocked a trading post; Blanton built and stocked a hotel. The couple would establish two further trading posts, but for the moment they sat back to see how their investment would fare.

For a while, it was touch and go. Across the Verdigris River, another settlement had been laid out around the same time as the Coffey/Blanton site. Named Parker, it seemed to thrive as the little post on the other side of the river remained stagnant, and there was a single and simple reason for that: Parker had been designated as an interim terminus for the Leavenworth, Lawrence and Galveston Railroad. With that designation, Parker quickly grew to be a settlement of 1,000 people and then, almost as quickly, became a ghost town. Examining the terrain, the railroad engineers decided the western bank of the Verdigris River offered better opportunities for railroad construction than the eastern; Coffey and Blanton's little settlement was now designated as the new terminus. Coffey and his partner were prepared to have their settlement named "Walker" after the president of the Galveston Railroad. No, said that gentleman, we will call our new terminus Coffeyville.

In its last edition for August 1871, the *Western Home Journal* devoted part of its reporting to the opportunities now on offer in southeastern Kansas. Early on in its lead article, the paper's reporter made the point that "the town that is attracting more interest and investment than any other place in southern Kansas at the moment is Coffeyville." After singing the praises of the countryside in which the settlement was located, the writer outlined how "Coffeyville was laid out about three weeks ago and since that time 52 business houses have been erected and the foundations for 25 more laid." If this excitement had been generated before the Galveston Railroad had actually reached Coffeyville, readers were invited to speculate on just what the future might hold for Coffeyville.

To help with that speculation, and to celebrate the imminent arrival of the railroad, the article continued that "the freight depot is finished, the passenger depot has been commenced, the bridge across the Verdigris is fast approaching completion and the cars will be running to this point in ten days." Work on the roundhouse and repair shops was expected to commence in the next few weeks, and the reporter concluded by suggesting that the town would be the terminus of the Galveston Railroad "perhaps for years," and pointed out that the railroad was building extensive stockyards to the south of the town. It looked like a wonderful future, but the reality of the present was considerably different.

On Christmas night 1871, a dance was held at Coffeyville's Big Tent

Saloon. It seems to have been quite a festive affair with only one or two unsavory incidents. In the worst of these, a male patron was shot and wounded in the right hip, and two women also received wounds to their hands in the same incident. Coffeyville was a frontier town in the West, and there were a lot of things that went with that. At the time, the town's main thoroughfare was known as "Red Hot Street," and Coffeyville boasted a full complement of drinking holes, gambling dens, and cathouses. As the railroads moved further to the south and west, however, Coffeyville was no longer a terminus, and the cowboys and gamblers were replaced by farmers and businessmen. Incorporated in 1872 as a town of 1,500 people—take that, Parker!—Coffeyville already boasted several churches and was looking to start a newspaper, a school, and perhaps even its own bank. Oil had been discovered by a resident digging a well within the town limits, but no one knew exactly what this might mean for the town.

Coffeyville survived infancy through a combination of foresight and favorable circumstances. To grow to adulthood through the trials of adolescence would require something more than that, a reason to grow and prosper, a vision and visionaries. Fortunately, some were already there, and others were on the way.

After all the work they put in to make certain their little trading post was successful, neither James Coffey nor Napoleon Blanton played a major role in the development of the town that trading post became. Both men stayed around for a time after the town was incorporated, and both men then ran for elected office, but with limited success, and then both men moved on. Coffey eventually moved on to Dodge City, where he died from pneumonia in 1878, just fifty-one years old, leaving a widow, five daughters, and a son. Blanton also moved away from Coffeyville, to Wichita, where he died as the result of a motor vehicle accident in 1913 when he was well into his eighties.

Both men were in Coffeyville to witness the town's first wedding, that of J. T. and Augusta Isham. J. T. was the brother of Henry Howell Isham, who was the driving force behind one of the pillars of the new town, Isham Brothers and Mansur Hardware Emporium. (The family had always pronounced their surname "Eye-sham.") Born in November 1836, Henry Isham came from a pioneering English family who had risen to some prominence in Connecticut. Henry was born into the New York branch of the family and had grown up learning the intricacies of trade and finance. After the Civil War, he settled down in Michigan, married, and opened both tin shops and hardware stores. Attracted by the possibilities he sensed were inherent in southeastern Kansas, he moved his young family to the unincorporated township of Coffeyville in 1871.

Isham opened a small hardware store in the bustling township and soon realized the possibilities in Coffeyville were far greater than he expected. First, he brought his brother J. T. Isham out from New York to help with the store, and when his eldest daughter, Frances, married C. W. Mansur in the mid-1880s, he brought his new son-in-law into the business. By then, the Isham Brothers and Mansur Hardware Emporium at the southern end and the eastern side of Union Street in what was becoming the town's central business district was one of the best-known businesses in the county.

The hardware store itself was one of the larger premises on Union Street. A solid single-story brick building with a large basement, it had heavy plate glass windows and two plate glass doors opening on to the Union Street sidewalk. Outside those doors, there was usually a display of sale items during business hours, all protected by a large awning over the sidewalk. On its northern side it was abutted by the First National Bank of Coffeyville, and opposite, across the street and facing the open space the townspeople called the town plaza, was Coffeyville's second bank, C. M. Condon and Company Bank.

Just a few doors up from Isham's Emporium, a large boot hung over the entrance to a much smaller store. If Isham's was famous throughout Montgomery County, that boot and shoe store, J. W. Cubine's, was famous throughout Kansas, throughout most of the western United States, and even in other parts of the world where quality working boots were required. The proprietor was John Cubine, born in Bland County in southwestern Virginia in 1845. When the Civil War broke out, the sixteen-year-old Cubine enlisted in the Confederate Army, joining Company F, the Bland Rangers, of the Eighth Virginia Cavalry. Young John must have been something of a soldier because in 1862, as Corporal Cubine, he was captured by Union forces during Stonewall Jackson's

Shenandoah Valley campaign. He was imprisoned in Camp Chase in Ohio until being exchanged shortly before the war ended.

If Cubine returned home to Bland County at war's end, it was not for an extended period. Young John had learned some leatherwork before the war, honed some of his skills in Camp Chase, and taken them to a new level after the war, first in Missouri and then in Kansas. After opening a boot and shoe store in Chatopa in 1874, Cubine moved west to the much larger town of Coffeyville and opened a small store on Union Street in 1876. There, he designed and produced the footwear that would make him famous, the "Coffeyville boot."

By the late 1870s, the popularity of Cubine's boots, and hence his business, was growing rapidly. He was making and selling at least two pairs a week, repairing several other pairs, and making and repairing shoes too. The success of the business threatened to overwhelm John, so he sought assistance from his family, and around 1879 his nephew George Cubine arrived from Virginia. In 1882, George married a local girl, Alice Keyton, a marriage that produced three children, two girls who would not survive infancy and a son they named Charlie. Despite the tragedies, John and George continued to grow their business and that business's reputation. By 1891, they were producing almost 400 pairs of Coffeyville boots a year along with other footwear, and those boots were being sent across the United States and around the world. Locally, among their best customers were the members of a large family who lived just outside Coffeyville, the Daltons.

Almost as well known as Cubine's boot and shoe shop was the livery business of the Kloehr family, run, in the main, by John Kloehr. (The family then, and their descendants today, pronounce their surname "Claire.") Their livery stables were across the plaza and in the next street away from Union Street and were based around a solid brick stable with adjoining yards and pens. Within the stables were individual stalls for almost seventy horses, space for others, plus a tack room, hay stalls, and all the other accoutrements of a successful livery business. Around half the horses stabled there were available for hire, the others belonging to either locals or visitors. They represented a success story for a family of millers from southern Germany.

The proprietor of the business, John Joseph Kloehr, had been born in the small Bavarian village of Aschachbad to Joseph and Mary Kloehr in 1858. For generations, the Kloehrs had been the village's millers, but that changed abruptly in 1870 when Joseph and Mary uprooted and took their family to the United States, settling in LeRoy, a small settlement in northeastern Kansas. After two years in LeRoy trying to make a success of a packing business, Joseph Kloehr moved his family south, to the new settlement of Coffeyville. There he built and ran the Southern Hotel, and there his son John grew to adulthood.

Young John proved to be a restless spirit in early adulthood. Leaving school as soon as he could, John tried his hand at several things. He worked for a while as a butcher and for a while longer as a cowboy, and even tried his luck as a prospector in Colorado before returning to Coffeyville. There, he began buying and selling horses, before, most probably with the financial support of his father, he opened his first livery business in 1882. That business had grown to a major enterprise, and John had been joined by his brother Charles, and by 1892 the livery business was just one of John's interests. Early in his business life, John married a girl from Indiana named Katie Huff, a successful union that had produced four children. On top of all that, John had served as an alderman, a school director, and, for a while, as a deputy sheriff.

For John Kloehr, apart from his family, just about everything else was an interest rather than a passion. He loved Katie and their children dearly, but it was a love they shared with the other passion in his life—shooting. Not only was Kloehr president of the town's shooting club, but he was also the best shot in that club, with his only serious rival being Henry Isham. Regarded as a crack shot with a rifle, for a time he was also the state's champion trap shooter. In fact, in and around Coffeyville, the only shooter the locals believed could match John Kloehr was Bob Dalton.

A measure of Coffeyville's success was the fact that, by 1892, it was home to not one but two banks. The oldest and most traditional of the two was in a modest brick building twenty-feet wide and fifty feet deep next door to Isham's Emporium on Union Street. The First National Bank of Coffeyville had not started life with such a grand name more than a decade earlier. When it began operations in 1880, it had been known as the Ayres and Steele Bank after the two men who founded it, and the bank's success had been primarily due to the diligence of one of those two, Tom Ayres. Ayres had come to Coffeyville from Illinois where he had worked as a lawyer after being admitted to the Illinois Bar in 1871. He transitioned into banking later that decade, and his success was such that he was able to buy out the other backers of the Ayres and Steele Bank in 1885, renaming it the First National Bank of Coffeyville in the process.

Under Tom Ayres's tutelage, the First National Bank of Coffeyville grew into a local institution, as much a family-friendly business as a bank, and, continuing that theme, Tom had employed his son Bert in the bank plus another young man, Jack Shepard. There may even have been some other connection in that employment because, like Ayres, Shepard was from Illinois. There were two other notable things about Shepard. He almost never used his given name of William, and in early 1892 the twenty-six-year-old bank teller had married Elfrieda Hoffman, who had the distinction of being the first white female born in Coffeyville. About the only fly in the ointment had been that the year after he had incorporated his bank, competition arrived.

That competition was the C. M. Condon and Company Bank, a bank its owner had originally established in Oswego, thirty miles to the northeast of Coffeyville. When Condon's bank arrived in Coffeyville in 1886, it set up business across the street from the First National in what was arguably then the most desirable retail position in the town, the front of what was known as the Perkins Building, the grandest building in town, and possibly in Montgomery County, named after the man who may also have been the richest person in the county to boot, Luther Perkins.

A lawyer by training, Luther Perkins had arrived in Coffeyville soon after the town was incorporated and soon made an impression. He became the second judge appointed to the Coffeyville Court, succeeding William E. Zeigler, this honor coming after his election as clerk to the town's first council while also serving on its first school board.

Perkins was also successful in property dealing, which led to his most lasting contribution to the development of Coffeyville. He purchased a V-shaped block of land in the heart of the business district, where Walnut and Union Streets came together and overlooking the town plaza. Perkins then commissioned the design and construction of the building that would bear his name. He was quite specific about what he was looking for; the design should reflect the belief he shared with other civic leaders that Coffeyville had come of age and was a cut above those other Western cow towns. He wanted a building that would reflect permanence on the prairie and that would house not just professional offices and an opera house, but, at the front of the building the brand-new branch of the C. M. Condon and Company Bank.

When finished in 1891, it was the town's crowning glory. Constructed from red brick and ornamented with stamped metal panels inside and out, its two stories narrowed at the point of the V where Condon Bank was located. Light and airy, with large plate glass windows and two large plate glass doors, the southeastern opening onto Union Street and the southwestern onto Walnut. Inside, it was different from other banks, light-filled and seemingly spacious with an ornate carved walnut counter and a cashier's cage enclosed in iron mesh.

The bank's operations were controlled by Charles Carpenter, a native Tennessean, born in 1858, who had moved with his family to Oswego in Kansas in 1874. Carpenter was a graduate of Indiana University, ending there in 1876, returning to Oswego and joining his father's business. He soon switched to banking, however, starting as a cashier in C. M Condon's Oswego bank. In 1886, he moved to Coffeyville, becoming head of the new branch of the bank and vice president of all of Condon Bank's operations in Kansas. Earlier that year, like Jack Shepard, his friendly rival across the road, he had married, his bride being Miss Temple West. With such banks, and such bankers, it was easy to see why by 1892, Coffeyville was entitled to believe that it had arrived.

A visitor to Coffeyville in the fall of 1892 would have been in no doubt of this claim. A ten-minute stroll through the business district where Union and Walnut came together opposite the plaza would have included two large hardware emporia—Isham Brothers and Boswell's. Like its rival, the A. P. Boswell and Company Emporia was a large building, theirs' with both a basement and a second story. The lower front of Boswell's had plate glass windows and doors with a large iron awning above the sidewalk. The hardware stores were separated by Cubine's Boot Shop with its enormous boot hanging over the sidewalk. Nearby were the Barndollar Brothers Dry Goods store and Charles Smith's barber shop, where the longtime barber, his son, and Carey Seaman plied their trade.

Besides the obvious growth in Coffeyville's business district, other businesses were also flourishing. The town boasted a cheese factory, two sawmills and a flour mill, and several leathermakers. Coffeyville was also famous, in southeastern Kansas at least, for its brickworks, which would soon be producing hundreds of thousands of bricks. In addition to the oil discovery within the town limits, the first natural gas reserves in Kansas had been found not far from the city, for it was now a city, having been declared such in July 1887 when its population passed 2,000. Coffeyville was now both the administrative and commercial center for a vibrant farming and ranching hinterland, an area blessed with generally good land and generally good weather.

Underpinning the ongoing growth and success were the kind of people who saw Coffeyville as somewhere they could contribute to the community instead of just drawing from it. One of these was the town's senior physician, Dr. Walter Wells. Wells had been born in Maryland in 1843 and had moved west to Kansas in 1871, selecting the then boom town of Parker as the place to establish his practice. As Parker's fortunes declined and Coffeyville's rose, Dr. Wells simply crossed the Verdigris River and reestablished his practice in the new boom town. Other doctors had since moved to Coffeyville, but Wells, by dint of experience and longevity, was regarded as the town's senior doctor.

Equally influential in the bustling little town was David Stewart Elliott, owner and editor of the *Coffeyville Weekly Journal*. Prior to arriving in town, Elliott had tried his hand at several occupations, beginning with the military. The Elliotts were from Bedford County in central Pennsylvania, and David's father, also David Stewart Elliott, volunteered for service in the Union Army when the Civil War broke out. Posted to the West, Lieutenant David Stewart Elliott was killed when his unit was ambushed by William Quantrill's guerrillas at Baxter Springs in eastern Kansas in 1863. Young David had followed his father into the military and served in a Pennsylvanian infantry unit for three years and three months.

Elliott returned to Bedford County at war's end and studied the law, being admitted to the Pennsylvania Bar in 1869. He also married a young woman whose surname was Barndollar around the same time. While he practiced the law, Elliott also became involved in journalism, eventually editing one of the main newspapers in Bedford County. Like so many others, though, he was attracted by the opportunities the West seemed to offer, and in 1885 David Elliott took his family across the country to Coffeyville, Kansas, where his wife had relatives.

Elliott's dual career path continued in Coffeyville. He was appointed editor of the *Coffeyville Journal*, but left after a year, possibly because he disagreed with either the paper's editorial policies or its politics. Either way, he established a rival publication, which he called the *Coffeyville Weekly Journal*. Elliott also continued to practice as a lawyer, on one occasion representing Adeline Dalton in her divorce action against her husband, Lewis. He also threw himself into the social and civic side of life in Coffeyville, and at one stage was a member of sixteen lodges and fraternal societies in the town. In several of these, he rubbed shoulders with Charles Connelly, the police marshal of Coffeyville in 1892.

Charles Connelly was an accidental marshal, having been approached to take up a position that no one else in the town seemed to want. Coffeyville was a largely law-abiding town, but in early 1892, the town fathers had become concerned about what they called "the joints." In 1880, Kansas voters had approved the prohibition of the sale or consumption of alcoholic beverages in the state. Now, there were suspicions that a number of secret bars—the joints—were engaged in the sale of alcohol, which was being consumed on the premises. If alcohol was being consumed, there might also be gambling, and who knew what else. Hence the approach to Connelly, who some may have considered an interesting choice.

Connelly was part of a family that could trace its lineage back to Ireland and had moved via North Carolina and Kentucky to Parke County in western Indiana where Charles was born in November 1845. At the age of seventeen, he enlisted in the Ninth Indiana Artillery Battery, serving with the unit for the duration of the war. Connelly returned home after hostilities ceased and began a career as a schoolteacher. In 1867, he married Mary McCord, and the couple quickly had two children, a son they named Bert and a daughter they named Grace, before Mary passed away in 1874.

Two years after the tragedy, Connelly married Sarah Alexander, a union that also produced two children, a son who died in infancy and a daughter the couple named Jessie. In 1885, he moved Sarah and the three children to Kansas, first to Garden City, then to Independence, and finally, in 1888, to Coffeyville, where he took over as headmaster at the public school. He had little hesitation in accepting the position of police marshal when it was offered to him in May 1892. He successfully cleaned up "the joints" using a combination of persuasion and references to his friend, Montgomery County sheriff Tom Callahan, based over there in the county seat of Independence. The job done, by the fall of 1892, Connelly was looking forward to tendering his resignation and taking up a new job, first principal at the nearly completed Coffeyville High School.

Coffeyville was a vibrant and prosperous city as it entered the last quarter of 1892. That prosperity continued to attract investors and investments, young families and older men and women, all those looking for somewhere safe and quiet and comfortable. It was a prosperity and an opportunity that also attracted Bob Dalton, still looking for the one big job that would make it all worthwhile.

6 THE EDGE OF THE ABYSS

I

John Kinney's failure to put together a posse at Muskogee did not signify that the Dalton Gang would get away without pursuit, and elsewhere, large and determined posses were assembled and out after the outlaw gang. While those posses were being brought together, the express and railroad companies announced that they had placed a $5,000 reward, in addition to any existing rewards, on the head of each member of the Dalton Gang, for their capture and conviction. This brought the total amount for the gang's capture to $40,000, until then the largest reward offered for the capture of any band of American outlaws. The offers were unconditional; the reward monies would be paid for the outlaws, dead or alive. Then, in addition to the warrants already extant for robbery, new murder warrants were issued by the federal court at Fort Smith in Arkansas.

The posses that were formed were led by some of the best-known man hunters in the West, including Wells Fargo's Fred Dodge and deputy US marshals Heck Thomas, Bill Tilghman, and Danish-born Chris Madsen. Now they would all be out there hoping for more than a per diem, a traveling allowance, and the satisfaction of capturing the West's most wanted men. For them, there might also be a pot of gold at the end of the trail.

The gang they would all be chasing rode all night to put as much distance between themselves and the pursuers, eventually stopping at daybreak and setting up a camp at Blue Springs, east of the Grand River, deep into the Indian Territory and not far from the Arkansas border. There, after breakfast, a saddle blanket was spread on the ground and the spoils from the robbery divided up. The amount they had taken was far less than they had all hoped it would be, and once more Bill Doolin led the grumbling over the Daltons receiving a larger share than the others, but it was never more than just grumbling.

After resting for two days, the gang broke up into three groups, each of which headed out on a different trail. Grat Dalton, Dick Broadwell, and Bill Powers rode in the direction of Vinita, traveling by way of a fly-spot on the map called Big Cabin where they again split up to go their own ways. Doolin traveled with George Newcomb and Charlie Pierce in another direction, stopping at the small settlement of Carwosa, where they purchased guns and supplies. From there, they traveled farther into the Indian Territory, to a new hideout they had set up in the Sac and Fox Nation. Bob and Emmett Dalton also rode together, traveling across Osage country and heading west into the Osage Hills.

For the next two months, at their hideout in the Osage Hills, Bob thought deeply about what had happened at Adair, and of the implications of that for himself and for his compadres, refining many of the thoughts that had come to him as he led the gang away from the robbery. Bob and Emmett did not live in total isolation in their hideaway, and the select visitors they received kept the brothers informed of what was happening in the wider community. They were aware, for instance, that the gang was being blamed for the death of Dr. Goff and the crippling of Dr. Youngblood, that people were saying they shot the two medical men down like stray dogs when they rode through Adair after the robbery. Bob was aware, too, that every robbery—and most of the other crimes—that occurred in the Oklahoma and Indian Territories was now being attributed to the gang. Any grudging admiration, any wellspring of sympathy or support that they may have once enjoyed had now almost evaporated.

As his thoughts crystallized around what they should do next, Bob shared some of his concerns with his younger brother. Holding up and robbing trains had become far too risky; the trains were becoming too heavily guarded if they were carrying a significant amount of money, and not worth the effort if they weren't. To travel to and from potential holdup sites—and these would become increasingly distant—would mean traveling through country likely to be patrolled by posses, and where any of their movements that were spotted would certainly be reported. Finally, he had concluded that the lawmen were on the train at Adair because one of the gang's sometime confidantes had reported to authorities that one of the gang had mentioned the Katy and Pryor Creek in the same context.

There were now other considerations. Once again, their money was running low. In addition to their own personal expenses and sending odd amounts of money and loot to other members of the family, Bob paid occasional helpers, such as Jim Riley and Frank Broadwell, so there was an ongoing need for cash. This was a time, too, when authorities had let it be known that anyone assisting the Daltons would be arrested and sent to Fort Smith for trial. Finally, the eyes and ears Bob had in the wider community were passing information to him about the posses out looking for the gang, and he understood that it was now just a matter of time before one or more of them were caught.

So, it had to be one, big successful job, and then skedaddle to somewhere safe, safe and preferably a long way away. Unlike Charlie Bryant, Bob had no overweening desire to go out in a blaze of glory.

For Emmett, the weeks he spent alone with Bob at the end of the summer of 1892 were among the most formative times of his young adulthood. Both men were now outlaws, liable to be shot dead on sight for a reward, something that was driving him down toward a dark place:

> Posting a "dead or alive" reward for a man performs some dark alchemy in his spirit. It places him beyond the pale. He becomes fair game for every pot-shotting hunter. Like a harried beast he goes to bay, mustering his primitive faculties to meet the outward threat. In quite a real sense he belongs thereafter to the living dead; and when death hovers so close inhibitions are lifted from ancient and terrible proclivities. The blood price upon his head checks all inner growth towards normal humanity.

Seeing his younger brother starting down the same path as Charlie Bryant and so many others had taken prompted Bob to act. He chose to intervene, to jump in and show Emmett that all was not lost and that they could all still come out the other end if they could just be a little bit smarter than all those who wanted them dead.

They were not going anywhere yet, so they simply had to be very, very careful. Trust the family and be wary around anyone else. Be careful with alcohol and always have your six-shooter and Winchester handy. When out, remember to check to see that no one is behind you. Be ready to react instantly when possible threats appear. Finally, know what is around you, know what you are trying to do, and always maintain a strong self-discipline.

Bob also revealed to Emmett that he had thought long and hard and believed that the solution to their problems was to switch from trains to banks and, specifically, to the two banks in Coffeyville. Emmett later said that he was aghast at the idea when Bob first raised it, thinking it was a recipe for disaster. Bob spoke of hitting the two banks at the same time, raising enough money in one raid for them all to get away for the rest of their lives without having to constantly look over their shoulders. He also said that in doing so, they would be outdoing anything the James Gang and the Youngers had ever been able to achieve. That worried Emmett too, he later recalled, as it smacked of ambition overriding caution, and, as both Bob and Emmett knew, it was a bank raid that had destroyed the James/Younger Gang.

It was clear that Bob had thought the whole thing through. Speed would be of the essence in this job, and so he thought it would be best if he reduced the size of the gang this time. At Adair, trying to control the activities of eight men had proved difficult. For what he had planned in Coffeyville, Bob thought five men would be sufficient: the three Dalton brothers plus Broadwell and Powers. He would not use Newcomb or Pierce because he thought both were a bit too "soft," too ready to take things at face value and even too trusting. He would not include Doolin either because the big redhead was too volatile, had too quick a temper, and was likely to do something totally unplanned.

Both at the time and after, Emmett agreed with his older brother's reasoning, but suspected there might be more to the decisions than met the eye. Newcomb and Pierce were both good men to have around. They were excellent cowboys, handy with guns, and inured to the hardships that life on the run brings. They were also fun to have in the gang, and always good-natured and ready with a quip or a joke at the appropriate time. However, they were both gossips, and Emmett believed Bob suspected that one of them had been responsible for the law receiving the tip-off about a possible train robbery at Pryor Creek.

Excluding Doolin was also an easy decision for Bob to make. Doolin did have a quick temper and was impetuous, but he was also as physically tough as Bob and almost as smart. He would argue the toss over many of Bob's plans, and both men suspected that sooner or later things would come to a head over which direction and which actions the gang should take. Plus, whenever there was an argument over how the spoils of their robberies should be divided up, Doolin was always the one calling for an equal division, with Newcomb and Pierce his only supporters.

All in all, Emmett thought that Bob was really just recognizing the reality of how the gang was beginning to form into factions and acting before the whole thing fell apart.

Bob also looked to maximize their chances of success in Coffeyville. As he outlined his thinking to Emmett, the plan was to hit both banks, the First National and Condon Bank, at the same time. It would need to be early in the day, soon after the banks opened, so the maximum amount of money would be there, with not much time for any large withdrawals. Speed would also be crucial. Because the banks were just across the street from each other, they should be able to ride into Coffeyville, hitch their horses outside, rob the banks, and ride away not more than five minutes after they arrived.

Over the days and weeks in the Osage Hills, Bob continued to add refinements to the basic plan. The Dalton brothers were all well known in Coffeyville, but no one there would recognize either Broadwell or Powers. To maintain surprise until they had cleaned out the banks, the Daltons would therefore need to wear either masks or disguises. Afterward, they would ride hard to the southeast, an area they knew well and where Bob believed they could shake or scare off any pursuit. Having done that, they would ride down to the Cherokee Strip, where they would split up, Broadwell and Powers going in one direction, the Daltons in another.

Bob had a further layer to the plan, but at this stage was only prepared to share it with his brothers. At a predetermined point in the Cherokee Strip, the Daltons would rendezvous with Amos Burton, a Black cowboy they had known in their cowboy days. Burton would have a covered wagon and enough supplies for a long overland journey to the northwest, with all the men posing as farmers on their way to Oregon. Their real destination would be Seattle, and from there they would make their way, individually or as a group, to South America. At least, that was the plan.

Bob was also aware that time was not on their side. None of the eight gang members who were at Adair had been caught, but there had been a number of near misses, and this time the posses would not go home after two weeks. Their eyes and ears out in the Oklahoma Territory kept Bob up to date on the movements of the larger posses, particularly the well-armed and well-organized posse led by Fred Dodge and Heck Thomas. Those two were the lawmen Bob feared most, and when he learned they were preparing to move closer to the Daltons' hideout to the north of Tulsa, he knew it was almost time to move.

The five members of the streamlined Dalton Gang came together at a prearranged meeting point twenty miles west of Tulsa. The meeting spot was ideal, a limestone cave on the property of a man named Berryhill, above the point where the Cimarron River enters the Arkansas River. When they met there during the afternoon of Saturday, October 1, 1892, they were more concerned with money than with just about anything else.

It was a sometimes fractious get-together, opened by Bob asking all the others how much money they had. Emmett was down to his last $20, and between them the five men were able to muster $900, with Bob contributing most of that amount. That counting gave Bob the opportunity to put forward his plans for holding up the two banks in Coffeyville at the same time, taking enough money for them all to move away from Oklahoma and the outlaw life. His proposal prompted an immediate pushback; at least two of those present said that Coffeyville was united in its determination to see the Dalton Gang tracked down, captured, and suitably punished. At that, Emmett spoke up, saying he doubted if that was true; the family used to have many friends there.

Bob continued by saying they had the opportunity to do what none of the others—the Jameses, the Youngers—had been able to do. Emmett again asked why the two banks and why Coffeyville, but that may have been an agreed ploy, because Bob responded with both force and passion. They were being hounded, they were short of money, and they would never have a better opportunity than Coffeyville now offered. If they were scared, well, that was it, and they should now look for somewhere to hide for the rest of their lives. With the mention of the C-word—cowards—the argument was over.

II

The arguments over before they ever really began, the five men rode away from the cave late in the morning of Sunday, October 2 after covering up any evidence that they had ever been there. The men rode north, through the Osage Nation, avoiding all settlements and keeping a careful lookout for posses. They were forced to make one slight detour, however, when Emmett's horse went lame. They made a short side trip to the Mashed O Ranch, where the foreman was regarded as a friend. There, they were able to exchange Emmett's horse for another, a beautiful bay stallion named Red Buck that had once been owned by a deputy US marshal named Ed Chapman; $100 guaranteed the exchange and bought the foreman's silence, for a while at least.

They made camp that first night in the wooded hills to the north of Tulsa, on a secluded corner of the Peggie's Prairie Ranch, and once more Bob walked them through what was to happen in Coffeyville. Before he did, Emmett asked—or later claimed to have asked—once more why they had to hit Coffeyville, a town whose people had always been friendly toward the Daltons. It was a family rather than a gang discussion, and Bob and Grat shut it down quickly by saying they were both going and that he could do what he liked. When he thought through it, Emmett decided to ride with his brothers; he would be blamed for it anyway and, besides, he had just $20 to his name.

That matter resolved, Bob returned to the actual robbery. This time, there would be no tossing of coins or dealing of cards to determine who would do what during the robbery. The two banks were just across Union

Street from one another; Condon Bank significantly larger than First National. He thought they would hitch their horses either outside Condon or across the street from it. That meant that whoever held up the First National would have a greater distance to cover—not much, maybe twenty yards each way—and Bob had decided that he and Emmett would do that. Grat, Broadwell, and Powers would take Condon Bank. There were no questions; there were no arguments.

It rained the next day, Monday, October 3, something that was both a curse and a blessing. A curse because it was almost depressing to ride in the rain, it discouraged them from talking among themselves, leaving each of them very much alone with their own thoughts. A curse, too, because it kept them alone in their own little world, their horizons limited by clouds and rain and not knowing what was beyond that thick grey veil. That hid the world from them, but it also hid them from the world.

Bob and the others had been aware that the posses were drawing closer, something that had been one of the incentives for the Coffeyville plan, but had not been aware of just how close they were. The main posse, that led by Dodge and Thomas, had cut the trail of the gang the previous day and estimated that they were no more than a day behind the outlaws. In the rain that Monday morning, the posse watched in vain as the tracks they were following were gradually washed out. Late in the morning, the posse stopped and then split up; Dodge thought the Daltons were making for the Santa Fe Railroad and, taking a couple of possemen, rode off to warn them of what might be coming their way. Thomas continued with the remainder of the posse. They moved a lot more slowly now, and the Daltons pulled ahead.

They covered twenty miles that day, camping alongside California Creek as the light began to fade. At odd times during the day, Bob had spoken about the Coffeyville raid, and it was a theme he returned to as they sat around a small campfire that evening. By hitting the banks early, around 9:30 A.M. when they opened, they would be in the banks and on the streets before too many people were around, he said. That made it less likely that any of them, or anyone else for that matter, was going to get hurt. He mentioned again that this would be their last job, and that it promised to be a good one. Bob mentioned the James/Younger Gang's

Northfield, Minnesota, raid, and said he'd always wanted to match Jesse James—then raise him one.

As the talk switched to what they would do afterward, it was on the assumption that they would ride away with a lot of money. After they had rendezvoused with Amos Burton and his wagon, they now decided they would split up. Powers and Broadwell thought they may make their way down to Mexico and set themselves up there, for a little while at least. Bob and Emmett still thought they would go to the Pacific Northwest and then sail south, possibly to Mexico first and then farther south. Grat had thought about things, too, and now thought that maybe he would stay in the United States, give himself a new identity, and live somewhere in the West. Not California, though, because there were still too many warrants out for his arrest there.

They slept that night twenty miles from Coffeyville.

Law enforcement and local government also had sources out there in the larger and smaller communities in the Oklahoma and Indian Territories, and in Kansas and Arkansas. Those sources were throwing out little hints, titbits of rumors, suggestions, and innuendo. After three months, it was reported, the Daltons were preparing to strike again. This time it would not be another railroad, it would be a bank, and possible targets had already been identified: either one or the other of the two banks in Coffeyville, Kansas, or the single bank in Van Buren, Arkansas. For reasons still unclear, the Van Buren bank was considered the most likely of these targets, and law enforcement in that town was beefed up considerably. Just in case, one of the federal marshals organized for extra rifles to be sent to Coffeyville, without apparent explanation.

Coffeyville had heard rumors that the Daltons might raid the town, but those rumors appear to have been dismissed out of hand. No additional law enforcement officers were either asked for or sent, and neither of the town's two banks considered it necessary to employ guards. This seeming complacency was due in part to Coffeyville's continuing to turn its back on its cowboy past as it prepared to enter the twentieth century as a shining example of a modern western metropolis. In early October 1892, for example, the main streets in the downtown business districts were being ripped up before being macadamized and given a hard black surface.

The modernization had already begun, and the town plaza had been completely surfaced. Now it was the turn of the main streets in the downtown hub, including both Union and Walnut. New curbs and gutters were being installed along those streets before their surfaces were paved, and in preparation for the work, all hitching rails and horse troughs had been removed. Anyone looking to hitch their horse in one of the main streets while they conducted business nearby would now have to find an alternative hitching point. It might add a couple of minutes to that business transaction, but that was a small price to pay for progress.

The men continued riding north the next day, Tuesday, October 4, a fine and clear day with no hint of rain. Again, they avoided main roads and settlements and were generally quiet as they moved through the landscape. Around mid-afternoon they paused for a while on a timbered hill above Hickory Creek, about twelve miles from Coffeyville, moving on again as soon as the sun had gone down. In the semi-dark, they crossed into Kansas, and Bob led them to a property not too far from Coffeyville that had a wooded area alongside Onion Creek.

When they arrived at the property, Powers produced wire cutters and used them to cut through the barbed wired fence that marked the edge of a newly ploughed field. The men then rode, five abreast, across the field to the woodland that straddled Onion Creek, close to the exact center of the Davis farm. Reaching the trees, the men dismounted and led their horses into the woods, where each was tied to a separate tree. The men stretched their arms and legs and looked around at what would be their last campsite before the raid.

After a brief discussion, two of the men untied their horses and rode a short distance to an adjoining property where they gathered as much corn as they could collect in the grain sacks they carried. Back at their campsite in the woods, the men first fed and watered their horses and then had their own meal, hard-boiled eggs and some freshly baked biscuits they had cooked at their last stop. By the time they had finished, it was quite late, but Bob just briefly walked them through what would happen in Coffeyville one more time. Using maps and diagrams drawn in the dirt, he outlined their entry and exit routes and the town's major landmarks. Summing it all up, he said they should be leaving the city limits fifteen minutes after entering them.

He had a bit more that he wanted to say, but that could wait until the morning. Instead, he issued a few last instructions. It was already a cold night, and promised to grow even colder, but Bob said that the fire was to be kept as low as possible so it would not be seen by anyone passing by or through the area. He also said they would all stand watch during the night in two-hour shifts; he would take the first, and the others drew cards for their shifts. Emmett drew the low card, and therefore the dog watch, the last one before dawn. Finally, Bob instructed the others to go through their clothes and saddlebags carefully, looking for anything that could possibly identify any of them. That material—a photograph or letter, a receipt or a newspaper clipping—was unceremoniously dropped into the fire.

Later, it seemed to Emmett that his head had barely touched the saddle he was using as a pillow when he was shaken awake by Broadwell. It's 4 A.M. and it's your turn, he was told by the older man. He added that it was also damn cold, and if you stop moving, you'll goddamn freeze on the spot. It was good advice. Emmett kept moving and listening and thinking, and suddenly the sky was growing light in the east. The day had arrived.

III

It was still cold at dawn, but the sun had risen into a clear blue sky and promised to bring some warmth later in the day. The Daltons told the others that it would be a typical Indian summer's day in that part of Kansas. Their first task was to feed and water the horses and then themselves. They ate the leftovers from the previous evening, more hard-boiled eggs and biscuits that were becoming increasingly hard themselves. Grat washed his down with a swig of whiskey. It was then time to prepare for their day's activities, turning now to accoutrements and appearances.

Each of the men would be heavily armed when they rode into Coffeyville that day. Each would carry, at the very least, a Winchester rifle that they would initially put in a scabbard alongside their saddle, and wear at least one six-shooter in a holster; some would be armed with much more than that. In addition his Winchester, Bob armed himself with a .38-caliber Webley Bulldog revolver in a waistcoat pocket and a Colt .45 single-action revolver in a waist holster; for good measure, he tucked a Smith & Wesson revolver into the top of his boot. Emmett would take his Winchester and, in a pair of holsters around his waist, a matched pair of .45-caliber Colt double-action revolvers, weapons he found much easier to use than the single-action army revolver. Carrying them was an ammunition belt holding fifty rounds of ammunition for the weapons.

Grat, Broadwell, and Powers would have their Winchesters and their six-shooters, and all of them would carry 100 rounds of ammunition for their firearms. If necessary, they could fight a small battle at Coffeyville. To disguise just how heavily armed they were, the men would all wear their dustcoats on the road into Coffeyville.

Some people in the town would recognize Bob, Grat, and Emmett the moment they set eyes on them, but Broadwell and Powers were and would remain strangers to the townsfolk. To delay that recognition—and possibly to prevent the three ever being associated with what was coming—the Dalton brothers all wore disguises. After shaving, Bob attached a moustache and goatee beard to his face; Grat another false moustache, jet black, and side whiskers; Emmett opted for a full beard. They managed a mixture of compliments and insults before again settling down to business.

The men checked everything one more time, their weapons, their horses and saddles, and their campsite, looking for any incriminating material they may have left behind. A final quick look around, then up and into the saddles for the walk across the ploughed field and the ride into Coffeyville, now just a few miles away. Bob seemed to be in especially good spirits: "On to Coffeyville," he called to the others. "This is the last trick." It was 7:30 A.M. on Wednesday, October 5, 1892.

The morning was crisp and clear and slowly warming up as the five riders paced slowly down the road to Coffeyville. With their dustcoats and broad-brimmed, high-crowned black hats, they looked for all the world like a posse returning from a search or some other duty down in Oklahoma or the Indian Territory, which was exactly what Bob had intended. It was a morning made for early risers, and the little group of horsemen was spotted several times as they headed toward the town. Early on, a little girl on a pony followed them for a short distance after they left Onion Creek, she riding from one farmhouse to another as the five men rode out of sight. They rode past a farmer named William Gilbert, out in his fields early that morning; glancing across at them, he saw a posse going somewhere, and then returned to farming.

The landscape grew increasingly familiar to the Daltons. Within twenty minutes of setting off, on their right and half a mile distant, they passed the farmhouse where the three of them had lived for several years. For Emmett, "the big light-green house and the red weathered barn stood out clear and remembered in the still autumn morning." Then, an hour later, Coffeyville itself came into view: "We rounded a turn in the road and there it lay—Coffeyville. Sprawled out on a little mound in the prairie, peaceful and familiar in the sunshine. Here rose a church steeple. There was the school. The more pretentious houses. The stores ranked around the central plaza."

They rode slowly—they would need their horses in top condition in an hour or so—and as they drew closer to Coffeyville, they came across increasing numbers of people. Their coats and hats worked, because most of those they met would subsequently state they assumed the group was either a returning posse or perhaps a team of cowboys between jobs. All thought the group looked travel-worn. The occupants of one of the carriages they encountered later remembered that some of the men appeared to be wearing cheap disguises. Several travelers who saw the group of horsemen later claimed that there were six riders, but five men left Onion Creek and five men entered Coffeyville, so it was an issue of memory. The riders were neither greeted nor challenged.

The country road they were following became Eighth Avenue when they entered Coffeyville, and as they approached the town they increased their speed to a trot, the horses raising little clouds of dust that hung in the air for a second, then settled. They also fell into a formation that saw the three Dalton brothers ahead in front and Broadwell and Powers a few yards behind. A short distance into town, Bob led the others into a left turn at the Episcopal Church at the corner of Eighth and Walnut. Ahead, they could see the town plaza and several businesses, but Bob could not see the one objective he was looking for, the hitching rail between the opera house and Condon Bank. In fact, he could not see any hitching rails at all—both sides of the street seemed to have been dug up.

"Some changes since we were here last," Bob said to his brothers as they rode down the street. The plan he had worked so long and hard on was starting to fall apart before it had been put into action. The safest and smartest thing to do would have been to keep riding, past the stores and banks and plaza, and then continue on and out the other side of Coffeyville. Equally, there was a real possibility that this kind of opportunity would not come their way ever again. So Bob continued to lead them, and just past the office of the Long-Bell Lumber Company, he turned into a small alley that ran east–west between Walnut and Maple Streets and parallel to Eighth and Ninth Streets.

The alley they rode into had no name and was used primarily to deliver supplies to the businesses that backed onto it. Its Walnut Street entrance, between the lumberyard and the two-story building, which housed Slosson's drugstore downstairs and Dr. Wells's professional offices upstairs, widened considerably a few yards past that entrance. There were already several men and horses in the alley when Bob led the others in, and they in turn were followed by a Standard Oil tank wagon hitched to a pair of horses and being driven by Pat Doran. Bob led his group 100 yards down the alley to an iron hitching rail at the back of a lot owned by Charles Munn, Coffeyville's police judge; just past the lot was the town jail.

The men dismounted, tied their horses to the rail, and looked around. They were just more than three-quarters of the way down the alley, with Maple Street perhaps twenty yards away. Between their hitching rail and the end of the alley was a blacksmith's shop and it, too, had a couple of horses hitched to an outside rail. Back down toward Walnut Street, they could see the Standard Oil wagon, its young driver now walking toward Slosson's. There were also several dumps of large stones along the widest part of the alley, curbstones waiting to be given a final shape by a stonemason. One such stonemason was actually examining one of the piles. Happily for the riders, no one seemed to be paying them too much attention.

Their quick check completed. The men got down to business. They took their dustcoats off, folded them and put them in their saddlebags. They removed their Winchesters from their scabbards on the horses and quietly checked them, then checked the various handguns they were carrying. All would hold their rifles in one hand by their sides, but both Emmett and Grat carried grain sacks in their other hands. Jackets buttoned and hats sitting squarely on their heads, the five men set off down the alley, the three Daltons leading the way, Broadwell and Powers following. They moved quickly, almost at a dogtrot, and with determination. Condon Bank was 130 yards away and the First National Bank perhaps an additional 30; one minute would see them there.

Just before the alley narrowed between the lumberyard and the drugstore, the men passed the stonemason, a recent arrival in Coffeyville, who was just finishing his examination of one of the piles of stones at the side of the alley. He had moved a number of stones to one side because he would soon be using them on Walnut Street; he glanced up, still deep in thought, as the five men walked past. He noted that they had their jackets buttoned up but he could still see the outlines of pistols underneath. It was the West, he figured, so it didn't seem too unusual. He stood up as they passed and followed them down the alley, past the Standard Oil wagon and out onto the street. The stonemason barely registered that they went straight ahead while he turned left onto Walnut Street.

Ordinarily on a weekday morning there would be three or four wagons parked somewhere around the edges of the newly paved town plaza, but this Wednesday morning there were at least half a dozen, possibly more. At least two of those wagons belonged to Charlie Gump, another relatively new arrival in town. Like several other self-made men in Coffeyville, Gump had been born in Ohio—in his case, Dayton—in 1860 and had moved to Kansas in the early 1880s. He had married there, in Oswego, in February 1884, his wife a native Texan who had been orphaned at just eight months of age. Charlie had started a small haulage business in Oswego, and in 1887 moved that business, and his wife, to Coffeyville. The move had been a success; the business was growing and, more importantly, in October 1892, the couple were expecting their first child.

Gump had won the contract for part of the paving works the town was undertaking, and it was his wagons that were hauling most of the paving stones and removing most of the overburden. That day, his teamsters would be cleaning up the debris the roadworks were causing, and he was there to both supervise and take part in that operation. When the five men entered the plaza, Gump was standing in an empty wagon parked at the edge of the plaza, having a conversation with town constable Billy Hughston. His eyes wandered across to the five men as they strode across the plaza, rifles in hand. He had a good vantage point and watched as three of the men entered Condon Bank, while the other two continued across Union Street and into the First National Bank. As Gump looked through the plate glass windows of Condon Bank, he saw the three men who had just entered raise their rifles, and he suddenly understood what was happening.

Had the five men glanced to their right as they left the alley, the Daltons at least would have seen a man they knew, Aleck McKenna, sweeping the sidewalk in front of the store he owned, McKenna and Adamson's Dry Goods Store. They may not have seen him, but he certainly saw them, and after an initial glance at the five, his eyes jerked back for a second intense look, all thoughts of sweeping now gone. He knew the Dalton family, they had been regular customers, and he knew that all of the Dalton boys had a particular look, a particular way of moving. And though they seemed to be wearing disguises, he was certain that at least one, and possibly more, in that group were Daltons. McKenna moved farther along the sidewalk to a spot where he had a clear view into Condon Bank and saw three men raise and aim their rifles. He, too, suddenly realized what was happening.

Parked further down the plaza, ice merchant Cyrus Lee was doing nothing, sitting on the driver's seat of his ice wagon, and thinking about nothing in particular. He, too, knew the Daltons, and he immediately recognized that there were at least two Daltons in that group of five. He was already moving when three of the men entered Condon Bank and was standing in his wagon when the other two walked through the door of the First National Bank. Cupping his hands to his mouth, Lee called out at the top of his voice, "It's the Daltons! It's a robbery!" It was a call that came back, almost like an echo, as McKenna and Gump joined in, warning Coffeyville that the Daltons had arrived.

Condon's Bank, Coffeyville, in the aftermath of the raid, peppered by rifle and shotgun fire.

The picturesque courthouse in Independence where Emmett Dalton's fate was determined.

The shared grave with Bill Powers's name misspelled and the iron hitching rail at the top left.

Emmett Dalton, Los Angeles businessman and advisor to Hollywood cowboys.

Elk Falls railway depot, typical of the stopping points the Daltons scouted and then targeted.

Posed shot of the dead gang members on a hay rack in Death Alley. Note the misidentification of Bill Powers—Tim Evans—and the cloth taken from Bob Dalton's and Dick Broadwell's pants by souvenir hunters.

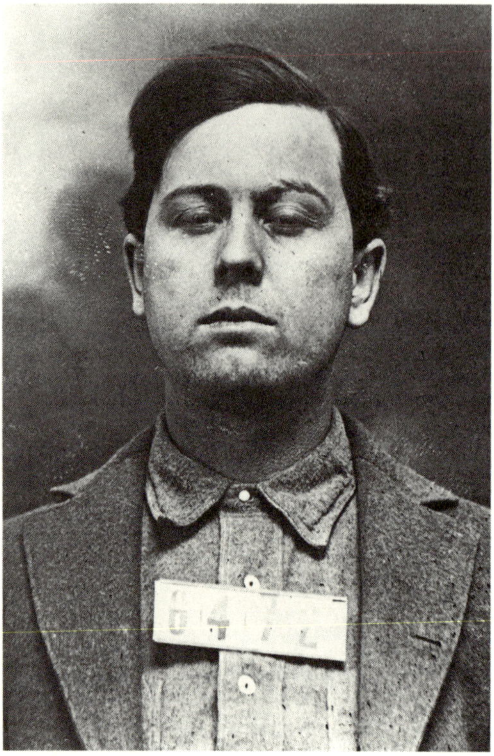

Emmett Dalton, barely recovered, on his first day at the "Castle on the Plains": the state penitentiary in Lansing.

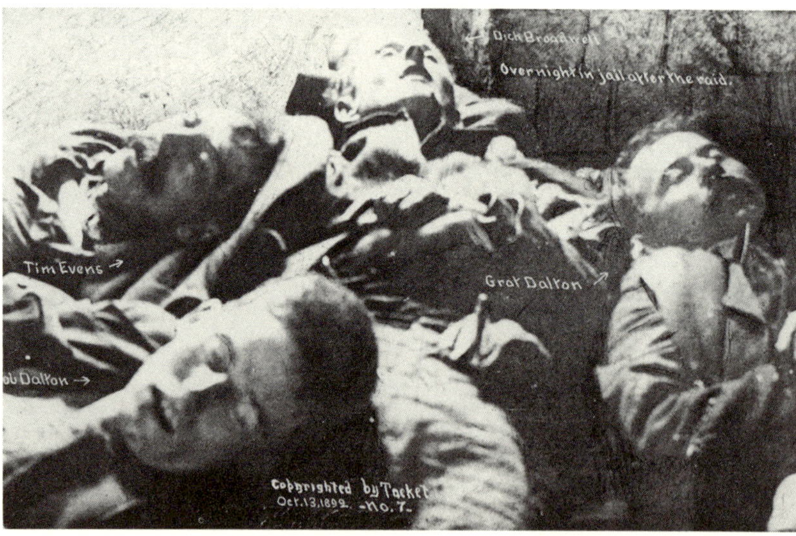

The reality: Four dead outlaws dumped in a jail cell.

7 BREAKING THE BANK

It started off just as they had planned. Grat led Bill Powers and Dick Broadwell in through the Condon Bank southwestern door, Grat raising his rifle and shouting at the top of his voice, "We have got you, goddamn you! Hold up your hands!" as Powers quietly closed the door behind him. The other two now also raised their rifles and looked at what they had standing before them, roundly abusing and threatening anyone who seemed to hesitate in following their instructions. Their entry had startled the staff and two customers who were now staring back wide-eyed at them. As they had discussed so often beforehand, the outlaws all now moved to their assigned positions: Broadwell just inside the southeastern door, and Powers close to the southwestern; both men kept their rifles up, covering staff and customers.

Charles Carpenter was the senior bank official present that morning, and when the men entered, he was hard at work, perched on a chair near the western end of the counter, preparing remittance documents for bank customers. Carpenter was so engrossed in his work that he did not at first hear the three outlaws enter the bank; he became aware of a loud yell and of the sound of jangling spurs, and when he looked up from the counter, it was to see the barrel of Grat's Winchester and to hear the outlaws' leader tell him to get his goddamn hands in the air. He did so immediately.

Elsewhere in the bank, young bookkeeper Tom Babb had just moved away from his desk near the southeastern door when the yelling started. Ducking down, he walked the few short steps to the open vault and went inside, seeking to make himself invisible behind a book rack stacked high with ledgers. The third bank officer, cashier Charlie Ball, was in his office in the northwestern section of the bank. The office had its own door opening onto Walnut Street, but the noises he heard were clearly different from the sounds of the workmen out in the street. They sounded like they came from inside the bank toward the front, and when he went out to investigate them, he found himself staring at rifles held by desperate men, and he put his hands up in the air and stood very still.

Near the southeastern door, Broadwell kept an eye, and his rifle, trained on the staff and customers standing with their hands in the air on either side of the center of the bank's famous walnut counter. He remained focused on them as Grat—still shouting and directing most of his vitriol toward Carpenter—walked around the end of the counter and through the small swinging door, carrying a grain sack in his spare hand and indicating to both Carpenter and Ball they should take the sack. At the southwestern door, Powers was keeping as careful a watch as Broadwell, but his concentration was broken when the door behind him was opened and two men walked straight in.

It would have been hard to know who was the most surprised, but Powers recovered first and swung his Winchester around to cover the new arrivals. He would not have known either man, but they were two of the bank's oldest and most regular customers. One was the town's moneylender, John Lewan, and the other a merchant named D. E. James. As the two men stood still and then raised their hands at Powers's direction, Grat snapped at them to get across the goddamn floor and stand with the goddamn others. It was a particularly bittersweet moment for Lewan, who had actually gone to the bank to warn the staff that he had heard that the Daltons were around.

Bob and Emmett increased their pace as they crossed Union Street and were almost trotting when they entered the First National Bank. Slamming the door behind them, both men immediately raised their rifles and yelled at the startled customers and staff to get their hands in the air and to goddamn do it now if they didn't want their goddamn brains blown out. In front of them they found five men: Tom Ayres, cashier and senior banker; bank teller Jack Shepard; and three customers, J. H.

Brewster, A. W. Knotts, and C. L. Hollingworth; with the bank staff behind the counter and the customers waiting quietly in front. When the Daltons entered, Shepard was sitting at his desk between the counter and the vault, while Ayres was behind the window in the cashier's cage assisting Brewster to transact some business.

Bob went straight around to the far side of the counter, opening the grain sack that he had brought with him; Emmett took up a position just inside the door, rifle leveled and an eye on the door. As Bob was telling Ayres—whom he called Tom—to fill the sack with all the money in the bank, Emmett turned to glance at the door and was surprised to see a face peering in. It was a forty-three-year-old local, Jim Boothby, who with fourteen-year-old Jack Long had been walking back from the railroad depot and were passing a livery barn when another local named Jesse Morgan called out to them at the corner of Eighth and Union. Pointing with an umbrella he was carrying, Morgan said, "They're robbing the banks!" Not knowing what to make of this, the two continued along Union Street until they stopped at a railing set in the sidewalk outside the First National Bank. As Long stared across at Condon Bank, trying to decipher the activity he could see within, Boothby peered through the door of the First National Bank.

Almost before Boothby's eyes had time to adjust to the light within the bank, the door was flung open and the busybody was confronted by Emmett's Winchester and its very angry owner. Emmett snarled at him, "Get in here, you son of a bitch," and pointed the way into the bank. Spotting Long beside Boothby, he tapped his Winchester against the glass in the door and said to Long, "Get away from here, son, before you get hurt." Long was already moving as Emmett closed the bank door, but he paused, stooped, and looked below the window curtains into the bank where he saw Boothby, Abe Knotts, James Brewster, and a man he didn't know (Hollingworth) standing with their hands in the air. He could see and hear both Dalton brothers, Bob now moving toward the bank's vault, Emmett near the counter, rifle covering the group of men now standing with their hands in the air and being roundly cussed.

Long then scurried along the sidewalk to Rammel's drugstore where he ducked into the doorway. It was a bit of a squeeze, though; bootmaker George Cubine was already standing there, looking across the road to Condon Bank, a short-barreled Winchester in his hand.

Neither group of outlaws in the banks appear to have been aware of the storm that was gathering behind them after they entered into the two banks. When Charlie Gump and Aleck McKenna shouted out their warnings about the Daltons and that the banks were being held up, men began running to the hardware stores on Union Street, Isham's and Boswell's, knowing that both stores carried supplies of arms and ammunition.

When the alarm was first raised outside his store, Henry Isham was seated at his desk toward the rear of the emporium, writing a receipt for the payment he had just received from a customer. Elsewhere, two of his clerks—Lou Dietz and Arthur Reynolds—were serving customers at the front of the store. When he realized what was happening, Isham apologized to the customer, then closed and locked his safe. He then went to the front of the store where he told Dietz and Reynolds to arm themselves and any other residents they knew who requested a weapon. One of the first to do just that was Charlie Gump, who asked for a shotgun and cartridges and who then sped off as quickly as he had arrived. While his clerks were handing out various firearms to others, Isham selected a Winchester for himself and then placed himself in a comfortable firing position behind an iron cooking range at the front of the store. There, he had a very good line of sight to both the southeastern side of Condon Bank and to the alley on the other side of the plaza.

Word spread quickly about what was happening, and numbers of townsmen made their way to the hardware stores. As Isham set up his firing position, Dietz and Reynolds handed out a variety of weapons to those who requested them. Gump may have been the first, but he was followed by a steady stream of others. From just a few doors away, Charles Brown, the fifty-nine-year-old owner of the C. K. Smith Barbershop, arrived and asked for—and was given—a Winchester rifle and ammunition. His assistant at the shop, Carey Seaman, was with him but did not require a weapon; he had been out on a hunting trip and had just retrieved his shotgun from his wagon. A quiet young man, the twenty-three-year-old Methodist Church chorister Lucius Baldwin, made his way around the plaza from his workplace at the Read Brothers general merchants store and asked for a weapon. He selected a Colt revolver and ammunition and walked away with them.

The scene at Isham's was repeated a few doors down at Boswell's Emporium. A young leathermaker named Parker Williams arrived at Boswell's and asked for and was given a Colt .44 revolver and ammunition. Williams, whose workplace was on the second floor above Cubine's Boot Shop, understood that shooting from a height was an advantage, and took himself and his revolver to Barndollar's Dry Goods store where he went upstairs and climbed out a window and onto the awning that stretched the length of the sidewalk in front of the store. Moving to the end of the awning, he realized he was in a perfect position to look, and perhaps shoot, into Condon Bank.

Shortly after Williams collected his six-shooter and departed for his firing perch, John Kloehr arrived at Boswell's, having made his way around the southern end of the plaza from his livery stables in Ninth Street. Kloehr had been asleep a few minutes earlier, having a brief nap on a cot he kept in his office, a nap disturbed by shouts and the sound of running feet as someone came into the stables shouting that Condon Bank was being robbed. There were no weapons at the stables, so he made his way quickly around to Union Street. At Boswell's, the sharp-shooter asked for a short-barreled Winchester but declined the cartridges he was offered. Instead, he looked through the ammunition drawer for specific cartridges and, when he found them, picked out a box and headed outside.

The *Coffeyville Journal* later reported, "There was not a single solitary armed man anywhere upon the square or in the neighbourhood," but that was not entirely true. Carey Seaman was able to collect his shotgun and ammunition from his wagon at the rear of the store, and bootmaker George Cubine went to the back of his uncle's shop to collect the loaded Winchester rifle he was storing there. He had brought that rifle to work just a few days ago when he realized that his growing children were also inquisitive children, and he didn't want to leave any weapons within their reach. Now, he sought out the Winchester and stood for a while in Cubine's doorway before moving up to Rammel's doorway, which offered a better overview to both banks.

Around him a dozen or so other townsmen were doing the same thing. From where he stood, Cubine could see the display of farm tools, hardwood butter tubs, and the like on the sidewalk in front of Isham's and a similar display in front of Boswell's. Several men were settling into firing positions among the display goods at both. He could see Isham and one or two others peering out from cover just inside the store's doors and, farther along Union Street, he could see where two wagons had been quickly pushed together to provide both cover and a shooting platform. In front of Boswell's, too, he could see Kloehr in quite an exposed position. Not as exposed as Gump, though; the contractor was standing on the sidewalk in front of Isham's, arms cradling a shotgun and staring intently across the street at Condon Bank.

The men were now all in their chosen positions and were beginning to settle in, waiting for something to happen. It would not be a long wait.

The tableau that Jack Long had observed when he peeped under the curtain and into the First National Bank remained in place for a few moments longer. From behind the counter, Bob snapped out several directions. Emmett was to keep a close eye on their little band of prisoners; if any of them moved, he was to blow their goddamn brains out. Tom Ayres and Jack Shepard were to fill the grain sack he had given them with all the banknotes and gold that was on the counter and in the cash drawer. He would see what else he could find in the bank.

Behind the counter was a vault, and alongside that a short passage leading to the rear of the building. Bob walked down that passage to an office at the back where he found Bert Ayres, Tom's son and the bank's bookkeeper, sitting behind a desk. The only other feature in the room was a door that, looking through a window, Bob could see opened onto a small lot with an alley behind that. The door was particularly impressive because it was protected by a second, a heavy iron grating security door with a spring lock on the inside. Quite peremptorily, Bob ordered Bert Ayres to the front of the bank, telling him that he was to help the others collect all the money the bank was holding. Back in the body of the bank, Bob also told the Ayres and Shepard that he would shoot anyone who didn't hurry up.

Back behind the counter, Bob ordered Bert Ayres to go into and open the vault and bring out all the money it contained. Quite defiantly, the younger Ayres said he would not be able to do that because he did not have the combination needed to open its lock. For a brief second, it appeared the situation would turn nasty, but Tom Ayres intervened, saying that he knew the combination and would open the vault. The Ayres were then told to go into the vault and bring out all the money it contained. The father and son then proceeded to do what they could to frustrate the outlaws, moving slowly and constantly talking down the amount of money the bank held. Tom Ayres was deliberately stalling for time; he had heard the yelling and seen the movement outside the bank and knew that the town was preparing to defend itself.

Tom and Bert Ayres then began a very slow transfer of money from the vault to the grain sack that Bob was now holding. He was all bluff, bluster, and business, recognizing what the two men were trying to do and saying that if they didn't speed it up, someone was going to die. It had the desired effect; instead of bringing out a single money bag at a time, they brought out several at one time and said they represented all the bank was holding. Bob snapped at Tom Ayres, asking if he was certain about that. Tom put his head back in the vault, calling back that there was a little bit of gold there, and asking Bob if he wanted that too; Bob's answer said it all, "Yes, every damn cent of it."

Tom Ayres brought out a small number of gold coins, which went straight into the bag, and again said that all the bank's money was now in the grain sack. Not prepared to take either of the Ayres at face value now, Bob walked into the vault and immediately called out to Tom Ayres, asking him what was in the bank deposit box in the vault. Ayres replied that the box contained title deeds, deposit slips, and the like; that was a lie because the box contained a number of gold watches that the bank was safekeeping for its customers. He then emptied silver coins from a money sack, letting them fall and spill across the floor, and made a final check of the safe in the vault. When he emerged, it was with two packages of banknotes, each containing $5,000, which he had found at the back of the safe. Holding them in front of Tom Ayres face, he asked the banker, "What's this?" in a voice dripping with sarcasm.

Then it was time to go. Bob thought that they had been there a little too long. A quick look at the counter and open cash drawer suggested they had taken all the money they were likely to get, so Bob told the Ayres and Shepard to go to the front of the bank and join the others there. He passed the sack to Emmett and then spoke to the prisoners they held. We're all going out through the front door, he told them, and I don't know what's out there, so keep your hands as high in the air as you can possibly hold them. Plus, he added, we'll be right behind you so don't try anything too goddamn smart.

With that, the door was opened, and the customers, led by Jim Boothby, stepped out onto the Union Street sidewalk. They all had their hands straight up, and the customers were followed by the bank staff and then Bob followed by Emmett. As he stepped out, Emmett glanced around and immediately called out to his brother, "Look out there, to the left!" As he did so, two shots rang out in quick succession.

The two main issues that Bob and Emmett faced in the First National Bank had been a degree of recalcitrance from the Ayres, father and son, and the unexpected arrival of Boothby and young Long. In Condon Bank, Grat faced similar issues but with different outcomes. Grat was a Dalton, but he was not Bob and, in many respects, he was not Emmett either. He was rushed and he was nervous, he was anxious, and he was unsure of exactly what role he—and everyone else—was now required to play.

When staff and customers in the bank were held in place by the rifles of the others, Grat hurried around behind the counter. Stepping out from his office, cashier Charlie Ball took in what was happening at a glance and, when the rifles swung in his direction, his arms shot into the air. Grat now handed the grain sack he carried to Ball, ordering him to hold it open. He then told Charles Carpenter to empty all the money from the cash drawer into it and any money that was on the counter. With Grat's Winchester pointed toward them and his threats to blow their goddamn brains out if they didn't goddamn hurry up, the men had no option but to comply. Carpenter did so with a certain nervousness; Ball was very calm, very collected.

At this point there was a moment that was almost comic relief. Luther Perkins, the town's richest man and owner of the building that housed Condon Bank, had been sitting in his office directly above that bank when he looked out a window and saw what he later characterized as "two armed ruffians" entering the First National Bank. Concerned that Condon Bank might also be at risk, he rushed downstairs to warn Carpenter and his staff. Perkins opened the door to the pointy end of Broadwell's Winchester and a group of men with shocked looks on their faces and hands in the air. Thinking quickly, Perkins didn't say a word but simply swiveled, pulled the door shut behind him, and retreated at speed, upstairs and back to his office.

By then, Carpenter had put all the money from the cash drawer and counter into the sack, prompting Grat to ask where the rest of the currency and the gold was kept. It was a question that wasn't really answered as Grat now directed Ball and Carpenter to walk ahead of him into the open vault. Inside were several objects; a Hall burglar-proof safe with its door open; a large, burglar-proof standing chest, closed and with a combination lock; three canvas bags and a large shelf stacked high with ledger books and document boxes. It also contained Tom Babb, who was spotted almost immediately by Grat. Told to come out of hiding with his hands in the air, Babb was given a rebuke and a threat and told to stand to one side and not move a goddamn muscle.

Grat asked what the canvas bags contained and was told that each one held $1,000 in silver $1 coins. Grat ordered Carpenter to empty them into the sack that Ball continued to hold. He did, but almost 200 pounds of silver meant that he had to put the sack down onto the floor of the vault. As soon as he did so, and as Carpenter continued to tip silver dollars from the bags into the sack, Grat ordered Ball to open the locked chest. Ball looked straight back at Grat and said that it would not be possible to do so, or at least not yet. He explained to Grat that the combination was controlled by a time lock and could not be opened before a certain time.

Grat asked the obvious question, what time would that be, son? Ball was equal to the task and answered that the chest could not be unlocked before 9:40 a.m. The follow-up question was equally obvious, with Grat asking what the current time was. Ball was up to that task, too, answering that he believed it was 9.30 A.M., perhaps a minute or two later. The time was actually 9:45 A.M. and the chest's time lock was set for 8 A.M., meaning it had been open for more than ninety minutes. Ball also knew that the chest contained $40,000 in gold and banknotes and he was not prepared to hand over that amount of the bank's money without some sort of effort to save it. To support the ruse, Carpenter went over to the chest and attempted to turn its large handle, which did not budge; Carpenter was trying to turn it in the wrong direction.

Grat said that they would wait but was obviously suspicious, and that suspicion quickly turned to a nasty combination of anger and nervousness. After thirty seconds, he snapped at the bankers demanding to know exactly what was in the locked chest. Before either could answer, he continued, "Goddamn you! I believe you are lying to me. I've a mind to put a bullet through you! Open it up or I will shoot you. You've been blowing too much about what you can't do. Where is your gold?"

Once again, Ball took the initiative in replying, telling Grat that there was no gold in the bank but that they had ordered a shipment, and that he believed it was currently being held in the office of the town's express agent. When Grat then demanded to know how much the bank's books showed they were holding at the close of business the previous day, Ball again answered calmly and authoritatively. He told Grat that when the books were closed the previous evening, the bank was holding around $4,000, made up of $3,000 in silver coins and approximately $1,000 in banknotes. When Grat again demanded to know what was in the locked chest, Ball told him it contained several bags of coins, mainly pennies and nickels.

Grat thought about this for a second and then told Ball and Carpenter to carry the sack to the front of the bank because it was now too heavy for one man to carry comfortably. It was now 9:46 A.M., and the men had been in the bank for six minutes. As the three men moved around the counter, they heard two shots fired almost simultaneously and a single gunshot almost immediately afterward. Then, after another brief pause—bedlam! A volley of shots rang out as the bank's windows were pierced by a dozen bullets, with glass flying alongside slivers of wood from the floorboards and furnishings. Without a word being spoken, everyone hit in the bank hit the floor.

Bob had planned carefully, thinking of various possibilities that could come to pass after they exited the bank. He expected that some townspeople might try to interfere with their escape but doubted that any opposition would be sufficient to prevent five determined and well-armed men from getting away from Coffeyville. He was also trying to take as few chances as possible and planned the exit accordingly. Everyone in town knew Tom Ayres, and would presumably not shoot him, so he could lead the party out of the bank, hands held high in the air. The other customers would be next, followed by Bert Ayres and Jack Shepard, and finally

Bob would exit ahead of Emmett, who would be carrying the grain sack with all the money.

The hostages would act as a shield, Bob reasoned, but only if the shooters were in front and ahead. Now, as Emmett left the bank, he glanced left and saw where the shooters actually stood. In front of Isham's, among the sale items and awning posts, he saw several armed men and, in front of Rammel's drugstore, were two men with raised weapons, one with a rifle, the other with a six-shooter, aiming them directly at Bob and himself. He called out a warning to Bob—"Look to the left!"—and just as the words left his mouth two shots rang out, followed in an instant by a single shot. George Cubine had fired his Winchester and an express messenger named Cox had fired a borrowed six-shooter. Both missed, Cubine's bullet smashing into the frame of the bank's front door and Cox's missing everything. The single shot was from Bob's Winchester, and his bullet found its mark.

Charlie Gump had taken up a firing position behind one of the iron posts supporting the awning outside Isham's and was staring across at Condon Bank when Tom Ayres led the prisoners out of the First National Bank. Seeing movement out of the corner of his eye, he swung around and was in the process of raising the shotgun to his shoulder when Emmett called out his warning and Cubine and messenger Cox fired at the Dalton brothers. In one smooth and practiced action, Bob swiveled to his left, bringing his Winchester up as he did so. As it passed hip height, he steadied the weapon with his left hand and fired a single shot. The bullet he fired struck Gump in the wrist, exiting at the base of his thumb. It continued on to smash the gunstock, driving wooden splinters into Gump's lower right arm.

The shotgun was knocked out of Gump's hands, and he yelled out in pain and surprise. The other shooters' attention was diverted and most turned quickly to see what had happened. When they looked back, it was to see a vacant sidewalk in front of the First National. The hostages were now running toward them, seeking shelter, but there was no sign of the outlaws. One or two shots were fired toward the front of the bank, but the shooters were now divided into two groups. One group of just two or three helped the wounded man back into Isham's, to the rear of the store where temporary treatment could be applied. The second group, most of the armed men, opened fire on Condon Bank. Those at Isham's were directed in their firing by Isham himself; those at Boswell's were being directed by John Kloehr. Both marksmen told the other shooters to not rush their shots and to choose their targets carefully. And then, when they fired, they should shoot to kill.

At the exchange of shots, Emmett jumped back inside the First National Bank, followed closely by Bert Ayres and Jack Shepard, neither of whom wanted to be caught in a crossfire. Bob was the last man in, and he slammed the door shut behind him. After a moment, he opened the door slightly and fired two quick shots off in the general direction of lower Union Street and the plaza, and several shots were fired back in return. It was at that point that Emmett realized that they might be in real trouble; in the past, just one or two shots kept the locals cowed.

Bob was all business. He looked out through the bank's front windows—up, down, and across—and saw enough movement to recognize that they would not survive out on Union Street. He then announced they would be leaving by the back door, and directed Bert Ayres and Shepard to the back room by pointing with his rifle. There he told Ayres to stand still and asked Emmett to retie the string around the top of the grain sack tightly so that nothing could fall out. He also told Emmett that he was now to look after the sack ahead of everything else, while Bob would look after the fighting. After telling Bert Ayres to stay exactly where he was until they were long gone, Bob told Shepard to unlock and open the back door and then the iron security grate. "Now," he said to Shepard, "you walk out there, slowly."

Among those shooters in and around Isham's was young Lucius Baldwin, probably feeling a little out of place among the older men in their firing positions with their rifles and shotguns. There was not a lot he could do out there, but he might be able to assist in another way. He knew there was an alley running behind all the stores on the northern side of Union Street and he presumed the First National Bank might have a back door that opened onto that alley. If he placed himself back there, Lucius would be able to call out a warning should the bandits try to escape that way. So, he made his way through Isham's and out through their loading area to the alley beyond. There he stood, eyes focused on the rear of what he knew was the bank building.

At 9:47 A.M., Grat, Powers, and Broadwell were still inside Condon Bank. Broadwell had opened the southwestern door for a quick look, an action that had attracted a burst of bullets. All staff and customers were now on the floor, trying to make themselves as small as possible. Crouched behind the counter, Grat asked Carpenter and Ball whether the bank had a back door and was told there wasn't one; the two doors at the front of the bank were the only points of entry and exit. Again, it was a lie. Charlie Ball's office had a door that opened directly onto Walnut Street, but Ball was not going to offer up that particular piece of information. A minute passed and Grat realized that they were in serious trouble.

8 THE STREET FIGHTER

I

Inside Condon Bank, customers and accidental visitors alike had dived for the floor when the first bullets smashed into the building; Dick Broadwell called across to the staff to get under the counter "or else you will get killed by some of those people." Both he and Bill Powers returned the fire that was coming into the bank from the shooters on the other side of Union Street, and for thirty seconds the interior of the bank was a cacophony of noise as the windows and façade of Condon Bank were repeatedly struck by rifle and revolver bullets and shotgun pellets; at least eighty projectiles hit the exterior of the bank. During those thirty seconds, the noise of Winchesters firing in the main area of the bank became deafening, the air quickly filled with acrid fumes and gun smoke.

The three outlaws in Condon Bank were outnumbered by armed townsmen by at least four to one, but the brief battle that was now underway was not quite as one-sided as the ratio might suggest. Grat, Broadwell, and Powers, like Bob and Emmett across the street in the First National Bank, were all professional shooters, men who relied on their skills with firearms to both survive and to make a living in their chosen profession of robbery. They worked constantly on those skills, with regular times being devoted to cleaning and maintaining weapons, sighting those weapons in, and practicing their marksmanship. By contrast, those shooting at them from the clusters outside the hardware stores were all amateur shooters, some weekend hunters, but most just men who had been taught how to shoot, but little more than that. The two exceptions were the competition shooters: John Kloehr outside Boswell's, and Henry Isham inside his family business. But now they were firing at moving targets and, moreover, at targets that were shooting back at them.

In the initial exchange of gunfire, both Broadwell and Powers fired half a dozen rounds each, a form of suppression fire to keep the townsmen's heads down and to give Grat a little time to figure out how best to get away from what was an increasingly dangerous situation for them all. The gun smoke in the bank made them more difficult targets—both Kloehr and Isham were urging those around them to hold their fire until they had a clear and recognizable target—but a number of those townsmen with their weapons were also quite visible to those inside the bank.

Store clerk Arthur Reynolds was firing his Winchester from just inside the door at Isham's, standing alongside young Charlie Brown, the son of the owner of the nearby barber's shop, and Jack Anderson, a carpenter who had been working two blocks away when he heard that the Daltons were robbing the banks. Reynolds spotted a man standing just inside the southeastern door and fired a single shot at the figure. It was Broadwell, and Reynolds's shot missed him but provoked an immediate response from Broadwell's gun. His shot did not strike Reynolds directly but ricocheted into his right foot, entering at the base of his little toe and exiting through his instep. Reynolds went down in great pain and was helped inside to join Charlie Gump at the rear of the store. The Winchester he dropped was picked up by Anderson, who then began to look for a target of his own.

Then, through the smoke and fumes in the bank chamber, Broadwell spotted Parker Williams at his roost on top of the Boswell awning. As he watched, Williams raised his revolver, took aim, and fired a single shot. At that range, and using a six-shooter, Williams's shot was more speculative than considered, but it did prompt another immediate response from Broadwell, who raised his Winchester to his shoulder and fired off two quick shots. The first of those missed everything, the second bullet ended up in the second-floor clothing department of the next-door Barndollar Brothers store. It was enough of a warning for Williams, who suddenly realized how exposed he was out there on the awning. Without further ado, he scrambled back toward the window and safety. Before he did so, he took one more look back into Condon Bank. He couldn't be certain, but he thought he saw one of the outlaws drop his rifle and grab his shoulder.

Williams was correct. As he took careful aim at Williams for a third shot, a rifle bullet crashed through a bank window and into Broadwell's left shoulder. He let out a cry and dropped his rifle before calling out across the bank to the others, "I am shot, I can't use my arm. It is no use, I can't shoot anymore."

When the hostages from the First National Bank scattered at the sound of gunshots, most of them ran for cover with the hope of putting everything they had just been through behind them. There was one exception, Tom Ayres. Filled with righteous indignation at what the Daltons had done to his bank, his staff, and his customers, Ayres rushed into Isham's where he asked for, and was given, a short-barreled Winchester rifle and ammunition. He then made his way out of the store and found a suitable firing position near the store's northern door. From there, he had a good, clear view of both his own bank, Condon Bank, and up Union Street and across the plaza. While others were taking potshots at Condon Bank, Ayres held his fire. He wouldn't shoot at shadows; he would wait for a real target to present itself.

After Cubine and Cox fired at the Daltons, and things went crazy in Union Street, young Jack Long knew he was in a place where he did not belong. Turning his back on the gunfight, he went into Rammel's drugstore, passing through the body of the shop and out onto the loading dock at the rear. The alley it overlooked was very quiet, especially in comparison to what was going on in front of the building, but there were still sounds reverberating up and down the alley. Though muted by the buildings, gunshots could be clearly heard, occasional shots now rather than the volleys that had opened the battle. Dogs—many dogs—could be heard, some barking and some baying, a sort of background noise that ebbed and flowed in harmony with the gunfire.

As Jack looked up the alley toward Eighth Street, he realized that he was not alone. Twenty yards away, standing at the rear of Isham's and looking toward the back door of the First National Bank, was Lucius Baldwin, who Jack knew was both a clerk at the Read Brothers store and a sweet-voiced chorister at the Methodist Church. But now Baldwin was carrying a six-shooter, held in his right hand and at his side. As Jack watched, Baldwin moved farther up the alley, now staring intently at the bank's back door, which had swung open and through which three men now walked. Jack recognized them, too, and had seen all three men when he peeped in through the First National's front window. The first man out worked at the bank; the next two were the men who held it up.

The sound of the dogs was the first thing Emmett noted when Shepard opened the back door of the bank. There were many of them barking, near and far, a sound that would reach a frenzy every time two or more guns were fired in succession. There was no gunfire at the rear of the bank where Bob reiterated what he had said inside, that Emmett was to look after the sack and leave everything else to him. With that, he told Shepard to open the back door and walk straight ahead, which he did. There was no calling out and no shooting, and Bob led Emmett out immediately afterward. There was no one in the open lot at the rear of the bank and no one in the alley ahead until Emmett glanced to the right and saw two figures. One was the boy who had almost walked into the bank during the holdup. He was watching them from the rear of Rammel's drugstore, but the boy was unarmed and posed no threat. The second was a young man standing in the center of the alley twenty-five yards away, holding a pistol in his right hand and now starting to walk toward them. Emmett hissed a warning to Bob.

Lucius Baldwin had not told anyone of what he planned to do. He was not a gunman, he was not a shooter, and he thought, perhaps, that the best thing he could do to help the town that had helped him so much would be to guard the alley at the rear of the Union Street stores. He did not expect the bank robbers to come this way; it would be too easy to trap them, and the alley led nowhere. He saw the inner door at the rear of the bank open, and then the iron grating door opened outward, and three men walked through it into the small lot that opened onto the alley. First out was Shepard, whom he knew, followed by two large men, both of whom carried rifles. Shepard did not seem distressed or even particularly concerned, so perhaps the two men with him were also there to secure the alley. If so, he had better talk to them to find out what was actually happening.

Bob and Emmett did not know the young man now walking toward them, carrying a gun in his hand. They stopped, and watched him approach, Bob calling out, "Boy, throw that gun down. I don't want to hurt you." A short distance away, Long clearly heard Bob's words, and he heard the outlaw repeat the call twice more. Baldwin continued walking, but now had a slightly puzzled look on his face. Jack saw the taller outlaw turn to his younger companion, the one carrying the grain sack, and say, "I've got to get that man," as Baldwin closed to within fifteen yards of the two men. Suddenly, the older man raised his Winchester to hip height and fired a single shot, which hit Baldwin in the left side of the chest and passed right through his body.

The impact knocked the young man backward, and he landed in the dirt of the alley with a thud.

Without a look back, Bob and Emmett headed north along the alley in the direction of Eighth Street. Behind them, Long rushed back through Rammel's to Union Street where he called out that Baldwin had been shot. Several men who had been inside at Isham's had also heard the shot and had gone out into the alley to find Baldwin in the dirt, critically wounded and unconscious. They lifted him up carefully and carried him into Isham's, where he joined the other wounded. None of the men saw anyone in the alley.

At the front of Rammel's, Long spoke to George Cubine. Pointing up Union Street to the north, he said, "George, they're coming this way."

Chaos reigned inside Condon Bank. Any movement seemed to attract several bullets from across the street, so just about all movement ceased. In front of the counter, Broadwell and Powers tried to make themselves as inconspicuous as possible while continuing to look outside in case the townsmen were preparing to rush them. Broadwell called across to Grat, giving him an update on his wound and what he could and couldn't do. It was that wound that finally forced the indecisive Grat into action.

Grat had remained behind the heavy walnut counter with Ball and Carpenter, the timber barrier providing all three with an additional layer of protection. Even Grat realized now that they had to get out of the bank through one of the two front doors. Using the southeastern door would expose them to every gunman on the other side of Union Street, and they would all be cut down within a few paces. The southwestern door was marginally better. The shape of the building would provide partial protection for a few yards, and then it would be a sprint across thirty yards of open plaza to the mouth of the alley where their horses were tethered. He called out to Broadwell and Powers, telling them what he planned, and then told Ball and Carpenter to take the grain sack containing all the money to the front door. As soon as their movement was spotted from across the street, another fusillade of bullets crashed into the bank and the two men dived back behind the counter.

Grat now acted swiftly. He ordered Carpenter to empty everything out of the sack and to not worry about the silver dollars, which were scattered across the floor. The two men were told to collect all the banknotes and any gold coins and put them back into the sack. A bullet cracked past Ball's head as he was doing this, adding a sense of urgency to the task. Grat also joined in, stuffing banknotes into his vest and coat pockets. Telling the bankers, probably unnecessarily, to remain on the floor, Grat hung the grain sack over his left arm and kept hold of his Winchester with his right. Keeping as low as he could, Grat rounded the counter and dashed across to the southwestern door where Broadwell, also crouched low, waited for him. And there, Grat's luck seemed to have finally turned. Across the street, a fresh round of firing broke out, but none of it seemed to be directed at Condon Bank; the shooters had found another target. Realizing they would never have a better chance, Grat opened the door and, with a yell, ran as hard as he could for the mouth of the alley, now so near, now so far.

II

After shooting Baldwin, Bob immediately moved on both physically and mentally. The young man had been a nuisance that had become a problem; he had dealt with the problem and gave it no more thought. The two young outlaws moved at speed now, jogging down the alley to the point where it intersected with Eighth Street. There, after turning left into Eighth Street, they almost literally bumped into a young boy named John Sibert, who had been attracted to the area by the sound of gunfire. In all innocence, Sibert asked the two men with rifles what was happening. The reply was probably not what he expected. Bob shoved him in the body, partially turning him around, and then growled at the boy to get away from the area or he was likely to get hurt.

A short distance down Eighth Street, they came to Union Street, a potential danger point, and Bob looked very carefully down the street before stepping into the intersection, Emmett a couple of steps behind. No one from farther down Union Street appeared to notice them, most seemingly concentrating on what was happening in Condon Bank. Both Daltons could see several armed men, clustered around the front of a number of stores overlooking the bank and the plaza, especially gathered in front of the two hardware stores. As the brothers watched, several of the shooters down there fired their weapons across the top of the plaza and into the bank.

Again, Bob came to a split-second decision. The rest of the gang was still obviously in Condon Bank and, if they were to have any chance of escape, he and Emmett had to provide some kind of distraction and even the odds a bit, if that was possible. Bob spoke briefly with his brother, then both men raised their rifles and fired two shots in quick succession, moving the actions in a blur. Forty yards away, the bullets found their mark. George Cubine, standing alongside Jack Long with Winchester in hand, was hit in the foot, left thigh, and the heart, and was dead before his body hit the sidewalk. The fourth bullet smashed through a plate glass window at the front of Rammel's drugstore.

From inside the doorway of his own shop, the senior Charlie Brown saw his friend Cubine fall to the ground and, leaving his own rifle behind, rushed out to his assistance. When he reached Cubine, Brown understood immediately that the bootmaker was dead, something that filled him with rage. He reached down and across Cubine's body to pick up the dead man's Winchester and was straightening up, preparing to fire, when two more shots rang out. One of them struck Brown in the chest, inflicting a mortal wound. Still conscious, and in great pain, Brown fell across the body of Cubine; one was already dead and the other would die within three hours. The second bullet hit the doorframe of Rammel's, narrowly missing Long. Daring a quick look, he saw that the outlaws were already moving again.

Bob and Emmett had continued across the street, and Bob paused on the western side and stood on the raised sidewalk for a final look back down Union Street. Movement caught his eye. Tom Ayres, now positioned with a Winchester among a display of saddlery and equine accessories, was raising his rifle and looking at Bob. In a smooth, practiced action, Bob raised his own Winchester and fired a single shot. Seventy-five yards away, Ayres reeled backward and fell to the sidewalk. The bullet had struck him in the face, entering below his left eye and exiting at the base of his skull. That wound should have killed him, but it didn't. As blood spurted like a fountain from his shattered face, an unarmed bystander named George Picker pressed down on the ruptured artery with his thumb, staunching the flow and saving Ayres's life. Others helped Picker carry Tom Ayres back into Isham's, where he joined the growing list of dead and wounded townsmen.

As Bob turned to rejoin Emmett, a grocer came out of his store on the corner and called across to Bob, saying he and the other man with him were killing innocent people. Emmett, a few paces away, called out a warning to the man and raised his rifle; the grocer hurried back inside. The brothers continued along Eighth Street on their roundabout route to their horses. They were jogging again, and they saw faces peering from doorways and appearing in store windows, sometimes shouting abuse and at other times looking on in silent rage. It was just all background, and the two men kept moving.

Bob and Emmett had done their job well. After Tom Ayres had been wounded and the brothers had disappeared somewhere to the west down Eighth Street, the men outside Boswell's and Isham's stopped firing for a moment, to reload and to check on their wounded, and to then consider what would happen next. It was the opportunity Grat had been waiting for, and he burst out of Condon Bank's southwestern door, ducking low and running for the mouth of the alley thirty yards away; Broadwell and Powers followed immediately behind. The lull in the firing was only temporary, and before the men had covered half the distance to the alley, a dozen guns were trying to bring them down. Previously intermittent, the firing briefly intensified, the crack and bang of rifles being joined by the deeper percussive booms of the shotguns.

At the range from which they were firing, it would have been a miracle if all the shooters missed their targets—and they didn't, with at least four bullets striking home. Grat was hit twice in the short sprint across the open space, Powers was struck shortly after he ran from the bank, and Broadwell was wounded a second time when midway across the plaza. All were hit in the back, and those watching noted that the impact of the bullets raised little puffs of dust on the man's jackets. The outlaws staggered when hit, but none went down, and, in an act of defiance as they entered the alley, each turned and fired a single shot at their tormentors.

Bob and Emmett continued west along Eighth Street, moving quickly but keeping an eye out for any possible trouble spots. They paused briefly to look down Walnut Street and, when they could see that no one was either waiting for them there or trailing behind them, ran across Walnut and on to another alley that ran parallel to Walnut and that Bob knew would take them straight to the alley where their horses were tethered. As they entered the alley, there was a burst of fire from somewhere behind them, and they realized that the others were now in real trouble.

Town police marshal Charles Connelly had joined the town's defenders at Boswell's Emporium shortly before the outlaws had broken out of Condon Bank, and after what had already been an eventful morning. Connelly and his wife had been up early that morning helping the eldest children, Bert and Grace, prepare for their day's adventure. They were to catch the morning train to Topeka, where they would spend the day at the State Fair before returning to Coffeyville on the evening train. The Connellys had seen the children off and then, as his wife went home,

Connelly had begun his day's work as marshal, visiting several businesses that had raised issues with him. He had been in an upstairs office in a neighboring building when the alarm was raised and made his roundabout way to Boswell's as the shooting erupted.

Now he had a hurried conversation with John Kloehr, the two men then joined by Carey Seaman, still angry over the shooting of his friends George Cubine and Charlie Brown. They thought the three outlaws who had run from Condon Bank were hiding somewhere near the entrance to the alley and would no doubt soon be joined by the two who had held up the First National Bank and then shot down several people outside Isham's. The outlaws' horses were believed to be tied up somewhere toward the far end of the alley for an escape out the other end, via Maple Street. If they could either block the other end of the alley or set up some kind of roadblock along it, they would have all five bandits trapped in a confined space, and those bandits would have just two options: surrender or die. The three men headed for the southern end of the plaza to put their plan into action.

As they made their way along Ninth Street, Kloehr carrying his Winchester and Carey Seaman his shotgun, Kloehr asked Connelly if he was armed. No, said Connelly, but he would call into the jail where his Colt six-shooter was hanging from a peg on the wall. Kloehr said he might need a weapon before then and suggested the marshal call into Swisher Brothers machine shop to see if he could borrow a firearm there. Thirty seconds later, Connelly rejoined the other two, now also armed with a short-barreled Winchester rifle. The three men continued along Ninth Street.

Even before he entered the alley, Grat understood that he had been badly wounded, and he immediately looked for somewhere, anywhere, that would offer him some protection and the opportunity to assess what he should do next. He found a degree of sanctuary behind the outside staircase at the Slosson's building, and he ducked in behind it. There, he came to the realization that if he and the others were to make it back to their horses and ultimately get away from Coffeyville, they would have to do something about the townsmen shooting straight into the alley from the safety of their firing positions outside the two hardware stores. Grat carefully and laboriously reloaded his Winchester, and then stepped back into the alley and fired several times in quick succession at the shooters on the far side of the plaza.

Grat's shots may not have been aimed properly but they were not without effect. One, well wide of the intended target area, narrowly missed a group of onlookers in front of the Masonic Block on Ninth Street. Others were better directed. Isham's clerk, Lou Dietz, had been shooting into the alley from behind a cast-iron stove at the front of the store. Standing up to have a clearer shot at the alley, Dietz was struck by one of Grat's bullets. It was his lucky day—the bullet struck a spanner that Dietz was carrying in a pocket. The impact knocked the clerk over, and he would be sporting a nasty bruise for several days, but the young man was otherwise unscathed.

Grat's shooting had one other effect. It was still a relatively windless day and the gun smoke from his firing remained in the alley, not particularly thick but making it just a little more difficult for those shooting into the alley to see their targets clearly.

Broadwell had been wounded in the shoulder while in Condon Bank and then struck in the back as he ran across the open plaza. Then, just after he entered the alley, he was struck by another bullet, this one fired by a realtor named Joe Uncapher, shooting from his office on the second floor of the Perkins Building. Broadwell, too, knew that he was badly wounded and looked for somewhere to stop and assess his injuries, and then regain his energy for a final dash to the horses. He found an entrance into the Long-Bell lumber yard and sat down alongside a large stack of timber. He thought he might rest there, for a little while at least.

Powers had also been hit in the back as he ran for his life across the plaza and was struck again, this time in the arm, when he was just a few paces into the alley. The impact knocked him off balance but not down, and he swiveled and fired a shot of his own before finding temporary refuge in the doorway of the McKenna-Adams store. There he carefully reloaded his Winchester. It would now be another race, this one to the horses he could see tethered perhaps fifty yards away. He almost made it. Just ten yards short, he was hit again and knew it was a bad wound and that he must seek shelter. There was a door, but it was locked and no one answered his desperate knocks. As he stepped back into the alley, another bullet struck and knocked him down; he would not get up.

Neither Bob nor Emmett had seen any of the other gang members since they had entered Condon Bank, but believed they could gauge their progress by the increase and decrease in firing from in and around the plaza. That became more difficult to judge, however, when they entered the alley running off Eighth Street that would lead them to the alley where their horses were hitched. That first alley was a private laneway used to service a row of brick buildings facing Walnut Street, and it was those buildings that absorbed and distorted the sounds of the gun battle taking place just a short distance away.

Around three-quarters of the way along that alley, at the rear of the Wells Brothers General Store, Bob and Emmett stopped and watched in amazement as the store's rear door opened and out stepped fourteen-year-old Bobby Wells, the son of one of the store's owners. Young Wells was holding a small .22 pistol in both hands, and, when he saw the Dalton brothers, he waved the pistol in the air and called out, "What're you fellers doing here?" in his best attempt at an adult voice. Bob stared him down, before advising the boy to get back inside again if he wanted to stay out of trouble. As the boy lowered the gun and stepped back to the door, Bob emphasized his message by tapping Wells on the backside with the barrel of his rifle; Emmett aimed a kick and a curse in his general direction.

The firing from the far side of the plaza seemed to pick up again as the Daltons approached the end of the laneway they had been following, but before they could ascertain the reason for this, Bob spotted movement toward the rear of Slosson's drugstore. As he watched, a rear ground-floor window opened, and Frank Benson, the store's manager, began to climb out. He was carrying a pistol in one hand and looked for all the world like a man planning an ambush. In one sharp movement, Bob raised his Winchester and fired off two shots in rapid succession. Neither shot hit Benson but they shattered the window he had just raised. Benson tumbled back inside and would take no further part in the battle.

When the brothers entered the main alley, they turned to their right expecting to see the others at or on the horses, but there was no sign of anyone in that direction. A quick glance to the left showed why, and they witnessed the other three in their desperate race for the alley and their desperate attempts to find shelter within it. Bob immediately chose to do whatever he could to help the others. He first called out to them that he had the loot and was going to keep it. He also called out that he and Emmett would provide covering fire for them all to get back to the horses and get out of that goddamn place. It was likely that his calls went unheeded and unanswered. The other three were hoping to survive more than for any escape; the appearance of two more targets in the alley had led to an increase in the volume of firing.

In the circumstances, it had to be every man for himself. The alley opening onto the plaza also opened onto a dozen or more shooting positions, and human movement in the alley attracted the attention of those shooters along Union Street. Only men with experience in the Civil War had a point of comparison for the firing: "The bullets, as they passed up the alley, had the peculiar zip that accompanies a minie ball." Before those bullets took a human toll, they caused mayhem among the horses in the alley. The fire from Union Street killed Bob's and Powers's horses before the men had any chance of reaching them and spooked every other horse in the area.

The other, surviving outlaws' horses reared and plunged, straining against the leather that tethered them to the railing. Further down the alley, at least one of the horses tied up outside the blacksmith's shop broke free and galloped off; fortunately, it galloped down toward the Maple Street end rather than back up toward Walnut Street, the area where the five outlaws were now fighting for their lives. There was more than enough mayhem there already. The paired horses pulling the Standard Oil wagon were becoming increasingly restless amid the smoke and dust and noise of a gun battle. Disturbed and restless, pawing the ground and snorting, they began to move in their traces and, if they took off in a panic, the wagon could crush anyone in the alley. Recognizing the danger, Grat shot one of the horses through the head, ending any chance of a runaway wagon.

The outlaws would all try to make their own ways back to where they had left their horses. Bob and Emmett, the two who had not been wounded, were also the only two to act in concert. They spoke to each other, identifying spots that might be out of the firing line, with Bob firing off a shot down the alley whenever the opportunity presented itself. The brothers mostly hugged the buildings and fences on the northern side of the alley, talking to each other and looking out for the others. As they were providing cover for their comrades, they moved relatively slowly, but they saw both Grat and Powers move past them and were level with Broadwell when another burst of firing from the other side of the plaza commenced after a brief lull. Then shots came from somewhere behind them, and Bob realized they were being outflanked.

Kloehr, Seaman, and Connelly, now fully armed, continued west along Ninth Street to a point where they believed they would be level with, or a little ahead of, the three outlaws who had escaped from Condon Bank and fled down the alley. The three were also unaware that Bob and Emmett had also now entered the alley and, even if they had been aware of that, it would not have altered their plan. All three would cut through to the alley at separate points; all three would shoot down any outlaw who went past their ambush position.

Seaman was the first to stop. He believed he had seen one of the bank robbers go into the Long-Bell lumber yard, and he knew that there were a lot of potential hiding places in that yard. He would approach it slowly, hoping that his presence, and the potential arrival of others, would flush out whoever was hiding there. Kloehr said he would continue to his livery stable and move straight through it to the alley at its rear. There he believed he would be in front of the outlaws and could wait for them to come to him. Connelly said that he would also cut through to the alley, but would use a vacant lot about halfway down its length. That should put him behind the three men, and he and Kloehr would have them trapped between their two positions.

What Connelly and the other two hadn't realized was that the outlaws' progress along the alley had been slower than they had anticipated. The three Condon Bank robbers had been wounded, seriously wounded, and they moved at a painstaking walk from fragments of shelter to fragments of shelter rather than at anything resembling a normal walking pace. Each had paused after entering the alley and each was now moving slowly toward where they had tethered their horses.

When Connelly stepped into the alley through a gap in the fence at the rear of the vacant lot, he turned left and expected to see the three outlaws at or near their horses at the railing. Instead, he saw a nearly empty alley and two groups of horses tethered a few yards apart. Just a few yards behind him, Grat had watched as the lawman climbed through the fence and turned to look to the west. As he did so, Grat raised his Winchester to his shoulder, aimed, and fired a single shot, which hit Connelly in the center of his back. The marshal slowly sank to his knees before pitching forward onto his face. He did not move.

The sudden appearance of Connelly, and his almost immediate fall to the rifle of Grat, caused another fusillade to be fired into the alley, and it seems probable that several bullets in that fusillade struck home. Grat received another arm wound, and it is likely that this volley ended Powers's life. It also prompted Grat to turn around and fire another shot in the general direction of the plaza. In doing so, he provided an almost ideal target for marksman Kloehr, standing back in the shadows at the rear of his stables. Kloehr also fired a single shot from his Winchester, the bullet striking Grat squarely in the throat, breaking his spine and killing him instantly. Grat's body fell almost alongside that of the dying marshal, and Powers lay a few feet farther along the alley.

Shooting continued from the men at the front of the Union Street hardware stores, but in single and double shots at vague shapes moving along walls and fences trying to jump from shadow to shadow in the smoky confines of the alley. Bob and Emmett were almost silent now, trying to navigate the last couple of dozen yards to where a number of their horses still stood. They had seen the bodies of Grat, Powers, and Connelly, but in those desperate moments were unable to either check if any were still living or begin to mourn if they were not.

Bob believed that some of the shooting came from a lot higher than street level and knew that sharpshooters on roofs would be able to pick them off at will. It was another unacceptable risk, and one he knew he would need to deal with. First, he would need to know where those sharpshooters were, and so he stepped out of the shadows and into the alley, just a little.

Emmett had a clear view of what happened next. As Emmett looked, his brother stiffened and staggered but, before he could move to help him, Emmett himself was struck in his upper right arm as he attempted to raise his rifle to provide covering fire. The Winchester dropped from his now useless right arm. Now in semishock, Emmett leaned over to pick it up with his left hand. That action complete, he turned to his brother. Bob had semicollapsed onto one of the piles of cobblestones that had been dumped in the alley. His back was resting against a timber fence, and he was looking straight ahead, saying nothing and perhaps not seeing anything.

From where he now sat, Bob could see across, up and down the alley, and through the drifting gun smoke spotted Kloehr just inside his livery stables. Slowly, laboriously, painfully Bob stood up and shuffled two or three feet to prop himself up against the wall of an old barn where he raised his rifle to his waist and fired a single shot at Kloehr. The shot went wide, striking the wall of another building. In reply, Kloehr raised his own rifle and fired a single shot that struck Bob squarely in the chest. The impact knocked him backward, back onto the pile of stones where he sat down, more heavily this time. His back rested against the fence and, with blood flowing from his mouth and nose, he dropped his head forward, chin resting on his chest. He did not move.

Emmett was also moving slowly now, but was moving with determination, clear in his intent to get to the horses and to then get away. With his right arm hanging uselessly by his side, his Winchester held tightly in his left hand and the grain sack hooked over his left forearm pressed against his chest, Emmett covered the last few yards to where Red Buck was tethered as bullets whispered and cracked around him. In the last few strides, he was joined by a second figure, Broadwell, who had made his own pain-riddled journey along the alley. Broadwell was there, and then he wasn't, knocked down by another bullet. He let out a groan, rolled onto his back and stood up before staggering the last few steps to his horse.

Alongside him, Emmett had reached Red Buck, where he put his Winchester in its scabbard and hooked the grain sack over the saddle horn. Emmett was hit again as he prepared to climb up into the saddle; the bullet struck his hip from behind, passing through his cartridge belt and narrowly missing two shells, before continuing through his body and exiting through his groin. The pain was intense and for a moment Emmett thought his leg was paralyzed. Feeling, and more pain, returned almost immediately, and he was able to swing up into his saddle seconds after Broadwell had climbed up into his. Both men's horses were now skittish and, as his horse began to prance around, Broadwell leaned toward Emmett and said, "I'm hurt bad." Then, clutching the saddle horn and the reins, Broadwell dug his spurs in and took off, westward down the alley.

Almost immediately, and with blood flowing into both boots, Emmett set off after Broadwell but, after Red Buck had taken just a few steps, Emmett reined the horse in. He had realized that Bob had not followed him and, turning to look back down the alley through the drifting smoke, he could see several bodies. Three were still lying in the dirt of the alley and appeared to be dead. The fourth sat on a pile of curbstones, back against a fence and head resting on its chest. That fourth figure was Bob, and from that distance, Emmett could not tell whether he was alive or dead.

It was not a decision Emmett had to even think about. He turned Red Buck and galloped back down the alley, bullets whip-cracking past his ears. As he pulled up next to his brother and the stones, Bob looked up. Emmett saw now that he was bleeding from his nose and mouth and that he looked tired, very tired. As Emmett reached down to his brother with his good left hand, Bob looked up and said simply, "It's no use Emmett." Rubbish, thought Emmett, there's always another day and nothing has ever or could ever stop his brother, and so he leaned over even farther. Then there was a loud roar and another loud roar and Emmett could feel himself lifted, and then he was falling and everything had suddenly gone very quiet and still.

Seaman knew that the wounded bandit who had sought refuge in the lumber yard had escaped; his search had failed to reveal anyone hiding there. And, even though he didn't know where the bandit was now, he knew where he was heading, and so made his way toward the point where the robbers had tethered their horses. He crossed a vacant lot and reached a hole in the fence opposite a pile of curbstones. One of the bandits—badly wounded, perhaps dead—sat on the stones, slumped against a fence. Before Seaman had time to process what he saw, another bandit arrived on horseback and leaned down toward the first man. Believing the horseman was going to try to hoist the other man up onto his horse and that, if he did, they might both escape, Seaman raised his shotgun to his shoulder and from a distance of five yards fired one barrel and then the other into the back of the horseman.

Had Emmett been sitting upright in the saddle when Seaman shot him with twenty pellets of buckshot from close range, he would have been dead before his body hit the ground. However, because he was leaning over, the pellets struck at an angle, causing extensive damage but not necessarily fatal. The impact left Emmett feeling completely numb but conscious, and he understood that what began as a lean was now an uncontrollable fall. In that fall he somehow dislodged the grain sack, and it landed in the dirt alongside him. All he could think of was to say, "I'm killed," and he was not certain that he even said it aloud.

From where he landed, Emmett could see Powers, facedown and dead in the alley, his arms thrown out wide so his body was in the shape of a cross. He could also see his brother Bob, still propped up on the curbstones and struggling to breathe. Somehow Bob managed to find the strength to raise his Winchester and steady it with his left hand. Finding a target that only he could see, Bob fired a single shot, then lowered the rifle, closed his eyes and was no more.

That was the final shot the outlaws fired in the battle. Emmett lay there conscious but neither willing nor able to move. The cracks and booms of rifles and shotguns gradually ceased, and the terrified whinnying of horses faded away. The background shouts and even the hubbub of everyday noises, voices talking and boots walking on hard surfaces also faded for a brief moment, and for Emmett there was almost complete peace and silence. That was broken by the barking and baying of dogs, dozens it seemed, barking as hard when the guns ceased as they had when the guns were firing. That, too, would gradually fade just as the gun smoke in the alley lifted. Emmett was aware of all those things as he lay there, and then became aware of numbers of people moving down the alley to where he and Bob lay in pools of their own blood.

As the fighting centered around the banks continued, residents not involved gravitated to the scene of the action, and a small crowd gathered in and around the southern part of the town plaza. With the end of the shooting, the crowd moved across the plaza and into the little thoroughfare that would forever afterward be known as "Death Alley." Emmett heard them coming, heard their bootheels on the cobblestones of the plaza, and heard them shuffling through the dirt and dust of the alley. When the first figures came into view, he raised his left arm in the air, briefly and tentatively, in a gesture of surrender. Among the angry, violent faces looking down at him was one he recognized, David Elliott, someone he and the others knew as "the Colonel."

It was to Colonel Elliott that he offered his weapons, and it was from Colonel Elliott he heard the words that would calm the restive crowd. Many in that crowd wanted to lynch Emmett and were talking about finding rope and selecting an appropriate tree. Elliott put an end to such talk: "We will not hang a dying man," he said.

As the angry townsmen gathered around the bodies in Death Alley, Broadwell toppled from his horse and fell to the ground half a mile away. Shortly afterward, he died from blood loss and, not too much later, his body was found by the posse sent out to look for him. They later reported that Broadwell's horse was grazing peacefully alongside its dead owner. Broadwell's body was found an hour after he, Powers, and three Dalton brothers rode into Coffeyville determined to leave their mark on the annals of the West and pull off that last, big job that would set them up for the rest of their lives.

9 AFTERMATH

There were a few moments of almost complete silence, broken only by the distant baying of dogs, before the normal sounds of Coffeyville began once more. People called out to one another, horses snorted and whinnied, and the noise of boots and shoes walking the streets and sidewalks once more became clear to those who listened. Someone had noted the time—9:51 A.M.—when the first call went out that all the bandits were down. Individually or in small groups, the citizens of Coffeyville reassured one another that they were all right, that they hadn't been shot accidentally or deliberately, and then many of them walked to where all the action had ended, the unnamed lane that would now be known as Death Alley. Some came from the firing positions they had taken up on Union Street, but many more came from the south side of the town plaza where they had gathered to watch the unfolding drama. Leading them was David Elliott, far enough ahead to accept Emmett's surrender and prescient enough to observe everything around through his reporter's eye for later retelling.

"It is simply impossible to describe the scenes that followed," wrote Elliott. "Excited and indignant men, weeping women and screaming children thronged the plaza and crowded the alley in which the last scenes of the fight had taken place." Elliott was prepared to describe those scenes, and, just as important, he was prepared to exercise the degree of authority that his military service and standing in the community afforded him. While doing just that, his instincts for a story, for intelligence about what had happened in that alleyway, kicked in. Elliott walked the length of Death Alley and catalogued for later use what he saw there. Scattered along the thoroughfare were Winchester rifles, fallen men and pools of blood, and hats that had been lost in a last, desperate struggle for life. There were dead horses, and guns that were still smoking. Most of the fallen there were dead, three in an almost direct line along the alley. A fourth, Charles Connelly, was alive, barely; the fifth, Emmett, was able to offer up a gesture of surrender, but appeared likely to succumb to his wounds sooner rather than later.

A closer examination garnered further information and the beginning of a narrative for Elliott's story. Bob and Emmett lay close together—one dead, one dying—and between them lay a grain sack full of money. Not far away, just a couple of steps, lay the inert body of Connelly, face down in the dirt. Further down the alley was Grat, clearly dead and still wearing the false whiskers that had done little to disguise his identity. Next was the body of Bill Powers, the bandanna he had used as a disguise in Condon Bank now hanging loosely around his neck.

There would soon be a closer examination of the dead and dying in the alley. The bandits' false whiskers were removed, and Elliott would noted that "they were all closely-shaven, had on clean and comfortable clothing and were booted and spurred with the style so prevalent in the West." Also revealed were several anomalies and surprises. Grat was found to have stuffed more than $1,000 in banknotes into the pockets of his jacket and waistcoat, and between his waistcoat and shirt. The Winchester rifle he had dropped when he was shot dead had obviously seen a lot of recent action; in contrast, the two Colt revolvers in their holsters had not been fired at all.

Powers, lying dead farther along the alley, had also fallen with his Winchester by his side. It, too, had signs of considerable recent use, but it was empty. The two Colt revolvers he also carried had not been fired, and there was absolutely nothing on his person that would assist in his identification. The same was found with Bob and Emmett; heavy recent use of the Winchester rifles they had both carried—both rifles were still hot to the touch—but again revolvers unused. Each man was wearing an ammunition belt, but only the rifle ammunition had been used; all had also reloaded at least once. It had been a gunfight of rifles rather than six-shooters, and the side with the most rifles had won.

There was rough talk in the crowd. Several rowdies spoke loudly about lynching the only outlaw still alive, but they were talked down, first by Elliott and then by older and wiser heads, who said that the man was dying and that the Christian thing to do would be to let him pass in peace. Next, someone—and again it was most probably Elliott—called out to leave the dead where they were, try to do something for the living first before assigning several men to see that the bodies were not interfered with until proper arrangements had been made. The crowd had at first stood back a bit and seemed content to let a few poke fun at the bodies of the bandits. Some of the braver souls then moved forward to stand alongside them, several reaching out to touch an outstretched hand or a fallen rifle. And then someone called out that the photographer was on his way.

The other authority figures arrived almost simultaneously. Montgomery County sheriff John Callahan had been elsewhere in Coffeyville when the fighting erupted, and it was all over before he arrived on the scene. He was well known and well respected, and immediately took charge of the scene in Death Alley. Hot on Callahan's heels was the town's senior physician, Dr. Walter Wells, whose consulting rooms were nearby, upstairs over Slosson's drugstore. While Callahan tried to organize the crowd of bystanders, Wells quickly checked the bodies, confirming that Connelly and Emmett were the only two still living.

At that, Callahan quickly organized two groups of men to carry Connelly and Emmett back down the alley and then upstairs to Wells's rooms. It was done quickly and, in Connelly's case, gently and with as much care as possible. Unfortunately, it was to no avail, and the marshal died as he was being carried down the alley. Emmett at least made it to the end and then up the stairs to a spare room in Wells's offices.

Behind them, Callahan seemed to be fighting a losing battle against souvenir hunters in the alley. At first prepared to poke, prod, and comment, many in the growing crowd in Death Alley were now encouraging one another to do more to find a souvenir, something they could take to show that they were there on the day that would most likely become the most famous of all days in Coffeyville's history. At first, some just cut hair from the manes and tails of the outlaws' dead horses, plus the other dead horses in the alley, others used their pocketknives to cut small patches of material from the clothes of the dead men. It quickly became something of a cottage industry; before Callahan was able to restore a semblance of order, the entire right sleeve of Grat's jacket had been cut off and both legs of his trousers were cut off, piece by piece, almost up to his knees.

Now frustrated by those guarding the bodies, the souvenir hunters looked elsewhere, many returning to the dead horses, now mostly bereft of hair. Horseshoes were pried off and then the hooves themselves were cut into small pieces and carried away. The saddles attached to the horses fared no better, picked apart strap by strap and string by string. Then, when it seemed that all the souvenirs were gone, some enterprising young men began scooping up horse manure in any container they could find and scurrying away with that, too.

There was an ongoing buzz in the alley, but relative calm in Dr. Wells's consulting rooms above. Wells was still conducting his examination of the wounded outlaw when he was joined by the town's two junior physicians, William Hall and James Ryan. The wounded man, in a lot of obvious pain, had gone through a number of changes of mind. He had first insisted that his name was Charlie McLoughlin, but, with his false whiskers removed, several people who knew him identified him as Emmett Dalton, so now he freely admitted that was indeed who he was. He had also asked several times to be handed over to the townspeople to be dealt with in whatever manner they thought appropriate. Now Emmett submitted to a medical examination without complaint.

The doctors concluded that Emmett had literally been shot out of his saddle. At least eighteen buckshot pellets had struck him in the back; because of the angle at which they had struck, none had penetrated deep enough to threaten any vital organs. Some could be removed, and others could safely be left there. The doctors also found three bullet wounds, two in his right hip and groin, the entry and exit wounds of a single bullet that passed through Emmett's body. The bullet did not appear to have struck any organs or major blood vessels, and the doctors believed both wounds would heal with time and care.

The third bullet wound was more problematic. Another single bullet had smashed into Emmett's right arm, just below the shoulder. Penetrating deep, it had shattered the bone in the upper arm before passing out the other side. The doctors were confident they could effect some repairs, but were also of the opinion that they would not be able to remove all the bone splinters. They doubted that Emmett would ever regain full use of that arm and suspected that necrosis and blood poisoning were inevitable. In his weakened state, Emmett would almost certainly die if that occurred. All three agreed that amputation was the best option, but, when they explained their reasoning and recommendation to the young man, he rejected it outright and would not reconsider it at all.

Emmett did agree to let the doctors clean and dress his wounds, but, as they were doing so, there was some kind of disturbance in the office outside. Walter Wells went out to see what it was, only to be confronted by a small mob who demanded that Emmett be handed over to them for lynching. Wells said that he wouldn't be able to do that; the young man was then unconscious and was also undergoing surgery to remove some of the lead the townspeople had pumped into him an hour or so earlier. Emmett's prognosis was not good, and besides—this asked with a twinkle in his eye—could anyone there ever recall a patient of his surviving his surgery? That question did the trick. The laughs outnumbered the grumbles, and the men trooped out of the office and downstairs to the alley below. Wells returned to the spare room to try to stitch a young man back together again.

The commotion in Death Alley was subsiding but only slowly and seemed to ratchet up again when the photographer and his equipment arrived. The photographer was an eighteen-year-old named John Tackett, a young man who had arrived in Coffeyville two years earlier with three siblings and a mother who opened a photographic studio in the downtown business district. Tackett may have been young, but he knew how to take a photograph. As he set up his camera, he asked for some assistance and soon a hayrack of sorts had been put together on the south side of the alley. Eager volunteers carried and placed the bodies of the four dead bandits—Broadwell's had been recovered and brought back—and Tackett took a series of photographs that would come down through the ages: four dead outlaws, bodies posed, and eyes closed, dead near the scene of the last great bank robbery of the Old West. And there, peeking through a hole in the fence behind the bodies, is the face of a small boy, an unwitting witness to history.

As the volunteers had moved the bodies into position, one of them had found if you raised and lowered Grat's arm, blood would spurt from the gaping wound in his neck. This amused some ghouls for a short while, but then Callahan directed those volunteers to take the bodies down the alley to the town jail where they were laid out on the sidewalk for additional photographs before being dumped unceremoniously in a cell for later identification. To prevent further interference with the bodies by souvenir hunters, Callahan organized for them to be guarded by the late marshal's deputies.

While all this was going on in and around Death Alley, elsewhere in Coffeyville its citizens were beginning to count the cost of what had happened between 9:30 and 10 A.M. that morning. There were a number of deaths to enumerate: George Cubine, Charles Brown, and Charles Connelly were dead, and Lucius Baldwin was dying. The young man was still alive, barely, conscious and able to speak of what had happened to him. He said he had spotted two men in the laneway behind the First National Bank and had just naturally assumed that they were townsmen like him, also looking for a spot to outflank the bank robbers. He heard one of the men call out to him, but in the high emotion of the moment, with the background of other shout and gunshots, he didn't really listen to what the man said. The next thing, he was on his back in the dirt, and dying.

Baldwin passed away shortly after midday, the eighth and last fatality from the gunfight. Three others suffered quite serious wounds—Charlie Gump's hand and Tom Ayres's face would require a lot of medical treatment, and neither man would ever regain full use of the wounded area. Emmett's wounds were life-threatening, and in the immediate aftermath of the fight, even the doctors treating him believed he would be lucky to survive. There were several others wounded to a lesser extent, and veterans of the Civil War believed the ratio of dead to wounded exceeded anything they had experienced in that conflict.

There was a toll taken on horses. The oil tanker team were both down and dead, as were two other horses farther down the alley. Another was so badly wounded that it had to be put down.

All business in Coffeyville ceased for the day when the gun battle ended. The crowds in Death Alley slowly thinned out, but for the rest of the day small groups of townsmen and women gathered on street corners and in the plaza to talk over their own and others' experiences that morning. Individually or with friends or neighbors, they walked between the various battle sites and marveled at what they or someone else would find there. An examination of the two sides that formed the front section of Condon Bank revealed at least eighty bullet holes and many pockmarks from shotgun pellets. Across the road, there was not a single mark on the front of the First National Bank.

Those who took an interest in such things estimated that there were fifteen active shooters involved in the gun battle and that somewhere between 200 and 300 bullets and shotgun cartridges were fired. In the twelve to fifteen minutes during which those shots were fired, no one who could be considered an innocent bystander had been struck by any of those projectiles. The four Coffeyville residents who had been killed were all carrying firearms when they were shot, but only one, George Cubine, had fired a shot before they themselves were shot down. It could have been very different. A bullet from one of the outlaw's rifles hit the timber beneath a window in Isham's store then passed through and narrowly missed a box containing fifty pounds of dynamite before lodging in a display stove.

The whole object of the raid had been to rob two banks at the same time, and that part had been successful, for a while at least. More than $25,000 had been taken from the First National Bank and probably something less than $2,000 from Condon Bank. Grat had dropped the grain sack containing part of the Condon Bank takings when struck by a bullet as he ran toward the entrance of Death Alley; it was recovered and returned when the shooting ended, as was the $1,000-plus Grat had stuffed into his pockets. The grain sack with the money from the First National Bank was also recovered from where it had fallen between the bodies of Emmett and Bob. Later that day, both banks conducted a careful audit; Condon Bank recorded a loss of $20, but the First National Bank ended the day with $1.98 more than it had when it opened.

When the dead and dying had been taken to either their homes or a funeral parlor, some semblance of order was restored through the efforts of Callahan and his deputies, both town and county. Lookouts and guards were posted at key points, and the county coroner was telegraphed with some details and a request to prepare for a number of inquests. As the sun went down, the little groups broke up and people started to head home. Those who thought deeply about what had happened that day may have looked at a pile of rocks that Charlie Gump's teamsters had dumped outside Condon Bank on Walnut Street. They had been dropped there just the previous day as part of the guttering and curbing of the downtown area the town was undertaking. Before dumping the rocks, the teamsters had watched other workmen remove the hitching rail, often used by the bank's customers, one that had stood there for years.

As the crowds of locals began to drift away during the afternoon, their replacements began to arrive in Coffeyville. The first telegram detailing the raid had been sent at 9:42 A.M., before the gang had actually finished their robbery and some minutes before the climax of the raid in Death Alley. That telegram contained the first words in what was to become a torrent of newsprint about what happened that day. Within hours, telegrams were pouring into Coffeyville, by the dozens and then by the hundreds, sent by newspapers across the United States and beyond, requesting more and more details about the robberies and the gun battle. One especially enterprising reporter tracked down Cole Younger and another Jesse James's brother Frank. Both were asked their opinions of the Coffeyville raid, and both were dismissive of the Daltons. Interestingly, neither expressed the slightest surprise that the gang had been destroyed in the raid.

The first and subsequent telegrams from Coffeyville also prompted a flood of official telegrams in response, most of them from county, state, and federal agencies, some asking for more details and some offering various types of support. The telegrams also prompted numbers of people to plan an urgent trip to Coffeyville. When the news reached Parsons, Kansas, a small town forty miles northeast of Coffeyville, the local representative of the Katy—the Missouri, Kansas and Texas Railroad—set about organizing a special train and a posse of fifty armed men to help out in Coffeyville. They arrived later that afternoon and were a welcome addition to Coffeyville's already overstretched resources.

When the news spread by word of mouth, Kansans from outlying farms and nearby villages and towns walked or rode into Coffeyville. They were joined by the sightseers who packed the regularly scheduled afternoon train in a great visitation that saw about 2,000 outsiders visit Coffeyville that day and the next. The banks and the town plaza remained points of interest, but the focus of every visitor's attention was and remained Death Alley. Hundreds of feet tramped from one end of the laneway to the other and hundreds of hands touched fences and stones and hitching rails, just as hundreds of eyes darted backward and forward as people tried to envision the carnage that occurred there just a few hours earlier. Anything that hadn't already been souvenired disappeared.

Law officers who had been looking for the Dalton Gang also responded as soon as they learned what had gone down at Coffeyville. One of them, the delightfully named Ransom Payne, arrived in town later that afternoon, telling anyone who would listen that he had been on the trail of the outlaws for the past fifteen months. On his orders—he was a deputy US marshal after all—the outlaws' bodies were stripped and washed before being dressed again, following which Bob and Grat were strapped to boards. With volunteers holding those boards upright, Ransom had a series of photographs taken of himself standing between the two men he claimed to have been chasing for so long. Payne was considerably less successful in confiscating the bodies and having them shipped to California so he could claim the reward money on offer for them there.

Down in the Indian Territory, Wells Fargo detective Fred Dodge learned of the affair when the posse he led with Deputy US Marshal Heck Thomas called in at one of the Indian agencies. Dodge and Thomas were surprised to learn that only five of the gang had been involved in the raid, because they knew that Bob Dalton could call on at least twice that number. They told the posse what had happened and led them on the trail back to Kansas. As they rode, the two men wondered what those other gang members would do about Coffeyville.

Upstairs in Walter Wells's spare room, Emmett had survived the repair work done to his many wounds by Wells and his two assistants. He was still in a critical condition but seemed a bit better than he had been when carried up the stairs. There was now something important that Sheriff Callahan had asked him to do. It was to identify the bodies of his dead companions and, although he knew it would be distressing, Emmett was prepared to go ahead with it. In a scene witnessed by Wells, Callahan, and at least one reporter, the bodies were brought—one by one—from the jail and upstairs to Wells's offices.

The first body brought in was described as "a tall young man, raw-boned with prominent features." Two men held the body upright in a way that allowed Emmett to see it from his cot. In a voice that quivered with emotion, Emmett said quietly, "I identify that as my brother, Bob Dalton." Observers thought he might be about to break down, but he steeled himself before once more becoming visibly upset when the second body was brought in. He was able to identify that corpse as being his brother Grat Dalton, adding that his brother was thirty-one years old. There were elements of confusion over the identification of the last two bodies because Emmett said he had only known both men for a few days. The third body was Bill Powers; Emmett identified him as Tom Evans, but he said the man had also used the alias Tom Hedde. Finally, Dick Broadwell's body was brought in, and Emmett identified him as Jake Moore, adding that he was sometimes known as "Texas Jack."

The identification complete, Emmett seemed to revive somewhat, and he began to talk, apparently just recalling things as they came to him. Looking around, he said that his brother Bob had turned twenty-three on the previous May 13, going on to say that he had not spent very much time with his brothers until he met up with them at a spot to the south of Tulsa on October 1. He added that, when they met, Bob told him that he had been involved in the Adair robbery with Grat, Tom Evans, and Jake Moore. Furthermore, he believed that Bob had told him that both he and Grat had been part of a train robbery in California in January 1890.

Talking freely now, Emmett said that Bob had come up with the idea of a double bank robbery just the previous Saturday. All the men were short of money and believed that several of the posses they knew were out there searching for them were now closing in. The others had argued that a double robbery was just not feasible, but Bob insisted that it was. Emmett also spoke about the robbery, but he stumbled over words when he came to the part where his brothers died and began weeping silently. Emmett then seemed to apologize for not knowing anything more about Tom Evans or Jake Moore, but said he had only met them a few days earlier. He weakened, and once more muttered something about his dead brothers.

At this point, Wells and Callahan agreed that the young outlaw should be given the opportunity to rest up and asked those present to now leave him alone. The reporter present took one final look and later wrote that what he saw was "a young man on a bed who had just reached his majority. He had rather an attractive face, a mild, clear eye, good complexion, regular features and a voice as smooth and pleasant as a man often possesses. There was nothing coarse, or brutal or villainous-looking about him. A man would indeed have been hard-hearted, who could have witnessed that through which he went without feeling a pity in his heart."

Outside the invalid's room, Callahan and the others who had been listening to Emmett compared notes. In discussing what they had all heard from Emmett that day, they said it seemed that his story had changed slightly each time he told it. Each telling would be similar to the previous, but it seemed that his role in the Coffeyville raid was being minimized with each iteration. One opinion was that he was doing this because he knew there were still people out there who would be happy to lynch him. It was also pointed out that he had been unwilling to answer questions about where they had met near Tulsa and where they had stayed en route to Coffeyville. The reasoning behind this, they agreed, was a desire to protect the identity of anyone who had assisted them. It was all so sad, one opined, because not all that long ago, the Daltons were considered brave and reliable, and people felt safer when they were around, in the beginning at least.

There was general agreement that Emmett had probably had enough for one day, but there was one more requirement of him. As the afternoon became evening, a Coffeyville attorney named Henry Dooley visited Emmett to take a formal statement. Emmett was quite forthcoming in that statement, making it plain that both Bob and Grat had spoken openly about killing anyone who got in their way. His work there complete, Dooley departed the building, noting as he did so that Sheriff Callahan had placed a considerable number of guards around Slosson's building where Wells's offices and the ailing outlaw were located. He understood that they were not there to keep the prisoner in.

The almost contemptuous treatment the bodies of the dead outlaws had received continued during the afternoon and into the night. After being dressed, undressed, and dressed again, primarily so various sets of photographs could be taken, the sightseers and the souvenir hunters moved on, and the four bodies were once more carried to the town jail and dumped unceremoniously in an empty cell. Late in the evening, an undertaker and his assistants arrived and placed each of the bodies in a plain, black-lacquered coffin, which, according to some reports, were simple, reed-woven constructs, the cheapest coffins available. Those coffins were then laid side by side at the front of the barn near where their horses had been tethered. Even late at night, there were people who wanted to see them.

The open coffins remained where they were throughout the night and into the next morning. Full light brought more spectators, more dust and, when the day warmed up, hordes of flies attracted by the crowds and the smell of blood settled indiscriminately on both the living and the dead. Late in the morning, the undertaker returned to close the coffins and with the help of his staff loaded them onto a wagon. The wagon headed south down Union Street and onto the road that led to South Coffeyville and then on to Oklahoma. It stopped at Elmwood Cemetery, where the four coffins were carried to a common grave dug just outside the boundaries of the cemetery, allegedly because the locals did not want the men buried in consecrated ground. The coffins were laid in the grave and covered with dirt before the few people who had been there moved on to other things. A bent piece of iron piping was left to mark the grave; some said it was the actual railing to which the gang had tethered their horses in Death Alley. Others disputed this, saying it was nothing more than a piece of scrap iron the undertaker had picked up to mark the grave.

There were two other services in Coffeyville that day, both larger and more solemn than the lonely interments by the Elmwood Cemetery fence. In the town that day, all flags were flown at half-mast, and many houses and public buildings were draped with black crepe paper as a mark of respect for the town's dead. George Cubine's death in particular had hit a number of people hard; he was a well-known and highly respected member of the community, which closed its stores so everyone could attend his funeral. At 2 P.M., a service was conducted in the chapel at the Skinner Funeral Home, with part of the service conducted by members of Cubine's fraternal lodge, the Modern Woodmen of America. Following the service, a large number of mourners followed the cortege to Elmwood Cemetery where the body was interred after a brief graveside service.

That day, a large memorial service was also held in Coffeyville for Marshal Charles Connelly, a service also conducted in part by the Modern Woodmen of America, one of several lodges to which the Connelly belonged. Connelly's actual funeral was held the next day in the county seat of Independence. The Missouri-Pacific Railroad Company provided two passenger coaches, free of charge, for family and friends to travel to and from Independence for the funeral. Following a service there, Connelly's remains were buried in Independence's Mount Hope Cemetery.

The other two Coffeyville residents killed in the raid were buried elsewhere. The body of the youngest, Lucius Baldwin, was returned to his mother in Burlington, Kansas, where he was buried in the town's Graceland Cemetery. The oldest victim, Charles Brown, was also returned to his hometown of Rapid City, South Dakota, where his widow saw him buried in that town's cemetery.

There was an unusual coda to the funerals. Several days after the Thursday burials, two of Dick Broadwell's relatives, his brother George and brother-in-law E. S. Wilcox, arrived in Coffeyville to claim his body. Both men were successful and respectable businessmen from the Broadwell hometown of Hutchinson, Kansas, and soon arranged for the exhumation of Dick's body and its return to Hutchinson where, dressed in expensive clothes and placed in an expensive coffin, Broadwell was reinterred in the family plot in Hutchinson's main cemetery. George Broadwell chose to remain silent, but Wilcox was prepared to speak to local reporters, telling them that the whole family was shocked when they learned of Dick's fate. They had not heard from him since May that year and believed him to be a law-abiding cowboy who neither drank nor gambled. Wilcox also made noises about recovering Broadwell's horse and the $90 that had been found on his body, but quietly dropped that idea when reminded of what Dick and the others had done to the town.

Emmett spent a difficult night in Dr. Wells's spare room. The men deputed to guard him reported that he had been restive all night and had appeared to be in considerable pain. Wells himself cleaned and redressed Emmett's wounds the next morning and believed that, even though the young man was still in a very serious condition, he seemed somewhat improved both physically and mentally. In discussions with Sheriff Callahan, it was also agreed that Emmett's treatment could best be continued at another location. That location was the Farmers' Home, a guesthouse/hotel that had previously been patronized by the Daltons when they made surreptitious visits to Coffeyville.

Around noon that day, Emmett was carried the relatively short distance to the Farmers' Home on Eighth Street and placed, under guard, in the front room of the two buildings that made up the guesthouse. It was an interesting trip, made through the numbers of people who had come to try to catch a glimpse of him and some of whom would also stand outside his temporary home at odd hours over the next few days for the same purpose.

At the Farmers' Home, Emmett remained under close guard, those guards being a company of private citizens organized by the town's deputy sheriff. For the first couple of days of his confinement, the only visitors Emmett was allowed were the doctors treating him, officials, and family members. One of the latter was his oldest brother Ben, and Emmett—still uncertain whether he would actually survive his wounds—opened up to Ben about some of the crimes the Daltons had been implicated in. He told Ben stories his brother would later repeat to reporters, one of which was that he, Bob, and Grat were behind the train holdups at Wagoner, Leliaetta, Red Rock, and Adair, but that they were not involved at Alila. Grat, in fact, had a watertight alibi for that one, but the brothers believed that someone was paid to perjure themselves to implicate the Daltons.

Another of those to visit him was James Charlton, the county attorney for Montgomery County. Charlton and his wife had been visiting Kansas City when he received a telegram informing him of the Coffeyville raid. He immediately returned to Coffeyville and began working with local authorities on a case he knew he would be required to prosecute.

As part of that process, Charlton visited Emmett at the Farmers' Home and spoke to him on several occasions. Against all his instincts, Charlton found that he could not help but like the young man and feel some sympathy for the position he found himself in.

To those who guarded or visited him, Emmett seemed to continue to improve on a daily basis, an improvement mostly reflected in his mental state. After just a couple of days, reporters were also allowed in, and Emmett seemed quite comfortable talking to them. He was also willing to talk quite openly about life as part of the Dalton Gang. To one reporter who asked about rumors that the Daltons had a treasure hidden away somewhere, he retorted that the story was rubbish: "If there had been a hidden treasure we would all have been alive today." He also said that Bill Doolin, Charlie Pierce, and George Newcomb were not part of the raid because their characters did not fit in with how Bob had planned to carry out the Coffeyville raid. That plan had included tethering their horses to the hitching rail in Walnut Street so they wouldn't be spotted until they were inside the banks. It would also mean they would make a quick getaway. Bob had also bought the horses and six-shooters they were to use in the raid.

Over time, the guards noted something interesting about Emmett. Given to introspection and even melancholy if left alone for long periods, he would really perk up for visitors, be they family or friends, law officers or reporters, and would remain buoyant for quite a while afterward. It was almost as though he enjoyed being the center of attention.

In some respects, Emmett's room in the Farmers' Home was like the eye of a storm, an oasis of calm while the elements raged outside. It was a front room and on occasion the guards would draw back the curtains to give Emmett a glimpse of Eighth Street and the outside world. What he mostly saw, though, was groups of people looking back in at the man who was then quite possibly the most famous individual in the United States. What he couldn't know was that many of those people harbored genuine fears about what might become of their town.

Five members of the Dalton Gang had entered Coffeyville and four had died there. Rumors had put the size of the gang at up to a dozen, and perhaps more, meaning that there could be almost ten more desperadoes out there somewhere, plotting the destruction of the town and its inhabitants. The tension was ratcheted up another notch when John Kloehr reported that someone had put a letter in his letter box, which threatened Kloehr with death and promised the destruction of the town that housed him.

At around the same time as someone was posting a threatening letter to Kloehr, well to the south in the Indian Territory, Amos Burton decided that he had waited long enough at the rendezvous point and that he had held up his end of the bargain. He had waited long and faithfully for the Dalton boys, and he understood that if they hadn't shown up by now, they wouldn't be showing up at all. He packed up the campsite, loaded everything into the covered wagon, and rode off the pages of history.

The Dalton family in Oklahoma learned of the Coffeyville raid and the death of two of its members through the good offices of Deputy US Marshal Chris Madsen. He rode out to Kingfisher and on to Bartlesville to inform Adeline and Ben Dalton about the deaths of Bob and Grat and the serious injuries Emmett had sustained before passing the same information to Bill Dalton and Eva Whipple. Then he rode on to Coffeyville to see if he could be of any assistance there.

Before Madsen departed, Bill Dalton had asked him if he thought it would be considered appropriate for Adeline to visit Emmett in care in Coffeyville, and Madsen, surprised at the question, said he could see no issues with a mother visiting a son who was perhaps dying. That travel would not take place for almost two days after Madsen delivered the news. Bill Dalton later said that the delay was due to safety concerns—he did ask about his own possible reception in Coffeyville—and also his mother's ill-health. A more likely reason was that Bill was weighing up whether or not there was any evidence linking him to the raid. Ever the operator, Bill continued to look at all the options available to him.

The Daltons' visit to Coffeyville had Bill Dalton's fingerprints all over it. On the Friday morning after the raid, he accompanied his mother, brother Ben, and sister Eva Whipple, moving by road and traveling via Guthrie, Oklahoma, where Bill found time to speak to a local reporter.

They were traveling to Coffeyville, he said, to collect the bodies of his dead brothers and return them home to Oklahoma. The subsequent report painted an unflattering and inaccurate picture of the spokesman for the Daltons, describing him as being short and stout, an ex-member of the California legislature and a prominent citizen of that state until he was arrested after his brothers robbed a train. It was a taste of the media attention the raid had generated.

Arriving late Friday morning, the family went straight to the Farmers' Home for an emotional reunion with Emmett. No doubt shaken by his wounds and his appearance, they must have been somewhat reassured when Emmett told them that he had been treated far better than he had expected to be. After the visit, and as they went about making their own arrangements to stay in Coffeyville, the family was sought out by many of the newspaper reporters who had made their own way to Coffeyville. Ben was prepared to speak to at least one, telling a journalist from the *New York Times* that he had been ill in bed when he had learned of his brothers' fate. He said that he and his mother had not seen his outlaw brothers for almost two years, and during that time did not know where they were or what they were doing. Ben concluded by describing himself as a simple farmer and saying that neither he nor his mother bore any ill-will toward the people of Coffeyville. They were simply doing their duty, he added. The Daltons mourned their losses, but they felt equally sorry for the families of those who had died defending the town.

During their time in Coffeyville, Ben Dalton remained calm and dignified, his mother and sister quiet and dignified too, descriptors that could never be attached to Bill Dalton. Speaking very loudly and very often, the most that Bill would concede was that the gang had been wrong to try to rob the two banks. But, he said, adding a caveat to even that statement of the obvious, when people were trying to shoot you—in the West at least—you were entitled to shoot back. Even more antagonistically, he suggested that the bodies of the dead outlaws had all been looted, and that he was considering the option of suing Coffeyville for the money and possessions he believed had been taken; $10,000 seemed an appropriate amount.

As it turned out, inventories of what had been found on each of the bodies had been undertaken. Bob's included his several firearms, the accoutrements for his horse, a gold watch, and $900. Bill's next move was to try to have himself declared administrator for the estates of Bob and Grat. A lawyer from Sandusky named Luther Perkins said he would assist Bill in his various legal battles on a contingency basis, but that arrangement seems to have fallen through when Bill was informed that he would have to lodge a bond with his application. When neither he nor Perkins was able to do so, the administrator's role remained with Sheriff Callahan, the legally responsible officer anyway.

By the end of the weekend, Coffeyville was sick and tired of most of the Daltons and what they had brought and simply wanted them all gone. They would have to wait a little longer.

If Sheriff Callahan could have been certain of the outcome, Emmett may not even have been in Coffeyville when his family arrived that Friday. Although it would not have been a comfortable trip for his prisoner, Callahan had hoped that Emmett would have been well enough to travel to Independence on the Friday, because moving him there would address several concerns the lawman had. Callahan was not one of those who believed that Coffeyville was at risk of a retaliatory raid by the Dalton Gang members still at large. The town had done well in the original raid, and a considerable number of reinforcements had arrived since then. He was more concerned about people who were still in Coffeyville. Rumors of lynch mobs would simply not go away, and the town's wounds were still very raw. He personally would have risked Emmett's health and put him on Friday's train to Independence, but there was credible information suggesting the train would be stopped en route so that Emmett could be taken off and hanged.

So Callahan opted to wait a few days longer, to allow passions to cool and allow him to organize a proper escort party as Emmett's health continued to improve. There were a couple of developments in those few days. F. Joseph Fritch, a lawyer from Independence who was also acting as an attorney for Montgomery County, lodged a formal complaint with Justice of the Peace George Gilmore alleging that Emmett Dalton had murdered Lucius Baldwin. A preliminary hearing of the matter was scheduled for January 16, 1893, in Independence. Within two days, Bill Dalton had been able to raise enough money from family and friends to convince Fritch to now act as a legal advisor to the Dalton family.

As a backdrop to all of this, several of Coffeyville's more prominent citizens had approached Sheriff Callahan urging him to move Emmett to Independence as soon as possible. Not only was his presence a constant reminder of what they had lost, that presence was also starting to attract "undesirable elements" to the town. Dr. Wells confirmed that Emmett would be uncomfortable but was probably well enough to travel. On October 11, Emmett was carried in a makeshift cot from the Farmers' Home to the Coffeyville train station, armed guards led by Callahan placed in front, behind, and on both sides. Under this heavy guard, Emmett traveled aboard the scheduled service to Independence, his brother Bill elsewhere on the train, plotting his next move. At Independence, Emmett was carried to the Montgomery County Jail, where he was placed in a small ground-floor cell that had been specially prepared for him.

Back in Coffeyville there was an almost audible sigh of relief. Although the town could never return to what it was like before the raid, there was a sense that they could go on, move forward. They could now look forward to a time of closure. The main story now doing the rounds was that, as the only surviving bandit, Emmett would be charged with four counts of murder. He may have escaped the lynch mob; he would not escape the hangman.

10

THE STATE OF KANSAS V. EMMETT DALTON

I

Emmett Dalton's move from Coffeyville to Independence was a transfer from a fishbowl to a fish pond. It took him from being the main game in a small town to being part of a larger game in a larger city. From being bed-ridden in the front room of a boarding house to a special room in a large county jail. It was not a move that seems to have caused the young man too much discomfort or too many regrets. His time in the Montgomery County Jail was remembered well in the main local newspaper:

> When in confinement here, Emmett made friends with everyone he met . . . was genial and gentlemanly in his bearing and was not given to swaggering or boasting, though his determination and bravery were evident enough. That a young man as well-endowed by nature with the elements that win friends and would have assured him success in any honourable calling should have drifted into a course of life that made him a greater menace to the peace and order of society that the most callow and depraved criminal that breathes the free air of Kansas today seems a thousand pities.

When he arrived in Independence, Emmett was still not well, and would have struggled had he been required to stand trial before the end of 1892. However, though physically frail, his mental state was constantly lifted by the dozens of flowers that always adorned his cell, most sent by admiring young women. One of his regular guards in the coming months was another young man, an Independence local named Billy Smith. The two young men talked at length, and Emmett again related to Smith the details of how the Dalton family came to turn to crime. Emmett spoke of how his brother Bob was owed $1,200 for all his work and expenses, but a US marshal named Walker would simply not pay him his wages. Bob and Grat then decided to levy their own fines on those they arrested. It was a short step from there to peddling the whiskey they seized. When they were caught doing this, they simply jumped bail and took off. Emmett also gave Smith some details about their holdups, always insisting that the Coffeyville raid was the first time they had robbed a bank.

Emmett also had several conversations with another jailer, a senior turnkey named Sparke. During their conversations, Emmett first offered Sparke $250 and, when that was rejected, $500, to let him escape. Sparke rejected the offers and brought them to the attention of Sheriff Callahan.

Bill Dalton would hang around in Independence, visiting Emmett on occasion, but generally behaving like a fish out of water. There were reports of him drinking heavily and of all-night card games where he was often successful, reportedly winning $500 in a single game. He was also free and easy with his opinions, talking about his brothers and what they might and might not have done, and what they might and might not do. And then, after a few days, he was gone.

In a move that appears to have surprised everyone, the case of the *State of Kansas v. Emmett Dalton* was the first to be called on the morning of Monday, December 19, 1892, in Independence's District Court. Emmett had not recovered sufficiently to be able to walk the short distance from the county jail to the courthouse, so he was carried in a chair that had been fastened to two poles, with a deputy sheriff named Morgan and a court bailiff named Hamilton acting as porters. Escorting the prisoner were deputies Tom Earnest and Harris Fairleigh in front and Callahan and town marshal Griffey behind. All were heavily armed.

There were only a few spectators present in the court for the opening of the case, but when word spread about who was facing trial, courtroom numbers swelled; a final estimate was that up to 200 people attended that day. Those who were present noted that Emmett looked tired, almost worn-out. When Judge Jeremiah "Jerry" McCue asked him if he was ready to face trial, Emmett's response was that no, he was not ready. When McCue then asked him if he was ready to enter a plea to the charge of murder, Emmett once again said that he was not. Then asked if he had a lawyer, Emmett answered in the negative for the third time. He did add that he had consulted with the attorney Joseph Fritch, but that had been on other matters.

Fritch was actually in court that morning and was given permission to address the bench, informing Judge McCue that he would be traveling by train to Coffeyville later that morning and would therefore not be able to represent Emmett.

McCue then asked Emmett if he would be able to raise enough funds to employ an attorney, something Emmett said he believed he would be able to do. McCue himself then addressed the court, saying that his wife was ill, very ill, and he would not be able to hear any cases that week. With that, he adjourned Emmett's case for seven days, until 9 A.M. on the following Monday. At that, Emmett took his place in the sedan chair and was returned to the county jail, now accompanied by his armed escort and dozens of curious onlookers.

The District Court was opened again at 9 A.M. on Monday, December 26, 1892. It was a brief session; Judge McCue informed the court that his wife's condition had deteriorated, and he would not be hearing cases that week either. He then adjourned Emmett's case until Monday, January 16, 1893, and closed the court.

Emmett would have struggled physically had his trial been held in December, but by mid-January all who visited him commented on his recovery. His right arm was still proving troublesome, but he had regained some movement in it. His hip and groin wounds had improved, too, and although it was painful, he was able to walk around his cell unaided. His spirits were also lifted by visitors, one of whom, the Independence city attorney, James Charlton, would become a regular visitor.

Charlton obviously enjoyed spending time with the young prisoner, and almost half a century later could clearly recall many of their conversations. Emmett told Charlton, somewhat disingenuously, that the Coffeyville raid was his first offense and that his brother Bob had tried to keep him from going along with the others on that fateful morning. However, Emmett had a premonition that Bob would be killed, and he was determined to be there if his brother was fated to die. When Bob fell in the alley, Emmett's only thought was to return to help his brother escape the death that was all around them. He rode back and was about to haul Bob up onto his horse when he was hit by what he described as "a shower of buckshot."

Charlton found Emmett to be an intelligent young man who had a great sense of humor. He visited Emmett one day shortly after there had been a department store burglary in Coffeyville and two of the burglars had been caught with a quantity of silk they had stolen. The two were taken to the Montgomery County Jail and lodged in a cell on the floor above Emmett. When Charlton visited the next morning, Emmett thought he may have been there because of the Coffeyville burglary. From his cell, he called out, "Mr. Charlton, the silk department is upstairs."

James Charlton developed a soft spot for Emmett, even though the young man was sometimes sparing with the truth. Then again, it is unclear if Charlton explained to Emmett that he was a key part of the prosecution team and that he would be doing his very best to see Emmett convicted of murder and then executed.

Just over twenty miles to the south, it was taking a while for things to return to preraid normality in Coffeyville. It just seemed at times that tying up one loose end would lead to the unraveling of several other threads. One of the first tasks that law enforcement undertook after the raid was to send patrols out into the hinterland to determine whether or not there were other gang members or supporters out there. One patrol, operating to the south in Oklahoma, claimed to have found a relay of horses left by the gang at the ranch of an acquaintance at Double Creek, twenty miles north of Tulsa. The gang planned to leave the horses they had taken to Coffeyville there and continue their getaway on fresh horses.

However, of the horses seized, one had been purchased legitimately by Dick Broadwell and two others had been bought properly but with some money still outstanding on them. A fourth horse was identified as being recently stolen from a man near Tulsa, who wanted it back. Not so, Emmett would say, "I bought that horse legitimately and I will go to court to argue my ownership." The law had the horses; the various owners wanted them back.

The Coffeyville raid received extensive coverage in newspapers across the United States and elsewhere around the world, and the reports were certainly sensational if not always accurate. They also contributed to what was rapidly becoming a tourist boom for Coffeyville. At first, those sightseers were primarily from Montgomery County, but within a week, people from all over Kansas and Oklahoma began to arrive, and the railroads that serviced Coffeyville were all reporting record numbers of passengers. For a while, it seemed like a new home industry might be emerging, one that promised to be both long-term and sustainable.

Several efforts were also undertaken to both recognize the bravery of the group who would become known as the "Coffeyville Defenders" and to try to compensate the families of those who died during the raid. The day after that raid, the American Bankers Association announced that it was establishing a fund to support the families of those who had been killed or wounded; within a few days, $20,000 had been pledged. The next day, Friday, October 7, a citizens meeting held in Coffeyville formed what they termed a "relief committee," also for the purpose of raising funds for the affected families. An appeal letter was drawn up and sent to banks, railroad companies, and express companies, the traditional targets of the Dalton Gang. The response was both prompt and impressive, and within a few weeks an additional $13,000 had been raised and disbursed. The widows of Charles Connelly, George Cubine, and Charles Brown, and the mother of Lucius Baldwin, were all given $1,650 as a first payment; lesser amounts were paid out to the wounded.

There was also the question of the official reward money that had been posted for the death or capture of the gang, and on Sunday, October 9, Deputy US Marshal Heck Thomas and Wells Fargo's Fred Dodge arrived in Coffeyville to assist in that process. Thomas and Dodge set up stakes in Death Alley to mark where the various outlaws had fallen, measured angles and distances, and took statements from those who had been directly involved in the gunfight. Dodge spoke to John Kloehr, who was becoming increasingly uncomfortable at being cast as the real hero of the raid, so much so that he was now asking the reporters to use the name "Jim Spears" when referring to him. Kloehr told Fred Dodge that, in Death Alley, he had aimed at Grat Dalton's head but had undershot and hit him in the throat instead. Interestingly, he did not claim to have killed Bob Dalton at that point.

Thomas and Dodge also held a town meeting to give all witnesses to the raid a chance to speak, but could do little else because they, and the posse they hastily put together, had to ride quickly to the south to investigate some disturbing reports that had been received.

The threatening letter Kloehr received had been signed, "The Dalton Gang," and Thomas and Dodge were responding to reports that the former members of the gang had come together somewhere in Oklahoma or the Indian Territory and were preparing a raid of their own. In Independence two days after he had brought Emmett to the Montgomery County Jail, Callahan received a telegram from Dodge, sent from Wharton in the Indian Territory. Dodge said that he, Thomas, and their posse were pursuing a group of outlaws who were supposedly looking to free Emmett. Dodge added that if the posse found them, they would kill them all. He also thought the posse may need to visit Coffeyville, and asked Callahan to let local authorities know so they wouldn't be mistaken for the outlaw band.

The news had an immediate effect in Coffeyville. The two banks there immediately closed, and at least a dozen townsmen again armed themselves with borrowed firearms. A telegram was sent to the marshal of Parsons asking for twenty-five armed men to be sent to Coffeyville and another dispatched to Kansas City requesting an additional ten Winchester rifles for the town's marshal's office. Further warnings, probably echoes of the first, would soon be received along with possible sightings of the outlaw band from locations all around Coffeyville and southeastern Kansas. A rail coach at the town's railroad depot was turned into a miniature fort, and the town was blacked out for several nights with armed guards posted at key points. Finally, an enormous bonfire was constructed in the town plaza to provide illumination should the outlaws attack at night. But, like Amos Burton before them, the town waited a few days for an outlaw band that never appeared, even if it existed, and then it moved on.

When several days had passed and the outlaw gang had not appeared, Coffeyville slowly returned to something approaching normality, but the raid and its aftermath continued to feature largely in the town's life. There were further efforts at reward and compensation. On October 20, the Kansas State Bankers Association held a meeting in Topeka to look at additional rewards for those responsible for the destruction of the Dalton Gang. The fund quickly grew to $18,000, with an additional $2,000 set aside to fund the prosecution of anyone who attempted to defraud the benevolent fund.

There were serious calls for Kloehr to run for governor of Kansas, and in Chicago a group of bankers decided to make a more concrete expression of the gratitude that most bankers felt. They commissioned, and subsequently presented to Kloehr, a highly decorated gold badge, in the form of a carefully crafted star with a diamond in the middle. Inscribed in a gold ribbon at the top were the words, "The Emergency Arose, The Man Appeared." The badge, four inches long and almost as wide, was rumored to have cost anything from $350 to $1,000. The Winchester Repeating Arms Company, whose products had been responsible for much of the carnage at Coffeyville, also stepped forward, giving Kloehr a presentation model Winchester 73 rifle, suitably inscribed as a gift to Jim Spears.

There were other echoes of the raid. In December, David Elliott was forced to give up the revolvers Emmett had surrendered to him after a lawsuit for their return was lodged by none other than Bill Dalton. The following month, Sheriff Callahan auctioned off Bob's and Grat's personal possessions. Various firearms, horse equipage, and personal jewelry went under the hammer, with Kloehr buying Grat's horse and Bob's saddle. The auction raised just under $300, enough to cover several outstanding debts the brothers had left behind them, with the remainder to go to the victims. These were all small but significant steps toward returning the town to normal. The biggest step would be the successful prosecution of Emmett Dalton, and there were a few more hurdles before that could occur.

II

One of those hurdles was Bill Dalton. His behavior, never especially predictable, became increasingly erratic in the weeks after the Coffeyville raid. The publicity surrounding what had taken place would have been especially grating for Bill. Whichever way you looked at it, from Bill's perspective anyway, the raid had been an unmitigated disaster and—what grated the most—was that he and Bill Doolin had known it would be, which was why they had walked away from Bob's plan almost as soon as he outlined it. Now two of his brothers were dead and a third was critically ill. Emmett, if he survived, would either be hanged or could expect to spend the rest of his life in prison.

Whether he knew it or not, Bill's name and reputation would now make it almost impossible for him to pursue an honest living, something he had seemed intent on doing since he had come back from California. Those dreams may have become a thing of the past, but Bill seemed determined to keep going by simply throwing himself into everything. He was the driving force behind bringing his mother, brother, and sister to Coffeyville to see Emmett before he either died or was locked away for a long, long time. In Coffeyville, he was everywhere, trying to organize legal representation and trying to lay claim, too, to anything that could be linked to Bob, Grat, or Emmett. Eva Whipple and Ben Dalton returned to Oklahoma when Emmett was moved to Independence, but Bill took their mother to the county seat, for a few days at least, before he took her back to Oklahoma. Then he just seemed to disappear for a while.

On October 18, 1892, masked bandits held up a Missouri-Pacific Railroad train at Caney, Kansas, eighteen miles west of Coffeyville. At least four bandits took part in the robbery, and those four would subsequently be identified as Bill Doolin, George Newcomb, a newcomer named Ol Yantis, and someone who may have been Bill Dalton. The pattern of the robbery was a familiar one, with the train's crew being jumped at a small wayside stop and shots fired into the express car until the messenger surrendered. Doolin was rumored to be the gang's leader and, if so, he and the others would have been disappointed in a robbery that yielded less than $100.

Two weeks later, during the afternoon of November 1, three masked bandits robbed the bank at Spearville, Kansas, several days ride to the west of Coffeyville. The three bandits got away with $1,700 and rode hard to the south in the direction of the Texas Panhandle, pursued in part by a posse, which they ultimately lost. Suspicions, later confirmed, suggested that the three bandits were Doolin, Newcomb, and Yantis. Once well clear, the three split up and went their own ways. Yantis returned to Oklahoma where he was eventually traced to his sister's farm. A posse arrived and in a subsequent gunfight, Yantis was shot dead.

And then Bill did it again. He let it be known that he had been appointed a deputy US marshal by Jacob "Black Jake" Yoes, then US marshal for the Western District of Arkansas, based at Fort Smith. He also let it be known that he had a warrant for the arrest of Ed Chapman, the former deputy marshal who had claimed ownership of the horse Emmett had ridden to Coffeyville. The stories Bill spread would subsequently lead to another, false report that Bill had tracked down and killed Chapman.

Finally, the stories Bill started would lead to the attorney general of the United States, William Miller, sending a formal letter of disapproval to Marshal Yoes. Both Yoes and his Kansas counterpart responded to the attorney general saying that the entire story was a fabrication. Yoes said that his predecessor had employed Grat, Bob, and Emmett in various capacities, but he had not and would not employ Bill.

Throughout January and into February 1893, rumors of Bill forming his own gang and planning to rescue Emmett circulated throughout southeastern Kansas and northern Oklahoma. When asked about them, Sheriff Callahan discounted the idea, but he did say things would have been different if you were talking about Bob or Grat rather than Bill. No doubt he also thought that all the rumors, the to-ing and fro-ing, and frequent disappearances of Bill were not doing Emmett's cause any good at all.

III

On October 14, 1892, two warrants had been issued for the arrest of Emmett Dalton. One warrant was for the murder of Lucius Baldwin and the other was for the murder of George Cubine. It was the start of a legal process that would see the State of Kansas attempt to try, find guilty, and punish the only survivor of a murderous assault on two banks and the town of Coffeyville by a band of well-known outlaws. That survivor could not understand why he was being tried for murder. He would freely admit that he had taken part in the robbery, he would freely admit that he had fired his Winchester rifle in the aftermath of that robbery, but he was adamant that he fired high on each occasion, to scare rather than harm, and would fight the murder charges as far as they could be fought.

The January 16, 1893, court case set down by Judge McCue in December saw Emmett appear in the Justice Court in Independence, the hearing being held in the Consultation Room of the courthouse. There he would appear before Judge Gilmore. The general public seemed unaware of the proceedings, but the local newspaper certainly was not and sent their best reporter to cover the proceedings. He would do a very thorough job.

This time, Emmett was able to walk unaided from the jail to the courthouse, accompanied by just Callahan, and neither man attracted any attention. Emmett was neatly dressed and, to the reporter at least, appeared to have almost completely recovered from the wounds he had suffered at Coffeyville; he walked with a slight limp but there was nothing to suggest his right arm had been almost crippled. Once inside, he sat quietly in the Consultation Room, glancing around and occasionally whispering to his lawyer.

That lawyer was again Joseph Fritch, the former schoolteacher who had taught himself how to read and write as an adult, and who had come to the law after marrying the daughter of a judge. The prosecution was led by the experienced William Ziegler, assisted by James Charlton.

Fritch opened the proceedings, immediately moving that the indictment be quashed on the grounds that there was a case pending in another court against the defendant, charging him with the identical offense he was about to be tried for. In that other case, scheduled to be held in the District Court and in which a preliminary hearing had already been held in Coffeyville, the defendant had been charged with the second-degree murder of George Cubine. In the case for which they had gathered today, the defendant was charged with first-degree murder. Fritch suggested the confusion would be ended if the current hearing was quashed. Judge Gilmore disagreed; the case would proceed.

The first witness called was Thomas Ayres, described as the cashier at the First National Bank of Coffeyville. Ayres was obviously still suffering from wounds he had received during the gunfight. The reporter noted that "his face remained misshapen, his hair was whitening, and he had deep lines on his face." Attorney Fritch immediately objected to the calling of Ayres, once more revisiting the argument about two trials. Once more, too, that objection was overruled, and Charlton was allowed to walk the witness through the events of that October day in Coffeyville. When Charlton was finished with Ayres, Fritch declined the opportunity to cross-examine the witness.

Several additional witnesses were called: T. H. Brooks, the Coffeyville agent for the Wells Fargo company; Kirby Long, a clerk in Barndollar's store; and William McCoy, a Coffeyville merchant. After Charlton had led each through their recollections of the raid, Fritch was offered the opportunity to cross-examine the witness. On each occasion, he declined that opportunity. Charlton then told the court that the prosecution had subpoenaed several other witnesses, but in the circumstances would not be calling on them to appear. No additional arguments were offered, and Judge Gilmore ordered Emmett to be held for trial without bail.

Emmett was adamant that he had not killed anyone in Coffeyville and was equally adamant that, because of that, he would never plead guilty to murder. The only plea he would consider, beyond not guilty to everything, was a plea of guilty to manslaughter or accidental killing it if was made plain that his only contribution to the deaths that day had been to be in the company of men who did kill and who were killed in turn. He was almost unshakeable in that belief. His next court date had been set; he would appear in the District Court in Independence on March 7, 1893, to answer the single charge of the murder of George Cubine in the second degree. The information against Emmett had been filed in the District Court on February 24 by County Attorney Ziegler, who would conduct the prosecution, once again assisted by Charlton. The trial judge would be McCue.

When Emmett appeared before the District Court on the morning of Tuesday, March 7, 1893, he could only walk with the assistance of crutches. It may have been a flare-up of the hip and groin wounds he had sustained at Coffeyville, or it may have been an attempt to garner some sympathy in the courtroom. If the latter, it was doomed to failure. The main courtroom in the Independence courthouse that morning was crowded, and the reporters noted that many of those present were residents of Coffeyville who had made the short trip to the north to see justice served.

When asked by Judge McCue how he pleaded to the charge, Emmett announced that he would plead not guilty. McCue then set the murder trial for the following morning at 9 A.M.. When asked about legal representation, Emmett answered that he lacked the funds to employ counsel. At that, the court appointed Fritch, his sometime legal advisor, as his defense counsel. The court then rose.

The pressure on Emmett to plead guilty now increased considerably. Fritch took his role as defense counsel seriously and had previously made inquiries about a possible plea of manslaughter within the legal fraternity in Independence, including possibly even Judge McCue. The response he received was unanimous; the events at Coffeyville were so egregious that second-degree murder was the least serious charge that could possibly be laid, and Emmett should be at least grateful for that. Fritch believed that a guilty plea to a second-degree murder charge would attract a maximum sentence of fifteen years, and that Emmett would probably not be required to serve more than two-thirds of the sentence. The most compelling argument, however, came from Ben Dalton. No details of that argument would ever emerge—perhaps an appeal to spare all the families more heartbreak—but whatever it was, it worked.

Tuesday's courtroom scene was repeated on the morning of Wednesday, March 8, with the same characters and pretty much the same audience. Only the script had been changed, and that by not very much at all. This morning, when Judge McCue asked the accused how he pleaded to the charge of second-degree murder, Emmett answered "Guilty." After a brief pause, McCue pronounced sentence, the maximum penalty of life imprisonment at hard labor in the Kansas State Penitentiary at Lansing. As Emmett, still standing and with tears in his eyes, started to protest that the sentence was unjust, Judge McCue ordered the prisoner removed and adjourned the court. Emmett Dalton had been granted his day in court.

What followed was a whirlwind of activity, and if Emmett had time to think about it, he would have understood that a degree of planning had gone into what began to unfold. Escorted back to the Montgomery County Jail, he was given a few minutes to collect his personal belongings while Callahan moved to finalize some other arrangements. Soon after he was returned to the jail, Emmett was visited in his cell by Charlton, who had come to say farewell and good luck to Emmett. Emmett was appreciative of the visit, and told Charlton "that he would show them he would be the best prisoner they had." An omnibus wagon had already been summoned for the trip to the Independence rail depot, and in the few minutes available to him, Emmett asked Callahan if his horse, Red Buck, could be sold and the proceeds given to Dr. McCulley, the physician who had been treating him in the county jail.

When they were ready, Emmett was handcuffed to his jailer friend Billy Smith and escorted by Callahan and a deputy named Marshall Griffey. It was just a few minutes in the wagon to the depot, where Ben Dalton was waiting to say goodbye his brother. Emmett broke down weeping when he saw Ben, but he recovered quickly. While he still had time, Emmett made some final arrangements. He gave Ben his scarf pin and asked him to take it back to his mother in Oklahoma. He asked Callahan to take his Winchester rifle as a gift, and asked the sheriff to see that his Colt revolvers were given to Fritch in appreciation of his efforts. Finally, he gave his white cowboy hat to Smith.

An hour after he entered the courtroom, Emmett boarded the train that would take him and his escorts all the way to Lansing, more than 170 miles away. Crowds of sightseers gathered at every station the train passed through, hoping to catch a glimpse of America's most famous outlaw and, whenever they stopped, strangers boarded and walked through the carriages for the same purpose.

The party reached Lansing station around 7 P.M.. A carriage was waiting to carry them the short distance to the state penitentiary, where Callahan officially handed his prisoner over to the warden. Callahan thanked Emmett for his behavior during the previous five months and there were handshakes all around. A new group of escorts led Emmett away.

PART III

TO THE GOLDEN WEST

11
THE CASTLE ON THE PLAINS

I

The Kansas State Penitentiary at Lansing was both a Western architectural wonder and an embodiment of penological principles that were already outmoded and certainly paradoxical even as they were being implemented across the advanced nations of Europe and the United States. Originally known as Peterborough Penitentiary, the construction of Kansas's main facility for prisoners convicted of crimes against state law began during the Civil War, using convict labor, but its first section did not open until 1870. When it did, it was a sight to behold. The main building in the prison complex featured turrets and false battlements. Its four-story central section housed both administrative offices and living quarters for the warden and his family. On either side of this structure, the north and south wings of the prison were just half the height of the central section, with each wing holding a four-tier block for a total of 344 cells.

Behind the main building, walls almost eight yards high enclosed the penitentiary's ten-acre main yard. Barely half a mile to the east were two notable landmarks, the Leavenworth, Lawrence and Galveston railroad tracks, and the mighty Missouri River. Train and riverboat travelers who glanced across to the west as they made their journeys believed the structure they saw resembled most closely a medieval castle that had somehow been transported to the middle of the Kansas plains.

From the time of its construction, Kansas authorities had wanted their state penitentiary to be first a self-supporting one and to ultimately return a profit to the state. That ten-acre main yard behind the high walls contained several thriving industries—wagon, shoe, harness, and furniture making, and a marble slab factory. The various workshops and factories were run by labor operators, who paid for the opportunity and who employed around 350 convicts.

Just outside the main wall, though, was another, smaller enclosure that contained the jewel in the penitentiary's crown, an operational coal mine. The prison complex had been built over a rich seam of coal, and a mine shaft was first sunk into that seam in 1879. Within a short time, there was enough coal extracted from the mine to meet all the penitentiary's requirements, with enough left over to supply other state institutions. By 1882, the main shaft extended 750 feet under the ground and coal valued at more than $40,000 had been extracted, making it by far the penitentiary's most valuable industry. It was also its single largest employer, with more than 100 prisoners working there every day from the mid-1880s.

Prisoners worked together during the day, ate in a communal dining area, and slept overnight in single cells. The prisoners also lived in a world of absolute silence and downcast eyes, wore identical striped uniforms, and owned no personal possessions beyond those issued by the prison itself. When they moved around the prison in their work gangs, they moved in lockstep, in single file with their right hand on the shoulder of the prisoner in front of them and their left hand by their side, right foot raised high and left foot shuffling as they walked.

This was to be Emmett Dalton's home for the rest of his life. When he entered that night in March 1893, he became the 950th prisoner in a facility designed to house 660 convicts.

After arrival that night, Emmett was photographed and interviewed, possibly by Warden Seth W. Chase himself, because Emmett was an extremely high-profile prisoner and Chase an extremely high-profile warden. Emmett was given a prisoner number—6247—and his details taken, the prison file recording him as being five feet eleven and a quarter inch tall, with dark brown hair, grey eyes, and a light complexion. All that he wore and carried was taken from him, and he was issued prison clothing and some personal items, including soap and blankets. He was then taken to the small, grimy cell that was now his home and where the prison routine was explained to him. There was one concession prison authorities had made to his physical frailties: he would not be assigned to work in the coal mine.

In the months and years to follow, Emmett came to know that cell like the back of his hand. His new home was in Cellhouse A, the first building built on the site in 1861 and barely modified in the intervening years. He would learn that each of the 222 cells in the cellhouse measured six feet wide, ten feet long, and nine feet high. Emmett was fortunate in one aspect: because of chronic overcrowding, some of those cells accommodated two prisoners in the same space. In his single cell, Emmett had a bunk that was six feet long and two feet wide, attached to the wall and capable of being swiveled up and down. In that cell he had his bedding, his uniform, and very little else.

Emmett would also learn how the penitentiary worked, about guards and trustees, good jobs and bad jobs, good behavior and bad behavior, and good prisoners and bad prisoners, and what awaited each. His injuries meant that he would start with a "good" job, working in the prison's tailor shop in one of those buildings out in the main yard. At first he was just issuing new and replacement "stripes," the prisoners' name for their uniform, before graduating to the role of actually fitting uniforms so that bespoke stripes could be made for those over- or undersize, or those considered worthy of wearing uniforms that actually fitted.

After two years in the tailor shop, Emmett was transferred to another "good" job, working in the prison library. It was a job he loved, because in prison he had become a voracious reader, and working in the library allowed him to nurture what would become a lifelong interest in William Shakespeare. And, despite the relative isolation and forbidding appearance in the landscape, the Kansas State Penitentiary remained part of a larger community with two-way communication between prison and community. For the prisoner at least, the prison library was at the heart of those communications. Working there enabled Emmett to learn the fate of the men he had once ridden with.

Just as Emmett was entering the Kansas prison system in Lansing, far to the south his brother Bill was moving on, literally and figuratively, from the life he had established for his family and himself in Oklahoma. A new outlaw band was established down there, a group known as the Doolin–Dalton Gang and that included several Dalton Gang alumni—Charlie Pierce, George Newcomb, and Bill Doolin himself. Although known as the Doolin–Dalton Gang, the actual leadership was supposed to have been determined by a ballot with the two Bills—Dalton and Doolin—being the only candidates. Legend has it that Bill Dalton received a single vote.

Irrespective of who was believed to be leading the gang, they went on a train-robbing spree in 1893, holding up another Katy at Wharton in the Indian Territory and then, leaving Oklahoma, held up other trains near the Kansas towns of Spearville and Cimarron. A fourteen-man posse caught up with the gang at Ingalls in Oklahoma on September 1, 1893, and in the shoot-out that followed, three deputy US marshals were killed, and Newcomb was badly wounded. One of the gang was captured, but the others escaped into the nearby hill country of the Creek Nation. While on the run, Bill—like Grat before him—became a heavy drinker and increasingly unreliable. He was caught up in several scrapes, most of which ended badly, including one in which Newcomb was again wounded.

After holding up a railroad station at Woodward in Oklahoma in March 1894, the gang met to divide up the $6,500 they had taken. Doolin, increasingly concerned over Bill Dalton's behavior, also thought it might be time for the gang to call it quits. Cut loose, Bill Dalton drifted down to Texas, where he formed a new gang with three other drifters. Their first job was at Longview, near the Louisiana border and, somewhat ironically, their target was the town's First National Bank. And, just like Coffeyville, the bank robbery quickly became a shoot-out between townsmen and outlaws. One of the robbers was shot dead in the clash, as was Longview's town marshal. Three other townsmen were also shot, two of them fatally. Dalton and the two surviving robbers rode west, hiding in canebrakes to elude pursuers, before crossing back into Oklahoma and splitting up.

Lawmen believed Bill Dalton was hiding somewhere near Ardmore in southern Oklahoma when money from the Longview bank robbery began circulating in the area. He was eventually tracked down when his wife, Jennie, and another couple named Houston went into Ardmore to purchase supplies, including a large amount of ammunition plus whiskey for Bill, but the whiskey was labeled as something else. The three paid a substantial amount of cash for their supplies, and that cash was also linked to the Longview robbery.

The next morning, a posse of nine men led by Caleb "Loss" Hart rode out to an isolated homestead near Elk in the Arbuckle Mountains and not far from the Houston's home. With the house surrounded and calls for his surrender, Bill Dalton tried to escape to a small ravine near the house but, in a brief exchange of gunfire, he was shot and killed by Hart. It was June 8, 1894. Jennie Dalton took her husband's body and her children back to California, never to return to Oklahoma.

Emmett learned of his brother's death not long after the event: "On 11 June, I received a letter from my mother telling me that, on 9 June 1894 my brother Bill was murdered near Ardmore in the Indian Territory by a bunch of cowardly United States deputy marshals. This being shortly after the Coffeyville trouble, people went on the theory that anyone could kill a Dalton and get a reputation as a brave man and not have to stand trial for it."

George "Bitter Creek" Newcomb and Charlie Pierce, the young, funny men of the original Dalton Gang, survived Bill Dalton but not by all that long. Western folklore has it that Newcomb was romantically involved with a woman named Rose Dunn, the original Rose of Cimarron, a woman who had several brothers, two of whom—Bill and Bee—were notorious horse and cattle thieves in Payne County, Oklahoma, to the west of Tulsa. Rose was probably just fifteen at the time, but it seems that she and George were in some form of relationship. Unfortunately for their future, when Bill and Bee Dunn were arrested for theft, they did a deal to avoid jail and agreed to provide authorities with details about the movements of the surviving members of the Doolin–Dalton Gang.

When the Dunn brothers also learned that there was a reward of $5,000 for bringing in Newcomb and Pierce, dead or alive, the outlaws' fate was sealed. In May 1895, a pretext was used to lure the two men to the Dunn ranch where both were shot. In one version, they were shot from an ambush when they arrived, another has them shot after they dismounted, and a third has them shot as they slept the night after they arrived.

It did not matter exactly where they were shot down. The two bodies were placed in the back of a wagon and covered with a tarpaulin before the brothers and their gruesome cargo headed off to Guthrie to deposit the bodies and claim the reward. Somewhere along the way, Bee Dunn heard a groan and saw movement beneath the tarpaulin. He climbed back into the body of the wagon and pulled back the tarpaulin. Despite horrendous wounds, Newcomb has been unconscious rather than dead, and was beginning to move and groan. Dunn shot him in the head and replaced the tarpaulin; the journey continued. In Lansing, Emmett was skeptical when the deaths were reported: "Very little was ever made public about the deaths of Pierce and Newcomb. The newspaper carried a brief account of their having been killed by a posse at the Dunn farm."

The last of the gang, Bill Doolin, later formed his own gang but with little success. Hounded throughout Oklahoma and the Indian Territory, a posse led by Deputy US Marshal Heck Thomas finally caught up with Doolin on August 25, 1896, with Doolin being killed in the subsequent gunfight. Many believed that it was Thomas who killed Doolin, but others said the shot that killed Doolin was actually fired by Bill Dunn. Irrespective of who killed Doolin, it left Emmett Dalton as the last outlaw from the last great outlaw gang of the Old West.

II

In May 1894, several newspapers in Kansas, Oklahoma, and Missouri carried a small report quoting Emmett as saying his hopes for an early release would improve if his brother Bill would just stop robbing banks. An indignant Emmett wrote to every newspaper that had carried the report. He dismissed all aspects of what had been written, saying the whole thing had been crafted to sell newspapers rather than to reflect on his hopes and aspirations. He also demanded that his letter of response be given the same prominence as the article that had provoked it; to the newspapers' credit, it was.

Despite his comments about Bill's crimes after he had been imprisoned damaging the chances for his early release, Emmett's first serious attempts to achieve just that commenced in 1897 at a time when the general public still felt that everyone was a little bit safer with Emmett behind bars.

On November 29, Emmett wrote a letter to George Hartley, then a bank president in Arkansas City, Kansas. A decade earlier, Hartley had been a federally licensed trader with the Osage Indians near the settlement at Pawhuska. According to Emmett, when the deputy's fees and reimbursements due to his brother Bob had failed to materialize, Bob turned all his financial affairs over to Hartley, a man all the Dalton brothers liked and trusted. Unfortunately, Hartley was also unable to recover the monies owed Bob by the US Marshal Service.

Hartley had moved to Arkansas City in 1894, and there soon became a prominent figure in the town's political, economic, and social life. Knowing this, Emmett wrote to Hartley, saying that he planned to make an effort to secure a pardon, and asked Hartley if his former acquaintance would be able to write a letter of recommendation for him. Emmett was making this request, he said, because Hartley knew as well as anyone "our troubles and the causes that led up to it." Emmett also asked Hartley for assistance in contacting Harry Richter, another trader who had been based at Pawhuska and who had gone on to bigger and better things. There is no evidence of Hartley's reply, if he did indeed reply to Emmett's letter. At that time, an association with Emmett Dalton may not have been in Hartley's best interests.

Emmett also had the nerve to approach Judge Jerry McCue for early release, writing a very well-crafted letter to the retired judge in 1897. McCue did reply to the letter, offering the sage advice that it was perhaps too early to consider such a course of action. It was advice Emmett seems to have heeded because there were no further attempts to seek a review of his sentence for two years.

In 1899, there were rumors circulating in Kansas that suggested the governor had now taken a personal interest in Emmett's case. The rumors were strong enough to prompt the citizens of Montgomery County to circulate a petition protesting any move to release Emmett. The petition garnered 800 signatures, including those of C. A. Connelly, son of the marshal who was killed in the Coffeyville raid; William Ziegler, the prosecutor who had sent Emmett to prison; and most of those in leadership positions in both Coffeyville and Independence. Not included was the signature of David Stewart Elliott, chronicler of the Coffeyville raid, Civil War veteran, and the man to whom Emmett surrendered his pistols in Death Alley.

When the Spanish-American War broke out in 1898, Elliott again answered the call. He sold his newspaper to concentrate all his energies on organizing and commanding Company G of the Twentieth Kansas Volunteer Regiment. His unit conducted most of its training in a store on South Walnut Street before shipping out for San Francisco and, ultimately, the Philippines. Shortly after their arrival there, the unit fought a sharp little battle at Caloocan, near Manila. The next day, February 27, 1899, Colonel Elliott was shot dead by a sniper. Escorted home by his two soldier sons, Elliott was buried with full military honors in Coffeyville's Elmwood Cemetery.

For Emmett, time moved in a different rhythm in the Kansas State Penitentiary. Rather than weeks and months, there were seasons and events: 1898, for instance, was the year he finally felt and moved easily enough to be able to discard the cane he had been using intermittently to assist his walking; 1896 was the year he finished up in the library and started working as a clerk in the main cellhouse; 1899 was the year his previous eighteen months work in the tailor shop was recognized when he became the shop's senior cutter. This meant that he was in a position where he could make suits and other clothes for prison officials in his spare time and be paid for his work. It was not a lot of money, but it would all add up, and would help him get started on the outside. That day was coming, sooner or later, of that Emmett was certain.

III

All her life, Adeline Dalton referred to her son Emmett as her baby boy. When that baby boy was sentenced to spend the rest of his life in prison, she took the sentence in her stride and with a grain of salt. Her baby boy would certainly have to spend some time in prison, but it would not be for the rest of his life, not if Adeline had anything to do with it. She had lived with a shiftless husband, had seen her birth family torn apart during the Civil War, and by the turn of the twentieth century had seen her sons Frank, Bob, Grat, and Bill cut down, all in the prime of their lives. In 1901, Adeline was in her sixties, well aware of the passage of the years and well aware of opportunities when they presented themselves. In 1901, an opportunity did arise, one that involved her birth family, and one that she was not prepared to let slip.

That year, in Minnesota, state authorities agreed to the parole of the Younger brothers from their life terms being served in the Minnesota Territorial Prison at Stillwater. One brother, Bob, had died in prison, but on July 10, 1901, Cole and Jim Younger walked out of the prison as free men. The commentary around their release would have given Adeline renewed hope of the possibility of her baby boy being released. Newspapers pointed out that society had entered a new century and "the wild environment of their bandit days is no more." Adeline was determined to seize the opportunity this presented to assist her own endeavors, and she hired Otto Eckstein, a forty-year-old Sedgewick County attorney from Wichita. Part of his role would be to organize letters of support and petitions calling for Emmett's release.

Eckstein did his job well. He procured positive testimonials from three former wardens of the Kansas State Penitentiary and somehow managed to convince Oklahoma governor William Jenkins to write to Kansas governor William Stanley asking for a pardon to be granted. Those who supported the campaign put out stories of how Emmett had opposed the Coffeyville raid but perhaps went too far by suggesting that he had also written to his mother asking her to help him prevent it happening. They were on safer ground when they emphasized Emmett's youth at the time of the raid, the influence his older brothers exercised over him, and the extremely good record he had won as a prisoner.

Eckstein also organized a petition calling for Emmett's release to be circulated for the citizens of Independence to sign, and it was this, coupled with the apparent desire of Oklahoma to tell Kansas what to do, that doomed this effort. Judge Jerry McCue refused to sign the petition, and all the town's law officers let it be known they were opposed to both the petition and Emmett's release. It became apparent that the people of Coffeyville were overwhelmingly opposed to Emmett's release, so the petition was not even circulated there.

It appeared that something might come out of all Adeline's and Eckstein's work when a first hearing of an application for the granting of a pardon to Emmett Dalton was scheduled for November 15, 1901. There had been so much organized opposition to any moves to free Emmett that the mere scheduling of a meeting was seen as a significant victory by his supporters. Adeline had told everyone that both she and Eckstein would attend the hearing, so it was a surprise to many when they withdrew the application just a few weeks before it was to be heard. They had learned that opposition to Emmett's release, at all levels of government, was overwhelming. Rather than try and fail now, they would wait for a more auspicious time.

In 1903, Kansas had a new governor, Republican Willis Bailey. Adeline took the opportunity to present the governor with a new petition calling for Emmett's release. It, too, was unsuccessful.

In early 1904, the Kansas legislature passed a new law enabling the directors of the Kansas State Penitentiary to act as a parole board, hearing applications for parole from prisoners within the state's prison system. Emmett was one of the first, making his own application to the board in May 1904. In it, he argued that he had always been a model prisoner and was then in charge of the prison's tailor shop. He also said that, if released, he would relocate to Kingfisher, Oklahoma, where he would help his elderly mother run her farm. Above all, he promised that he would not take to the stage or become involved in show business, as Cole Younger had done, feeling that Younger's actions may have damaged his own chances of parole. He may have been correct in this because Emmett's application was denied.

Emmett submitted another application for a parole to the board in December 1904. This time, he had tried to prepare the ground for a successful appeal by neutralizing some of the opposition that arose every time he or his mother had previously submitted an application. For some time, he had been regularly writing to all of the newspapers in Coffeyville, pleading his case. There were three points he consistently hammered in these letters. The first was that he was just a youth at the time of the raid, untutored in the ways of the world and in thrall to his older brothers. The second point was that if he was to be released, it should be while he was still able to make a living and a positive contribution to society. The third was that he wanted to take care of his elderly mother.

Opposition remained, and in Coffeyville it centered on Tom Ayres, now an attorney. Ayres was able to mobilize the town's business community to oppose Emmett's application, which was once again refused.

Emmett and Adeline's efforts to convince the wider public that he was a redeemed character worthy of release occasionally paid off. In August 1905, a prominent Western newspaper published what would today be called a puff piece:

> Emmett Dalton is a man of splendid physique. He has a round, boyish face and frank brown eyes. As he stood before me, tall and erect, there was a constant reminder of the sacrifice this man has made in his attempt to save a dying brother. Had it not been for his love and hero-worship of Bob Dalton, Emmett might have escaped.
>
> Thirteen years ago, Emmett Dalton, 20 years old [*sic*], was the constant companion of his brother Bob. Bob was a fearless, brutal, cruel, desperate outlaw who thought no more of taking a man's life than would a man who wishes to do away with a rabid dog. He had been a deputy US marshal and was dismissed because he robbed a prisoner and then allowed him to escape.
>
> Emmett never questioned the rights and wrongs of the Coffeyville raid; Bob asked him to go so he went.

Articles like this had no perceptible influence on Emmett's chances of parole, but his life inside had begun to change significantly anyway. His claims to be a model prisoner were not exaggerated, and in February 1907 he was accorded the highest level of trust in the penitentiary system. From that date, he was allowed to walk to Lansing, alone and with no guard overseeing his movements, if it was deemed necessary for him to do so. Excellent news from one perspective, it unfortunately coincided with a significant decline in his health.

In the twelve months leading up to February 1907, Emmett's right arm had become increasingly troublesome. He was able to move his fingers and retained some movement in his hand, but his arm itself had weakened to the extent that he could only move it if he used his left arm and hand to guide and support it. He could still write, but it had become a very slow and laborious process. He was being treated by the prison physician, Dr. Edwin Kanavel, who admitted Emmett to the prison hospital in early 1907. There he was visited by one of his former prosecutors, James Charlton, who subsequently told the *Coffeyville Journal* what he had learned.

Kanavel and other physicians with knowledge of the case had informed Charlton that the injured arm would have to be opened and the damaged bone scraped to prevent further decay and probable blood poisoning. Charlton learned two other things from the experts. The first was that if Emmett did not have the surgery, his right arm would have to be amputated. The second was that the delicate surgery that was needed could not be performed in the prison hospital. Emmett was aware of this and had put a proposal to the prison authorities. He believed his mother would be able to raise enough money to pay for the surgery, and if he was released from prison for the operation that would save his arm, he promised to return afterward.

Fortunately, and fortuitously, Kansas governor Edward Hoch visited Lansing in late June, and at a meeting with Emmett was sympathetic and promised to do what he could. That was the turning point, and in early July Emmett was granted four months of provisional parole, sufficient time to have the operation and recuperate.

Emmett's medical parole began at 3 P.M. on July 6 when he exited the penitentiary to catch the train that would take him to Topeka for the operation. For part of that journey, his traveling companion was Harry Richter, the trader from Pawhuska who had known the Daltons twenty years earlier and who, like banker George Hartley, had agreed to support

Emmett's campaign for release. Like Hartley, Richter had prospered in the days since Pawhuska, becoming a trained pharmacist, serving as lieutenant-governor of Kansas between 1899 and 1903, and, most significantly, had served three terms as a member and sometime president of the board of the Kansas State Penitentiary.

Richter's value was immediately apparent when the train arrived at Topeka. Emmett was neither willing nor prepared to speak to the crowd of reporters waiting at the station, and Richter stepped up, explaining to the reporters that he had met the Dalton brothers many years earlier: "That was some time before the Coffeyville trouble. Emmett used to come to the store with his brothers frequently. . . . He was a fine boy and I believe he would never have gotten into trouble if it had not been for his older brothers. He was a boy and they were grown men. He admired them and was an easy victim when they planned the raid on the Coffeyville banks. I hope the people of Topeka will treat him right for he has the making of a man in him."

From the station, Emmett was taken to the Copeland Hotel where he asked for a "plain, common room" for which he would be paying $2.50 a day. Emmett was disappointed that his mother was not there to meet him; her travel had been delayed, and she did not arrive until after the operation. He did, however, have brief meetings with several doctors, who examined him and then provided details about what his surgery would entail.

The surgery was performed at Christ Hospital two days later by Dr. John Outland, assisted by Dr. Lewis Powell and a third doctor named Ernest. It lasted almost ninety minutes and began when Outland made two incisions in the arm of the anaesthetized patient. The incisions, between Emmett's shoulder and elbow, allowed the surgeons to drain several pus cavities and remove particles of necrosis bone. The mark of the bullet that struck Emmett's arm could be clearly seen, and the main part of the operation involved the surgeons chiseling away half the bone for a length of around three inches. They considered the operation a success; neither of the main joints, the shoulder and the elbow, had been affected, and they were confident that Emmett would recover the use of his fingers and arm. In fact, they concluded, there was no reason to doubt that, in time, the arm would be as strong as it had been before it was injured.

Probably the best medicine Emmett could have been given to aid his recovery was the arrival of his mother in Topeka. Shortly after his operation, the *Coffeyville Journal* ran an article about the mother of the man many residents of that town still believed should have been hanged. It began, "Mrs. Dalton is a motherly woman, well-educated and refined with a soft, low voice that bespeaks the sorrow of her life. It is through her devotion to her son that he secured the parole, which has given him a chance to save his injured arm and may perhaps result in a permanent parole."

Emmett, recuperating, also felt comfortable enough to talk to the reporter about his mother and his life:

> She has been so faithful to me in my troubles, and I want to see her now that I am all fixed up and tell her how nicely I have been treated by everyone for it will make her feel so good.
>
> I was out in the country Monday with Dr. Outland in his automobile, out among the fields of ripening grain and growing vegetables and through the deep woods and the feeling of freedom which came over me was such as I never remember experiencing. It brought back memories of my boyhood days when I attended a country school and a longing for the freedom that was then mine.
>
> But who knows what there is something in life for me, and at any rate there is something comforting in hope and I guess that we all hope even though we sometimes feel that it is in vain.

It was Emmett being open and honest in public for, perhaps, the first time in his life.

Emmett's recuperation was steady rather than spectacular, and he was able to slowly move into a sense of what life might be like after prison. Having his mother at hand was a boon, but his surgeon, John Outland, also took a direct and personal interest in his patient's well-being. In addition to the outing in the Kansas countryside, Emmett described to the *Coffeyville Journal* how he came to see another first. One weekend, Outland drove Emmett to see his first-ever game of American football, a college game played at the University of Kansas. He said he was looking forward to the game: "I will see a battle, but of a different kind than I saw 15 years ago." Emmett also experienced real-life work. When he was well enough, he took on work as a night clerk at the Copeland Hotel, all part of an attempt to show authorities that he was ready for a permanent pardon, something Governor Hoch had suggested he was not averse to, and something prosecutor Charlton recommended after visiting Emmett in Topeka.

There was still considerable opposition to the idea. By 1907, Coffeyville had grown from a town of a little more than 2,000 people at the time of the raid to a city of more than 18,000. A town with two banks had become a city with four, Condon Bank and First National being joined by the State Bank and the Peoples' State Savings Bank. It was those four banks that led the opposition to a possible full pardon for Emmett. The situation in 1907 was not what it had been a decade or even five years earlier. The overwhelming majority of Coffeyville residents had not been there in October 1892, and they were living in a new century that offered boundless opportunities for everyone, ex-prisoners included. And perhaps the best indicator of public attitudes came from the *Kansas City Times*, which posed the question, "Coffeyville opposes a pardon for Emmett Dalton yet who ever heard of Coffeyville before the Dalton raid?"

As per the conditions of his provisional pardon, Emmett returned to the penitentiary at Lansing. That same day, and after considerable searching, a delegate from the state prisons administration finally caught up with Edward Hoch in Iowa, where he was on an official visit. The Kansas governor was offered a commutation order for Prisoner 6247, Emmett Dalton, and a pen. Without any hesitation, Hoch signed the order and returned it to the official. Emmett was now a free man, but there were still a few loose ends.

At the state penitentiary, Emmett went through a semireverse process to the one he had experienced fourteen and a half years earlier. He said his farewells and collected his belongings and the tidy little sum his tailoring skills had earned him over the years. The next day, he was back on the train to Topeka, where he was met at the station by his brother

Ben. That afternoon, Emmett was formally summoned to the governor's office; Governor Hoch had returned from Iowa. There was a nervous wait outside the governor's office and then a smiling Hoch emerged and greeted Emmett. Witnesses say Hoch spoke "tenderly" to the former outlaw before handing him a parchment scroll, saying it was a formal pardon, and shaking his hand.

There were two reporters from the *Kansas City Star* present for the occasion, and they agreed that Emmett's response was straight from his heart. He thanked the governor and promised to do everything in his power to be a good citizen. He then asked to be excused so he could go to the telegraph office to notify his mother of what had just happened. Outside, he told the reporters that he would remain in Topeka for a few more days until Dr. Outland cleared him to travel. He and Ben would then catch a train to Kingfisher, Oklahoma. He was going home.

12 OLD COWBOYS IN HOLLYWOOD

I

In his earliest appeals for a pardon, Emmett and his representatives repeatedly stressed that he would not seek to publicize his crimes or trade on his own or his brothers' notoriety by going into show business or any sort of organized public touring to make money. Now when the formal part of becoming a free man was over, Emmett and his parchment scroll went somewhere comfortable with the two reporters who had witnessed the simple ceremony in November 1907 and gave them the most complete account of his life and crimes that he had yet given:

> I was born in Cass County, near Benton, Missouri. I had three older brothers who went to the Indian Territory and finally my mother decided that she and I would follow. I was then 15 years old.
>
> All of my brothers were deputy US marshals. Everybody knows, I presume, what the social conditions of Oklahoma and the Indian Territory were nearly 20 years ago. There was a semblance of law, but as a matter of fact everything was as near wide open as anything could be. Shooting was common. The killing of a man was almost a daily occurrence. My oldest brother was shot in the performance of his duties by desperadoes. . . .
>
> One day when I was about 18 years old, I was with my brother Bob, who was then a United States deputy marshal. He started to make an arrest. The men resisted. Bob drew as they did and told me to "git." I

was just that young to not have enough sense to run so I drew my six-shooter and got into the game. We arrested the men and put them in jail. If I had run that day with Bob, the chances are that the Coffeyville raid would never have been pulled off and I would never have been asked to be one of the gang. But that performance in sticking to my brother seemed to make a great impression.

Did you ever have a brother you simply idolised? That was the way I looked to my brother Bob. In fact, to my eyes he was my hero . . . the fact that I refused to run under fire impressed Bob a heap. He spoke of it many times and said several times that some day he wanted me with him.

Fully a month before the Coffeyville robbery Bob spoke of the large amount of money the banks there were supposed to have on deposit. We had lived there for a while. In fact, I attended the public schools there. I was as well-known as any youngster in the town. Gradually Bob led up to the suggestion of robbing the banks at Coffeyville, mentioning that as I hadn't run before I probably would be game in this case. I discouraged the idea. The more I opposed, the more determined he seemed to be; I finally yielded. It was not so much that I wanted to turn outlaw, bandit and desperado, as it was that I feared Bob would consider me lacking in nerve.

Emmett then proceeded to give the reporters a detailed account of the Coffeyville raid, describing how, in the end, there were just five of them involved. He spoke of how they camped in a draw near Coffeyville the night before the raid, sleeping with their blankets on the cold ground. Nerves, he said, prevented him from sleeping very much that night, but when he thought about it, the plan was simple and foolproof. They would ride in, rob the banks, and ride out again. Besides, he was still strongly of the belief that as long as he was with Bob, everything would be all right. Their final plans were made the next morning, and by day's end the whole world knew what happened.

Emmett said he was bedridden for seventy-two days recovering from the wounds he suffered that day. The recuperation had given him a lot of thinking time, and he mused over the murder charges he faced, given that he had not harmed anyone that day. In fact, the only reason he had pleaded guilty to second-degree murder was because of the urgings of unnamed others. And here he was now at the end of the long journey that had begun that day.

It was an interesting story, and it made for interesting reading. Some saw it as an attempt by a relatively young man to explain the reasons behind his incarceration for two-fifths of his life, and it was certainly that. Others, perhaps more cynical, saw the extensive interview as Emmett Dalton road-testing a story and a delivery he could take to theaters and halls across the United States, cashing in on the notoriety his criminal past had brought him, and it was certainly that, too.

Emmett was a man in demand. Almost as soon as he walked out of Governor Edward Hoch's office, offers of employment started to find their way to wherever he was. In a follow-up interview with the *Kansas City Star* before he departed Topeka, Emmett said that several of the offers he had already received were for acting or stage roles, others involved working with carnivals or circuses. Emmett said he was adamant that such employment was not for him; he had moved well beyond that sort of thing. Rather, he thought he might spend some time with his family in Kingfisher before relocating to a larger place, somewhere like Kansas City perhaps.

During his time in prison, he continued, partly from various allowances credited to him and partly through the tailoring he had completed for private parties, he had made a substantial amount of money. He believed it would be enough to open a tailoring business and, again, he was considering a larger town—somewhere like Oklahoma City or Muskogee—if that was what most appealed to him. Tulsa was also a possibility because he had relatives there.

Tulsa won out. Oklahoma became the forty-sixth state of the United States on November 16, 1907, and possibilities seemed endless in the new state. Emmett did spend time with his family at Kingfisher, but after fourteen-plus years of having his life controlled by others, he opted to move away from what he may have seen as family obligations so he could live his own life. Initially, he moved to Tulsa and moved in with his cousin Scott Younger, and it was at the home they shared that Emmett was tracked down by reporters. Emmett was always up for an interview and was happy to speak again. He told them that he was taken aback by how large and modern Tulsa had become, now a thriving city of 16,000 people. Emmett told them he could remember the time when Tulsa was just a dusty little frontier town.

Emmett was also happy to explain that he and Scott Younger were looking at business options in Tulsa. One possibility was that they would open a butchery, another that they would open a tailor shop. The latter option was preferred, and after borrowing money from a silent partner, the cousins did open a tailor shop in Tulsa in mid-April 1908. Soon afterward, Emmett was caught up in the wave of boosterism sweeping the new state.

The biggest boosters in Tulsa were the members of the Tulsa Commercial Club, and in May 1908 the club organized what they called the Tulsa Booster Train, a moving advertisement that would travel to cities in the East and Northeast of the United States to sell Tulsa as a place of opportunity for individuals and businesses. It was a train in name and appearance. But the Booster Train, apart from the locomotive and tender, was composed of luxurious Pullman carriages carrying 150 Tulsa businessmen, a twenty-six-man band, and Creek, Osage, and Cherokee representatives. The train eventually traversed more than 10,000 miles, and the day's route and highlights were on the front page of the newspaper that was printed aboard and distributed each morning.

Emmett had been a Tulsa businessman for just a few weeks and was just the part-owner of a small tailor shop. But he was also a famous, and, one hoped, reformed, former outlaw, so his presence on the Booster Train made a certain amount of sense. He apparently tried to stay in the background whenever possible, something that proved impossible when the train rolled into Washington, DC. There, Emmett was pushed to the front, where he met President Theodore Roosevelt and presented him with a Tulsa Booster lapel pin. He also met the vice president, several members of cabinet, and several politicians who had asked to meet him. This firsthand experience of fame, as opposed to notoriety, was something he could ponder all the way back to Tulsa.

Emmett was a gifted storyteller, able to weave fact and fiction into a seamless whole. Some of the stories were totally false, with perhaps a small part distantly related to something that had actually occurred. If they were good enough, Emmett would repeat them, in both spoken word and in writing, over and over again until it seems that even he believed that a blatant untruth was an established fact. Take, for instance, the stories he told about the woman who would become his wife. They had been, he said, childhood sweethearts whose love for one another lasted through the good times and bad. She did not approve of what he did and waited patiently through the long years for his release from the state penitentiary at Lansing, Kansas. Her name was Julia Johnson.

Emmett had indeed known Julia when they were both teenagers, mainly because Bob Dalton took up with Julia's sister Lucy for several years. There is no material that suggests that Emmett and Julia were ever anything more than acquaintances. Then they went their own ways, Emmett to become a gang member, outlaw, and prisoner, Julia to become a serial bride. Her first marriage was in 1886 when the sixteen-year-old married Albert Whiteturkey, a Delaware Indian from their nation in the Indian Territory. The marriage seems to have foundered sometime during its first year.

In 1887, Julia married again, this time to Robert Gilstrap, reportedly a Cherokee who had been born and raised in the Cherokee Nation. Julia gave birth to a daughter they named Jennie May in 1887, but the marriage ended suddenly and violently on Christmas Eve that year when Gilstrap was shot dead in a gunfight with a Delaware named Frank Lenno in front of Lenno's store in Bartlesville. Julia and her daughter remained in Bartlesville, and in April 1903, she married again, this time to a hard-core criminal named Robert Ernest Lewis. Several times a convict, Lewis continued to live on the edge of the law, running a saloon called the Uno Bar in Bartlesville. In November 1907, two deputy US marshals went to the bar with instructions to close it down. A gunfight erupted with one of the deputies and Lewis both killed.

Bartlesville was forty-five miles north of Tulsa, and when Emmett was released, he went to visit some relatives there. During one of his visits, he met Julia and a romance developed between the two, a romance that led to their marriage at the First Presbyterian Church of Bartlesville on October 31, 1908, in a low-key ceremony. Emmett left Tulsa and his tailor shop to move in with Julia at the substantial house she now owned on South Cheyenne Street. They would soon add a full second story to the building to convert it into a boarding house. In addition to the home,

Julia brought a daughter and a stepson to the marriage. She also brought an entrepreneurial flair that would enable Emmett to take his stories—real and otherwise—to an audience far larger than anything he could ever have imagined.

II

Julia Dalton knew Emmett's story and the entire story of the Dalton Gang as well as anyone could, and she knew, too, that there were a lot of people in the United States who would be interested in that story, to understand just what it was like in the Old West now that the Old West had gone, never to return. The usual medium to tell the stories of cowboys and outlaws, lawmen and lynch mobs, had been the newspapers and magazines that had proliferated in the second half of the nineteenth century in the United States. Young men and old men, crowded into the big cities of the East and Midwest, lapped up the stories just as they lapped up the displays of the Buffalo Bill and Annie Oakley traveling shows. In the new century, there was a new challenge to the Wild West shows and dime novels—the moving pictures. The entrepreneur in Julia sensed an opportunity.

Western stories and the new medium were made for each other. Films with western settings were among the first of the "movies" produced in the 1890s, and Thomas Edison's film company produced short vignettes in that decade about Buffalo Bill Cody, Annie Oakley, and other famed Westerners. The genre really took off in 1903 when two films with copyrighted storylines appeared, *Kit Carson* and *The Pioneers.* The outstanding production that year was director Edwin S. Porter's *The Great Train Robbery*, an eight-minute shoot-'em-up produced in New Jersey for $150. The first decade of the twentieth century also witnessed the rise of the nickelodeon; by 1908, it was estimated that 10 million Americans a year fed money into the machine to watch short films.

As so often happens, circumstances then took over. John Tackett had been just eighteen years old when he took the photographs that would come to characterize public consciousness of the Coffeyville raid. In the intervening years, the Tackett family had built and operated a movie theatre in Coffeyville; located at the corner of Eighth and Maple, it was called the Tackett Theater. During those years, too, John Tackett had begun to dream of making his own moving pictures, with the Coffeyville raid an obvious starting point. In late 1908, Tackett met with Emmett to discuss the possibility of collaborating on a silent movie about the raid. Emmett—and Julia—listened and nodded.

In January 1909, Emmett and John Tackett formed a company to produce a film they called *The Famous Dalton Raid on the Two Banks of Coffeyville.* Their proposal attracted a backer, the Coffeyville Commercial Club, and it was decided the film would be premiered at the Alaska-Pacific-Yukon Exposition to be held in Seattle later that year. Shot on location in Coffeyville, the film would star Emmett and would tell the story of the raid through his eyes. Emmett would play himself and also his brother Bob, and act as technical advisor to ensure the historical accuracy of the film, or at least accurate to his recollections.

The film was a success. After its premier in Seattle, Emmett and Tackett took their film on the road, showing and promoting it wherever they went. Between shows, Emmett signed autographs and spoke of the follies of crime: "The sea of time is strewn with wrecks, and most of these wrecks are caused by men and boys not following the true chart in the voyage of life," was one of the sayings he trotted out after many shows. He also took with him a large and growing book of press clippings, which he would show in newspaper offices in the towns and cities they visited. While showing them to all editors and reporters, Emmett would also talk about "the pound and a half of buckshot and bullets" he claimed he still carried inside him. It was usually enough to guarantee another story and some more free publicity for the traveling show.

The film was not an unalloyed success. Out of respect to those who had suffered losses during the raid, it was not shown in Coffeyville, and several other towns banned it from being shown within the town limit. But, overall, it was even more successful than Emmett and Tackett had hoped. Eighteen months after swearing not to enter the industry, Emmett found he had show business in his blood.

A whole new world opened up before Emmett. He and Tackett followed *The Famous Dalton Raid* with a second film, *The Last Stand of the Dalton Boys* (1912), and then, two years later, a third entitled simply *The Dal-*

ton Boys. Emmett starred in all three, always playing himself and usually playing at least one of his brothers. He also began to write, at first just short news stories for the local newspaper and later longer articles about his life and times. At one point, he even worked as the editor of a Bartlesville newspaper, but his heart remained in the movie industry, and he began writing scripts for films he hoped to make.

Emmett also spent long periods on the road, touring his own and others' films, sometimes alone, sometimes with companions. Critics would describe seeing "a paunchy, ex bank robber talking with regret about his wasted past." At times it could be entertaining; Emmett often appeared on double bills with William "Devil Anse" Hatfield, patriarch of the Hatfield family and central protagonist in the Hatfield–McCoy feud. Emmett had produced a short film about the feud, and at their shows he would appear as the successful businessman that he was, while Hatfield would usually appear in an elaborate fringed jacket, embroidered sombrero, Winchester rifle, and a brace of pistols. What Emmett did with these shows was amusing and enlightening; what he did afterward was downright dangerous.

Increasingly, and like at least two of his brothers, Emmett turned to alcohol to help him cope with the life he was leading. At first it was a way of unwinding after a day of traveling, showing his films, and answering the same questions he had answered a thousand times before. Then the drinking became something more, a way of driving off the devils—real and imagined—that plagued him. Emmett was not a good drunk; at some hotels he would drink until first asked to leave, but then later had to be escorted out by local police. He would sometimes start fights and sometimes stagger out into the night to wake the next day in a jail cell rather than a hotel bed.

In early 1912, a police sergeant on duty at the Union Station in St. Louis spotted a middle-age man, dressed as a cowboy, displaying what the policeman thought were obvious signs of intoxication. With his companion, an older man, the cowboy was taken to the police station within the larger railroad depot where the cowboy introduced himself as Emmett Dalton of Bartlesville, Oklahoma, and described himself as an ex-bandit, ex-train robber, and ex-bank robber. He told the police that he was in St. Louis to speak to its citizens about his former life. He then introduced his companion as his cousin, Cole Younger. Younger was quiet and compliant and was released. Emmett was neither of those things and spent another night in his cowboy clothes in a jail cell.

Emmett probably reached his low point in Joplin, Missouri, the following year. Arrested four times for drunkenness in a single week, he was sentenced to thirty-one days' detention in the town's jail. From there, Emmett wrote a letter of complaint to the local newspaper, saying that his conditions in the jail were worse than he experienced in the Kansas State Penitentiary. The letter was published and was read by a Joplin resident named James Brown. Brown's father had been Charlie Brown, killed by the Daltons in Coffeyville more than twenty years earlier. Brown had once vowed to kill Emmett, but now chose to raise bail for him, believing that his father would appreciate returning good for evil.

Not too long after this, Julia told Emmett that his career and his life were going nowhere in Bartlesville. If they were serious about filmmaking, they needed to be near the burgeoning of the industry, and so the Daltons decided to move to Hollywood.

In 1914, Emmett and Julia moved from Bartlesville to Los Angeles where they leased a modest stucco house in the Hollywood Hills. It was a good time to be in and around Hollywood, which had become something of a magnet or both real-life and wannabe cowboys, attracted by the possibility of a career in the motion picture industry. Westerns had maintained their popularity, and Emmett was one of the few hopefuls who could legitimately claim expertise. Soon after settling in, Emmett started to gain small acting jobs and offers to assist in screenwriting. He also met and mingled with the biggest cowboy stars of the day—William S. Hart and Tom Mix—and was on first name terms with both.

Despite working in the industry and mixing with the top Hollywood cowboys, Emmett was always skeptical about how the West was portrayed. He would write, "Personally, I have met hundreds of bad men, hard men, shooting men, killers, both peace officers and outlaws, and I am yet to see the first notch on any of their six-shooters." He added that he had never seen anyone fan-shoot their pistol, shoot from the hip, or waste precious ammunition by firing two pistols simultaneously.

There were two things that would drive Emmett's and Julia's first few years in Los Angeles, and they were perhaps related. The first was to protect what Emmett thought was the Dalton brand. No story, no film about Emmett and his brothers and what they did would be permitted without Emmett's involvement or permission. If necessary, he would take out advertisements in newspapers warning against infringement of copyright and threaten direct legal action if he thought the Dalton name or stories about the Daltons were being used without his formal permission.

The second thing that Emmett was determined to do was to write, and possibly film, his life story. He took the first step in 1918 when he wrote five articles outlining his life up until then, and these were published in a magazine called *Wide World*. The articles were so successful that Emmett had them published as a paperback book. The book sales were less successful than he hoped, but Emmett may not have cared because he was working on a film of his life. Working with him on this was John Tackett, another who had now left his home to try to find success in Hollywood. Tackett agreed to coproduce the film with Emmett, who insisted that it be a true representation of the Dalton Gang, adding that he thought people were ready for "good, snappy Western historical pictures, based on fact." They would call the film *Beyond the Law.*

Preproduction started in 1918 and filming in 1919, at which point the Dalton/Tackett company issued a press release describing the forthcoming film as "a beautiful romantic love story written by and starring Emmett Dalton, last of the world's most noted outlaws, published in *Wide World* from May until September 1918. The first historical picture ever produced with any of the original characters." The release of the film should have let people judge for themselves Emmett's claims of historical accuracy.

The "beautiful romantic love story" starred Emmett as himself and in the roles of Bob and Grat. Starring opposite was eighteen-year-old Virginia Lee, born in Mexico and drawn to Hollywood, a young beauty who had already appeared in two films. In a later work on the early days of Hollywood, Lee was interviewed: "Emmett Dalton—when I met him—he was about 35 (He was actually 47 years old). I was 17. It was unbelievable the way he looked after me. He was a perfect gentleman, he wouldn't let anyone come on the set without their coat on. His wife took a shine to me. . . . I played the role of Ruth Lane Young, Emmett's sweetheart. We filmed it in different locations where it actually happened in the middle West."

The film had some success in New York and Los Angeles, but elsewhere results at the box office were disappointing. Part of this was no doubt due to critics finding Emmett's several performances in the film underwhelming. Undeterred, Emmett took the film on the road, concentrating this time on the larger cities where he would attract a larger audience, if only out of curiosity. He would once more appear at the end of the film, inviting questions from the audience and answering them with his usual mix of fact, fiction, and wishful thinking.

Emmett had starred in the 1917 film *Man of the Desert*, but critics found his acting wooden and unconvincing. When he received similar criticism after *Beyond the Law*, he chose to concentrate on other aspects of the industry, and from then on operated behind the camera. He wrote scripts for three more movies, *Across the Chasm*, *When a Man's a Pal*, and *The Wages of Sin*, none of which made any money. He also met and worked with Alexander MacDonald, a writer and reporter from Kansas City, who would turn several of Emmett's stories into successful novels. In fact, it may have been MacDonald who in 1919 wrote that Emmett had stopped shooting people and was now shooting movies.

As the 1920s progressed, part-time roles writing screenplays and a little bit of support acting became few and far between for Emmett, a potential development that Julia had seen coming sometime earlier. While Emmett was touring the country with his various film projects, Julia had been investing the money, such as into property, especially the development of new housing estates. Emmett, too, found that he had an interest in, and aptitude for, the world of real estate. He and Julia moved from property investment into construction projects involving property they had an interest in. In the 1930s, both Emmett and Julia turned sixty, a time when people generally start considering their retirement. They could do so with some confidence, thanks in particular to Julia's canny investments. In 1931, Emmett told a reporter, "Two land deals in Hollywood, California, brought me more money than our whole bunch ever made in deviltry."

From the mid- to late-1920s, Emmett began to introduce some social commentary into the little talks and larger lectures that accompanied his public appearances. There were two common themes in these talks, the first being the urgent need for reform in the prison and justice systems. To begin with, he believed the death penalty should be abolished, if for no other reason that it didn't work. He was able to point out that crime rates for capital crimes were increasing rather than decreasing, the opposite to what proponents of capital punishment argued would happen. His second theme was that the prison system was also failing the country, and until some kind of comprehensive vocational education was introduced in prison, prisoners going into the system would only come out as more hardened and professional criminals.

When prodded, Emmett spoke at length about the current crop of gangsters and outlaws. To begin with, he was not happy about the amount of publicity the hoods received, arguing that it made them out to be heroes to a certain class of society. He also disagreed with what he saw as FBI director J. Edgar Hoover's relentless quest for publicity as he fought what he called a series of crime waves. They weren't crime waves, Emmett argued, but simply newly enacted laws being broken. He even managed a dig at the criminals garnering all the headlines: "Can you imagine Jesse James or one of the Dalton boys with a bodyguard?"

III

For some time, Emmett had been thinking about writing the definitive story of his life, or at least the story that he wanted in the public domain. Beginning in 1930, Emmett started working with a Hollywood screenwriter named Jack Jungmeyer, putting down the storyline. He chose Jungmeyer because the screenwriter had been involved in several very successful Western movies and—Emmett being Emmett—there was always the possibility of the book going straight into film. Published in 1931 as *When the Daltons Rode*, it was a success despite the market for crime stories being dominated by tales of Prohibition gangsters and organized crime. On the back of the book's success, Emmett and Julia decided to revisit many of the locales he had known as a young man and had written about in the book. He and Julia also joked about their trip, labeling it their second honeymoon.

The Daltons toured Oklahoma and parts of Texas and Kansas, catching up with family, friends, and acquaintances. They visited Coffeyville, where they were well received, thanks in part to the efforts Emmett had made over the years to make some atonement for the raid. He caught up once more with Charlie Gump, with whom he had maintained intermittent contact. However, the main reason for the visit to Coffeyville was to do something about the grave in Elmwood Cemetery that held the bodies of his brothers Bob and Grat and Bill Powers. It was still marked by just the metal rail the gang were supposed to have used to tether their horses, and Emmett commissioned a local stonemason to make an appropriate headstone. Unfortunately, that stonemason omitted the "s" from Bill Powers's name.

From Coffeyville, the Daltons headed north to Lansing where Emmett hoped to meet some old prisoner friends at the Kansas State Penitentiary. It is not clear whether or not he did meet old colleagues. The couple then headed home to Los Angeles. Billed as a promotional tour for his new book and a second honeymoon, the trip to their old haunts looked very much like an older couple saying goodbye to faces and places they would never see again.

Emmett was getting old. He had lost relatives, close relatives, to sudden death; four of his brothers had died violently, and he had been close by when two of them were shot to death. All four had known, just as he had known, that sudden death was one of the risks they would confront when they chose to live a life outside the law. All the deaths had an effect, Bob's especially, but it was the other, unexpected deaths, that really hurt.

Emmett's sister Nannie—Nancy May—had died in 1901 when he was still in prison. She was just twenty-five years old when she passed away, married to Charlie Clute, with a little boy they had named Roy. Nannie had been given a smallpox vaccination, but something had gone wrong, and she contracted tetanus, which killed her. Roy had gone to live with Adeline and Leona, who would look after him and raise him well, but Roy would never know his real mother. His second oldest brother, Cole, had also died in 1920. Cole had remained in California for many years, and it was there that he contracted tuberculosis. He moved to New Mexico where he believed the climate might help, and it may have given him some extra time. Cole was sixty-seven when he died, and his body joined Nannie's in the family plot in the Kingfisher, Oklahoma, cemetery.

The death that hit home the hardest was that of his mother, Adeline, in 1925. Adeline had reached eighty-nine, a good total by any reckoning, but she had been the rock in his life through good times and bad, and her passing had left a heart-shaped hole in his life. What hurt, too, was that Adeline's death was reported quite extensively, and those reports always spoke of her outlaw sons and rarely of the strength she had shown in raising a large and boisterous family on the frontier. Then, just three years later, his younger brother Simon had died at fifty. No one ever thought that Simon would amount to much, he was a drifter and a dreamer, but he had volunteered for service in the Spanish-American War, and after that he still couldn't seem to settle down. He died in Oklahoma City in September 1928 from injuries he had received in a motor vehicle accident three months earlier.

If Emmett ever needed further evidence of the passage of time, or of his place in history, it would come back to him in the eulogies written whenever one of the Coffeyville Defenders, or someone associated with the raid or his trial, passed away. The first significant death in that cohort occurred in 1906 with the death of Henry Isham, whose hardware store had been the center of resistance and who had handed out firearms. Isham had remained in the hardware business in the years after the raid and, around the turn of the century, expanded his business interests by establishing a private bank. The hardware store remained his pride and joy, however, and it was there where, in 1906, he collapsed while serving a customer and died before the doctor arrived. Isham had been three days short of his seventieth birthday.

Tom Ayres's recovery from his facial injuries was slow and painful, and the year after the raid he moved to Sioux City, Iowa, for ongoing treatment and, possibly, to get away from the place where he was so severely disfigured. Ayres returned to Coffeyville in 1895, practicing as a lawyer and serving a term as the city's mayor. He also expanded his business interests, including a prescient investment in one of the region's first oil wells. Ayres's face always carried the scars of the wounds inflicted that day and parts of his lower face remain paralyzed for the rest of his life. Ayres never forgave those who had inflicted those wounds, including Emmett. Ayres died in August 1908 and was buried in Elmwood Cemetery.

Judge Jerry McCue's wife, whose illness interrupted the early stages of the state's legal actions against Emmett, took her own life in 1893. Two years later, McCue married his late wife's sister. The McCues moved from Independence to Kansas City in 1897, and Jerry continued to practice law there until struck down with Bright's Disease. Jeremiah McCue died in 1910.

John Cubine, developer of the cowboy boot that went around the world and uncle of the man Emmett was convicted of killing, died suddenly of heart failure at home in Coffeyville in January 1911. Charles Cubine, just six years old when his father George was shot dead, would become a well-known musician and singer. His mother, Alice, George's widow, remained in Coffeyville for the rest of her life, passing away there in 1935. John Cubine's son Claude took over the running of the family boot and shoe store when his father died. It would survive the end of the great cowboy era but not the Great Depression.

Charlie Ball, the Condon Bank teller whose quick thinking bamboozled Grat Dalton and potentially saved his bank tens of thousands of dollars, remained with Condon for the rest of his working life, becoming president of the bank in 1916. He died in 1922. Five years later, the city lost two of its better-known residents in the space of a few months. John J. Kloehr, the man who emerged when the crisis came, passed away at sixty-eight, and was buried in Coffeyville's Fairview Cemetery. Dr. Walter Wells died the same year. The avuncular Wells had probably saved Emmett's life twice on that October day. Once with his medical skills and a second time when his quickness of thought and sense of humor deflected a lynch mob.

A last little reminder for Emmett would have been the death in 1933 of the former teller, and sometime hostage, from the First National Bank of Coffeyville, Jack Shepard. Shepard had remained with the bank for a decade after the raid, rising to the level of vice president before leaving to pursue opportunities in the gas industry. In retirement, Shepard relocated to Missouri.

Emmett's own mortality became increasingly apparent. The last shotgun pellet Carey Seaman fired into him in October 1892 was not removed until 1923, and despite numerous operations, his right arm would never be complete again. The wound site would have to be regularly drained and was cleaned out and bandaged daily. Each day he would also take a "thick, sticky substance" to relieve the chronic pain he suffered. He kept this as well hidden as he could, carefully arranging his arms for photographs so that all looked normal. He also kept secret the fact that he was suffering from both diabetes and hypertension in the later years of his life.

There were some things Emmett wanted to do before he reached the end of the trail. He revisited his semibiography, *When the Daltons Rode*, making sure that it was as boisterous and adventurous as he could make it. Emmett thought it was a good story and knew that a number of Hollywood producers were just waiting for him to sign a contract for the film version of the story. Some good offers had already been forthcoming, but he had not been prepared to accept them. Instead, he quietly signed the movie rights over to his stepdaughter, Jennie Mae Perrier, along with some suggestions as to what she should do and what she should avoid.

Emmett also formed a long-distance, and unlikely, friendship with Charlie Gump, the road contractor whose shouted warning had set off the gun battle at Coffeyville. Like Emmett's right arm, Gump's right hand never really recovered from the damage caused by one of Bob Dalton's bullets, and at times it was more like a claw than a hand. But the men exchanged letters, and Emmett would come see Gump whenever he was in Coffeyville. Charlie visited Los Angeles in late 1935 and accepted an invitation to have Thanksgiving dinner with Emmett and Julia. Newspapermen were there, taking photos of two old men looking at firearms. Gump offered them a quote: "I always thought kindly of Emmett. He was the young one and his brothers dragged him into it."

Emmett also spoke to Gump that night, but it would be some time before old Charlie revealed what the old outlaw had said: "Emmett and I broke bread together last Thanksgiving Day. He said he hoped Coffeyville people had forgiven him, that he deeply regretted the tragedy."

Whenever Emmett and Julia dined out in Los Angeles, people would look. For several years, they were a staple of the social pages, but by 1936 they had virtually disappeared. This was due, in the main, to Emmett's health, which was failing. His physical ills were compounded that year when his brother Ben died on March 11. Ben and Adeline had been two pillars in his life since Coffeyville and the death of Bob, and they were now gone. Just over three months later, Emmett returned to religion, but not to the Presbyterianism of his youth. In August 1936, he was baptized into the evangelical Aimee Semple McPherson's Angelus Temple, and seemed to take some comfort from religion in his last months. Emmett's strength slowly faded away, he lost weight and then mobility. Weakening, his life slipped away and, following a stroke, he died peacefully at home on July 13, 1937, as Julia sat by his side and held his hand.

Emmett had planned for what was to happen after his death, but the planning seems to have been more in the way of conversations with Julia than in written instructions to be followed. Prayers for his immortal soul were offered up at the Angelus Temple, but the main service was held at the Forest Lawn Funeral Parlor in Los Angeles and was conducted, in part, by the Loyal Order of the Moose, a philanthropic fraternal lodge committed to the welfare of children and then only open to white men. Those in attendance were representative of Southern California at the time, and though none of his siblings were in attendance, two or three more distant relatives were there.

Emmett's death was widely noted in passing, but the newspapers and newsreels he had used so well were now dominated by stories of the missing aviatrix Amelia Earhart, so an era slipped by with hardly a hurrah.

Emmett had asked Julia for his body to be cremated and the ashes buried alongside his brother Bob in the Elmwood Cemetery at Coffeyville. It did not work out as he had hoped. After the funeral service, Emmett's body was cremated, and the ashes held at the Forest Lawn Mortuary until a decision could be made as to their disposal. Julia was prepared to go ahead with Emmett's wishes, but his sister Leona was not. All who knew Leona would describe her as a very strong and very pious woman, and one who usually imposed her will on those around her. Leona was determined that Emmett's ashes would be interred in the Dalton family plot in the cemetery at Kingfisher, Oklahoma. There he would lie in eternal peace with the "good" Daltons, rather than being interred at Coffeyville with the "bad" Daltons.

Emmett's ashes were dispatched to Kingfisher; they certainly weren't personally delivered by Julia, who seems to have stepped back from the whole process. The burial of Emmett's ashes in the Dalton family plot took place after dark one evening to avoid any casual onlookers turning up. Leona also insisted that Emmett's final resting place not be identified in any way until after her death.

Emmett Dalton was very much of his time and circumstances, not an innately bad man or someone whose character flaws would draw him naturally to the life of an outlaw. He became one of the "bad" Daltons because he was closer to Bob in particular, and Grat and Bill to a lesser extent, than he was to any of the "good" Daltons. In some respects, Emmett's was a story of redemption, of a young man who went astray, and who paid a terrible price for it. A young man who paid the price, took his punishment, and came out the other side able to make a positive contribution through his books and films, and through the life he lived in Los Angeles.

The one would not have existed without the other, and Emmett was never a man to think too deeply about things anyway. The reason he was such a good prisoner in Lansing was the same reason Bob Dalton valued his younger brother so much. Emmett understood best how to live his life in lockstep, arm on the shoulder of the man—or woman—in front, right foot high, and left leg shuffling as he went forward. There was more than enough sadness in Emmett's life, with even more in his death. Emmett idolized his brother Bob, and asked to be placed alongside him in death, in the position he had hoped to occupy throughout his life, at his brother's shoulder as they rode across the plains. It was not to be in life, or in death.

AFTERWORD

Show business being show business, later in the year after Emmett's death, *When the Daltons Rode* was re-released by the publisher and for the second time became a best-selling book. Shortly afterward, Jennie Mae Perrier negotiated the sale of the film rights to the book, which was made into a 1940 film featuring a stellar cast, including Randolph Scott as Emmett. Perrier remained true to her promise to Emmett and negotiated a role for Julia as a technical advisor to the film for a handsome fee of $10,000.

Julia did subsequently return to where she and Emmett had grown up. The first time was in 1940 when she traveled to Coffeyville for the world premiere of *When the Daltons Rode.* Around Christmas 1941, Julia returned to Oklahoma to visit family and friends, a list that included Leona Dalton. The following year, Julia married her fifth husband, John Robert Johnson, a fellow resident of Los Angeles who was thirteen years her junior. They married in 1942, but were not together long before Julia died on May 20, 1943, in Fresno, her death attributed to cardiac failure following a ruptured appendix. Julia's body was also cremated, and her ashes returned to Oklahoma where they were secretly buried in the Johnson family plot in Dewey.

Eva May Dalton Whipple died in Kingfisher on January 28, 1939, having moved there from Bartlesville to live with her sister Leona after her husband, John Whipple, died some years earlier. Out in California, Litt Dalton passed away on January 8, 1942. Eighty-year-old Litt, the last of the Dalton brothers, had been living on a state pension in Yolo for several years, his affairs being handled by his nephew and Bill Dalton's only son, Charles Coleman Dalton, who lived in nearby Lodi. In those later years, Litt was also a lot more willing to talk about his family.

At five feet, eleven inches, Litt claimed to be the smallest of the Dalton boys, telling listeners how "six of us boys lived something like mother wanted us to." Of his brothers Grat, Bob, Bill, and Emmett, he said "they had good upbringing, but the devil prodded them with his fork." He was also prepared to speak of those long-ago train robberies in central California, recalling how Grat was to have taken part in the Alila robbery, but that his horse had given out en route to join his brothers, so he returned to Fresno where he was able to establish an alibi. Bill did not take part in either robbery, but he assisted in planning them and helped Bob and Emmett to escape. Littleton left no one in doubt that he was one of the "good" Daltons.

After Julia Dalton's death in 1943, Leona finally approved a headstone for where Emmett's ashes had been buried. It read, "Here I lay sleeping, but not to remain. I look for the coming of Jesus again." Leona was the last of Lewis and Adeline's children, and her life ended in a Kingfisher rest home in April 1964.

When Emmett submitted one of his early applications for a pardon, and a countermovement was started by the city leaders of Coffeyville, a Kansas City newspaper issued the barbed jibe that, without the Dalton raid, who in the United States would ever have heard of Coffeyville? It was a legitimate question to ask, but it was also somewhat disingenuous; no one in Coffeyville asked for their town to become famous, and, in the beginning at least, the town paid a steep price for that fame. The Coffeyville raid did take place, eight people did die, and Coffeyville and its iconography have resonated down through the years. The raid and the fame that followed also affected the lives of all residents in the town that day, some more so than others.

The epicenter of the raid, the C. M. Condon and Company Bank at the front of the Perkins Building, remains where it has stood since originally built. It now houses the Coffeyville Chamber of Commerce and has been restored to near-original condition. In the aftermath of the raid, several glass panes from the main doors were removed and exhibited at the 1893 Chicago World's Fair by their maker, the Pittsburgh Glass Company, to illustrate the nonshatter texture of the material. It was an early hint at one aspect of Coffeyville's future. Condon Bank still operates in Coffeyville, but at a different location.

The broad structure of the Perkins Building still sits overlooking the plaza. The man behind the building, Luther Perkins, was given a terrible fright when he tried to enter Condon Bank when the robbery was underway. This may well have contributed to his decision to leave Coffeyville not long afterward to try his business hand elsewhere in Kansas and Missouri.

Isham's Hardware Store operates in Coffeyville to this day, as do Barndollar's and the First National Bank of Coffeyville, the latter in a different location. The old city jail was moved, brick by brick, to a new location in Death Alley, now a must-see attraction for all visitors to Coffeyville.

Many of those involved in the action that day, or in the legal process that followed, remained where they had lived and tried to continue their lives as though nothing untoward had occurred. Tom Ayres suffered horrific wounds, and townsmen Lou Dietz and Charlie Gump were also wounded. Dietz, the hardware store clerk, had a bullet pass right through his foot. Dietz recovered completely from the wound and went on to own a real estate agency and a home in the town. Like Emmett, he retired to Los Angeles, where he resided with his sister until his death in 1943. Gump also stayed on in Coffeyville, eventually finding work in his son's automotive shop. He was the only resident of Coffeyville to go out of his way to visit Emmett in California.

Joseph Fritch, Emmett's counsel and legal advisor, saw his law practice in Independence flourish after Emmett's trial, but it is hard to say whether or not there was a causal relationship between the two. Fritch later served as deputy clerk of the Kansas Supreme Court and as city attorney for Independence. Fritch's courtroom opponent, James Charlton, subsequently relocated to Bartlesville, Oklahoma, reacquainting himself with Emmett and Julia when they lived there. Charlton continued to practice law, serving as a circuit court judge.

One of the mountains in Fresno County, California, is named Dalton Mountain, and in a car park off a highway at its base is an historical marker: "In 1891, a posse shoot-out forced the infamous Dalton Brothers Gang from this mountain hideout. They made their way back to Kansas where they eventually met their fate at Coffeyville. The outlaws, long since gone, leave Dalton Mountain as their lasting valley legacy."

The story the marker tells is not 100 percent accurate, but it represents one small aspect of the much larger story of the Dalton brothers and their friends, and of the destruction of the last major outlaw gang in the Old West. Seems like there are places that deserve similar historical markers—the sites of all their holdups, and the sites of all their homes and hideouts. A major issue would be determining where the Dalton Gang started. In the Indian Territory or New Mexico, where the gang came into being? In Cass County, Missouri, somewhere near Benton, perhaps, where the boys grew up surrounded by mementoes and stories of a vicious civil war? When a Younger married a Dalton, or even when a young Lewis Dalton survived a battle he should not have under that hot Mexican sun?

So many markers and so many stories, all leading inexorably to the former cowtown of Coffeyville. For eight men, the story ended there, but the larger, more serpentine story did not end there. It ended in small and large burial sites in cemeteries across Kansas and Oklahoma and even California, and was finalized on Saturday, April 18, 1964, when a frail eighty-eight-year-old woman with a cleft palate passed away quietly. Leona Dalton had crossed the Kansas plains in a covered wagon and was laid to rest from the back of a horseless carriage. The last of the Daltons had gone, and their story had ended.

APPENDIX: THE VIEW FROM DOWN UNDER

The Coffeyville raid was widely reported in Australian newspapers, most basing their articles on a long telegram received from New York on November 5, 1892. Among the details included in that report were the following:

- Four outlaws entered Condon Bank where they were told by Mr. Ball, the cashier, that the time lock would not be opened until 10 A.M.
- They informed Ball and Mr. Carpenter, the teller, that they would wait, taking all the cash in the drawer while they waited.

A generally accurate description of the gunfight then followed, but the reports contained a number of inaccuracies.

- Grat Dalton was called "Grant" Dalton.
- George Cubine was called George "Cudine."
- Dick Broadwell and Bill Powers were identified as "Tom Heddy" and "an unidentified gang member."

The report stated that a sixth member of the gang escaped, but local authorities expected him to be caught before the evening. That gang member was named as Allie Ogee.

Reports from the scene suggested that if Emmett Dalton did not die from his wounds, he was likely to be lynched. Emmett had confessed that the gang had robbed the Katy at Adair the previous July, and had committed several other robberies.

The article was published in several newspapers, including the *Adelaide Express and Telegraph*, November 12, 1892, and the *Adelaide Advertiser*, November 14, 1892.

The *Hobart Mercury* ran a slightly different story on November 18, notable primarily for the number of errors it contained. It opened by describing the Dalton Gang as "train robbers, cattle lifters and murderers," saying that they met their fate at "Coffee Hill" in Kansas. The article described how six outlaws rode into town at 6 A.M., split into two groups of three, and simultaneously attacked two banks. Gang members included Bob Emmett and Pratian Dalton, Tom Evans, Texas Jack Moore, and Ollie Ozee.

As the gunfight approached its climax, "one man named Spears worked his Winchester rifle with such clock-like regularity that he killed Bob and Emmett Dalton and Texas Jack in quick succession at the entry to the alley. . . . Connolly, Tom Evans and Ozee mounted their horses and dashed out of town, but Evans was hit hard and fell dead from his horse half a mile away."

The report suggested the robbers took $90,000 from the First National Bank and $30,000 from Condon Bank, but that every cent that was taken had been recovered. It also stated that the Daltons were related to the James Boys, "the noted train robbers."

The same story appeared in a Brisbane newspaper, *The Week*, on November 18, 1892, and in number of regional newspapers in South Australia and Tasmania.

A decade and a half later, on December 5, 1908, a Sydney newspaper named *The Arrow* published a long article on the relationship between Emmett Dalton and Julia Johnson, perhaps in response to the news of the couple's marriage. It described how "the couple had grown up together and become sweethearts."

Julia, "a lithe, fearless slip of a girl," became the best horsewoman and rifle shot in the district before she had reached her mid-teens. Emmett, though not a natural criminal, was seduced by the dreams of his older brothers about how much they could make and how easily they could make it. This drove a wedge between the young lovers, and Julia broke off their engagement.

At Coffeyville, Emmett escaped as the gang was shot down one by one—Texas Jack, Joe Evans, and Grat Dalton—all to the blazing rifle of Jim Spears. Allie Ogee escaped, and Emmett made it to his horse, pursued by angry townsmen bent on vengeance.

The posse caught up with him two miles outside town, and after an exchange of shots, Emmett fell to the ground. Believing himself mortally wounded, Emmett made a full confession of his own and his brothers' crimes.

During his time with the gang, Emmett and Julia had rekindled their relationship even though she was now married to a man named Lewis.

Emmett survived, and during the long years of his imprisonment, Julia worked tirelessly for his release. Shortly before that happy event, Julia's worthless husband was killed in a shoot-out with US marshals. They were thus free to marry when he was released—and they did.

Over the coming years, small vignettes about the Daltons would regularly pop up in newspapers across Australia. Emmett's role in the movie industry and his friendship with noted Western stars, his writings, and, ultimately, his death were all noted in passing in Australia. Most reflected a degree of ignorance about the man and his life, but all recognized the Australian public's interest in the Wild West and its characters.

NOTES

PROLOGUE: ANGELUS TEMPLE, LOS ANGELES, 1936

p. 3 *. . . very silent and very empty . . .*
The descriptions of the Angelus Temple and the illustrated sermons are from the *Truth* (Brisbane), May 30, 1937, and the *Mudgee Guardian*, March 10, 1936, plus *The Angelus Temple*, American Experience, http://www.pbs.org/wgbh/americanexperience/features/sister-angelus-temple/.

1. BLOODLINES

p. 9 *. . . spared further embarrassment . . .*
See Euston for an interesting story about Elizabeth Simpson and her children.

p. 9 *. . . he transmitted these qualities . . .*
Dalton and Jungmeyer, 13.

p. 11 *. . . Lewis Kossuth Dalton . . .*
Young Lewis Kossuth Dalton's unusual middle name came from his father's admiration of Lajos Kossuth, a Hungarian revolutionary leader and fighter for democracy, who was widely admired in the United States. Two later children, Grattan and Emmett, were named after Irish nationalists.

p. 12 *. . . a young man named Cole . . .*
Among the legitimate children fathered by Charles Younger was Henry Washington Younger, the father of Cole Younger and the three brothers who would subsequently join him in an outlaw gang. Adeline was a child of Charles's second marriage.

p. 13 *. . . shrill with the cry of locusts . . .*
Dalton and Jungmeyer, 15.

p. 14 *. . . my eleven year-old mind . . .*
Dalton and Jungmeyer, 25.

p. 15 *. . . the new Mrs. Dalton . . .*
I was unable to find any further details, but a mother's death during childbirth was not uncommon at the time.

p. 16 *. . . he was by nature decidedly social . . .*
Dalton and Jungmeyer, 142.

p. 17 *. . . on top of whatever they were being paid . . .*
Art Burton, *Oklahoma's Frontier Indian Police*, originally published in *Oklahoma State Trooper Magazine*, 1996, http://www.lestweforget.hamptonu.edu/.

p. 17 *. . . Judge Isaac Parker's federal court . . .*
Parker is known to history as "the hanging judge," a somewhat ironic designation given that Parker himself was personally opposed to capital punishment.

p. 18 *. . . one archetypical figure . . .*
The Rennicks were a well-known family in the area of Missouri the Daltons frequented, and were regarded as a good family, prepared to always help others out.

2. ALONG THE OUTLAW TRAIL

p. 26 *. . . was returning to Texas . . .*
See Elliott, 40.

p. 28 *. . . a Texan of good birth . . .*
Tilghman, 28.

p. 29 *. . . and was offered work by . . .*
Shirley, 42. John Slaughter later left ranching behind and achieved greater fame as the sheriff of Cochise County, Arizona.

p. 30 *. . . some who looked to take advantage . . .*
Dalton and Jungmeyer, 301.

p. 30 *. . . a reata of firm friendship . . .*
Dalton and Jungmeyer, 36

p. 30 *. . . the language of the forty-five . . .*
Dalton and Jungmeyer, 37.

p. 31 *. . . he fired off two shots . . .*
Ohnick, 43.

p. 32 *. . . land around the small settlement . . .*
The Daltons' claims were located in what had been part of the Cherokee Nation, and the Kingfisher family were prominent members of that nation.

p. 32 *. . . recently married a businessman . . .*
Young Emmett had made quite a splash at the wedding, wearing his best clothes and a pair of matched Colt revolvers.

p. 34 *. . . and then shot it off . . .*
Shirley, 45.

p. 36 *. . . the wound healed . . .*
Dalton and Jungmeyer, 6.

3. WEST

p. 39 . . . *to the north of San Luis Obispo* . . .
Not far from the farm was the spot where film star James Dean was killed in a car wreck in 1955.

p. 39 . . . *who would do such a thing* . . .
Benziger.

p. 40 . . . *San Benito and Merced Counties* . . .
Ibid.

p. 40 . . . *the saloons in Fresno* . . .
Most accounts of this Californian interlude identify Emmett as being part of the action, primarily relying on contemporary newspapers misidentifying Bill McElhanie as Emmett Dalton. Emmett himself made it clear that he was not in California at this time.

p. 40 . . . *escape to the mountains* . . .
Myron Angel, "A Memorial and Biographical History of the Counties of Fresno, Tulare and Kern, California."

p. 41 . . . *Chris Evans and John Sontag* . . .
See http://www.hmdb.org, a Historical Marker database.

p. 42 . . . *three bandits were involved* . . .
Subsequent investigations showed that the express messenger actually fired the shot that struck Radliff, and he would be charged over the incident.

p. 43 . . . *accessories to the act* . . .
Salinas Weekly Index, April 2, 1891.

p. 47 . . . *it was all very dramatic* . . .
For other stories surrounding the legend of Grat's escape, see http://www.eshomvalley.com; Hunter, 14; and http://www.hmdb.org.

4. CATCHING THE KATY

p. 51 . . . *with the money Bob had given her* . . .
From the time he took up with Florence Quick, Bob seems to have deserted Lucy and their daughter. There are suggestions that Lucy died in the mid-1890s and the little girl was raised by relatives.

p. 52 . . . *the only man he knew* . . .
I found it impossible to locate primary-source reporting of this ambush, which suggests it might never have occurred. However, it is referred to in several secondary sources, Smith for instance, and William Tener Starmer is recorded as being killed on duty on at least one Oklahoma Law Enforcement Officers' memorial site.

p. 54 . . . *this was simply not true* . . .
The process that was supposed to be followed often was not. See details of subsequent robberies below.

p. 54 . . . *the regular railroad telegraphist* . . .
See Shirley, 54.

p. 54 . . . *in the heart of the Cherokee Nation* . . .
Wharton was renamed Perry in 1893 when that part of the Cherokee Nation was opened up for closer settlement.

p. 56 . . . *rode off into the night* . . .
Again, in one of several embroidered versions of the incident, the gang rode past the depot as they made their getaway. Seeing that the clerk had relit the office's lamps, and was now a perfect target, Charlie Bryant shot him dead.

p. 56 . . . *adding up to $1,745* . . .
Emmett later claimed that the robbery had netted the gang $14,000.

p. 57 . . . *fled to the Seminole Nation* . . .
Shirley, 59–60.

p. 60 . . . *a tiny flag stop station* . . .
The stop was apparently named after two daughters—Lelia and Etta—of a railway worker.

p. 66 . . . *profound stock of himself* . . .
Dalton and Jungmeyer, 142.

p. 73 . . . *all four were armed* . . .
Kinney, 162.

p. 73 . . . *coal pick in hand* . . .
Interestingly, the engineer had told Grat and Emmett that they had been prepared for trouble at Pryor Creek and relaxed when nothing happened there. Grat's reply was that they didn't want to disappoint them.

p. 74 . . . *some kind of toll* . . .
Dalton and Jungmeyer, 179.

p. 75 . . . *any sort of disturbance* . . .
A number of accounts tell a very different story, with the gang riding through town and unleashing a volley of bullets that, inter alia, brought down Goff and Youngblood. For several reasons, I consider those accounts fanciful.

5. THE PEOPLE OF THE MIDDLE WATERS

p. 82 . . . *ultimately, the Osage Nation* . . .
In the initial allocation, the future site of Coffeyville, although part of the Osage Nation, was actually designated part of the Cherokee Nation.

p. 84 . . . *brought him into contact with* . . .
Blanton's family was of French extraction. His grandfather loathed Napo-

leon, a person his father greatly admired. Christened James, he was renamed Napoleon Bonaparte Blanton when his grandfather died.

p. 85 . . . *more interest and investment* . . .
Western Home Journal, August 31, 1871.

p. 85 . . . *laid out about three weeks ago* . . .
Western Home Journal.

p. 86 . . . *a lot of things that went with that* . . .
Drake, 37.

p. 88 . . . *shortly before the war ended* . . .
See http://www.ksgenweb.com.

p. 88 . . . *he designed and produced* . . .
"Made in the Kansas town of the same name, the boot drew its inspiration from the English Wellington and US Cavalry footwear. Large, 'mule-ear' bootstraps aided a man in pulling them on. The term 'mule-ear' aptly describes the shape of the pullstraps stitched to the outside tops of the boots" (see Barbara Brackman, *Hyer, Justin and the Origin of the Cowboy Boot*).

p. 89 . . . *settling in LeRoy* . . .
Kansas seems to have been a popular destination for German immigrants, with one of the state's earliest newspapers being the Atkinson-based, German-language *Die Kansas Zeitung.*

p. 89 . . . *just one of John's interests* . . .
His father, Joseph, also found success in Coffeyville, building a mansion on 220 acres on the edge of town. He died there in February 1901.

p. 91 . . . *A. P. Boswell and Company* . . .
A. P. Boswell and his son George had arrived in Coffeyville to open their hardware emporium in 1876.

6. THE EDGE OF THE ABYSS

p. 95 . . . *the largest reward offered* . . .
Hanes, 54–55.

p. 97 . . . *the blood price upon his head* . . .
Dalton and Jungmeyer, 84.

p. 100 . . . *in their cowboy days* . . .
I suspect Amos Burton may be the same person as "Black Amos," a trail cook at the Double H Ranch.

p. 100 . . . *enters the Arkansas River* . . .
The cave would become known to history as the Dalton Cave.

p. 100 . . . *used to have many friends there* . . .
Drago, 109.

p. 101 ... *the argument was over* ...
Star and Kansan, October 7, 1892, provides Emmett's almost contemporaneous recollections of the meeting.

p. 103 ... *was beefed up considerably* ...
See Preece.

p. 104 ... *alongside Onion Creek* ...
The property was owned by a farmer named Davis, who knew the Dalton family but was not aware any of them were on his property.

p. 104 ... *the edge of a newly ploughed field* ...
This section is based on a detailed forensic examination undertaken later by law enforcement officials. See Elliott, 7–8, and Emmett's recollections in various publications and in his own books.

p. 106 ... *into the top of his boot* ...
The 1873 Colt Peacemaker, also called the Frontier Model, was officially known as the Single Action Army model.

p. 107 ... *ranked around the central plaza* ...
Dalton and Jungmeyer, 236.

p. 107 ... *neither greeted nor challenged* ...
The myth of the six riders has continued, and even grown, down through the years. Mark Pannill, for instance, believes that the sixth rider was Florence Quick, dressed as a man. Her role was to leave the main group and ride to the south of the town to aid their escape. He also believes she and Bob had previously scouted the salient sites in the town.

p. 108 ... *its young driver now walking* ...
Pat Doran was there to deliver an order of kerosene to the drugstore. He liked to gossip, so a fifteen-minute delivery usually took double that.

7. BREAKING THE BANK

p. 115 ... *he did so immediately* ...
Drago, 73.

p. 117 ... *assisting Brewster to transact* ...
James Henry Brewster was a stonemason, successful enough to form a company, the Continental Construction Company, that was then engaged in building the new sidewalks on Union Street. He was from nearby Independence. The other two were locals; Abe Knotts would subsequently become the town's deputy sheriff; Charles Hollingworth was a dairy farmer from just west of Coffeyville.

p. 119 ... *picked out a box* ...
See kayempea.net/adds/Kloehr.html.

p. 119 ... *a single solitary armed man* ...
Coffeyville Journal, October 8, 1892.

p. 122 *. . . to warn Carpenter and his staff . . .*
Some accounts have Perkins brandishing two revolvers as he did so.

p. 124 *. . . where is your gold? . . .*
From a postincident interview with Charles Carpenter; reported in Drago, 73.

p. 126 *. . . just one or two shots . . .*
Dalton and Jungmeyer, 240.

8. THE STREET FIGHTER

p. 132 *. . . George, they're coming this way . . .*
Based on Jack Long's and Emmett Dalton's recollections and what Lucius Baldwin reportedly said when he regained consciousness.

p. 135 *. . . something that filled him with rage . . .*
The fifty-year-old Brown was a native of Rochester, New York, and had left home at fifteen to try his luck on the California goldfields. After service in the Union Army and marriage in Michigan, he moved to Coffeyville in 1883, where he set up his business next door to Rammel's in Union Street.

p. 135 *. . . staunching the flow and saving . . .*
Picker, a farmer who lived just outside Coffeyville, later became a director of a town brickworks, Charlie Ball joining him in the venture.

p. 139 *. . . in his best attempt . . .*
Dalton and Jungmeyer, 249.

p. 140 *. . . the peculiar zip that accompanies . . .*
Elliott.

p. 140 *. . . Grat shot one of the horses . . .*
A number of writers, including Robert Barr Smith (129), have Dick Broadwell shooting both Standard Oil horses because they interfered with his aim. This appears to be based on a claim made by John Kloehr; see kayempea.net/adds/Kloehr.html. Given that Broadwell could not shoot because of the shoulder wound he sustained in the Condon Bank, I have discounted such claims. In his memoirs, Dalton and Jungmeyer (255) state that it was Grat who shot the horses.

p. 143 *. . . and perhaps not seeing anything . . .*
Dalton and Jungmeyer, 255.

p. 143 *. . . the shot went wide . . .*
In a later interview, Kloehr claimed, "his bullet went wide, glancingly striking the side of the alley, taking a tangent course and killing both the Standard Oil horses and entering my barn where it demolished a buggy wheel" (see kayempea.net/adds/Kloehr.html).

p. 146 *. . . in pools of their own blood . . .*
This section is, in the main, based on Emmett's and David Elliott's recollections of the sequence of events.

9. AFTERMATH

p. 147 . . . *the last scenes of the fight* . . .
Elliott, 28.

p. 148 . . . *the style so prevalent in the West* . . .
Ibid.

p. 156 . . . *identified him as Jake Moore* . . .
Star and Kansan, October 7, 1892. Authorities already knew the correct identities of Powers and Broadwell, and Emmett confirmed their real identities later that day.

p. 157 . . . *a pity in his heart* . . .
Ibid.

p. 158 . . . *loaded them onto a wagon* . . .
An Eye Witness, 223–224.

p. 158 . . . *buried in consecrated ground* . . .
Later, when the cemetery expanded, the grave was included in the cemetery proper.

p. 159 . . . *had done to the town* . . .
No one ever came forward to claim Bill Powers's body, and no relatives of his were ever traced, leading me to suspect that he may not have been using his real name.

p. 160 . . . *to implicate the Daltons* . . .
St. Louis Globe-Democrat, October 16, 1892.

p. 161 . . . *all have been alive today* . . .
Kansas Weekly Capital and Farm Journal, October 13, 1892, http://www.daltondatabank.org/Chronicles/Emmett_Dalton.htm.

p. 161 . . . *had also bought the horses* . . .
An Eye Witness, 230.

p. 163 . . . *after his brothers robbed a train* . . .
Star and Kansan, October 10, 1892.

p. 163 . . . *died defending the town* . . .
New York Times, October 8, 1892.

10. *THE STATE OF KANSAS V. EMMETT DALTON*

p. 166 . . . *seems a thousand pities* . . .
Star and Kansan, March 22, 1893.

p. 169 . . . *the silk department is upstairs* . . .
Works Progress Administration, Charlton interview.

p. 171 . . . *a raid of their own* . . .
The most likely author of the letter was Bill Dalton, who had left with his mother for Independence the day before the letter was delivered to Kloehr.

p. 172 *. . . and then it moved on . . .*
Right up until 1894, rumors persisted that the rump of the gang would return to Coffeyville to raze the town.

p. 176 *. . . deep lines on his face . . .*
Star and Kansan, January 20, 1893.

p. 176 *. . . for trial without bail . . .*
A court document, No. 728, dated January 17, 1893, lists the thirty-one witnesses the prosecution intended to call, among them Bill Shepard, Bert Ayres, John Kloehr, and Fred Dodge. The document itself was found in the late 1980s after apparently being misplaced.

p. 178 *. . . granted his day in court . . .*
Later estimates suggested that it had cost Kansas $500 to hold and try Emmett. Had the trial continued, the cost would have been considerably more. McCue fell ill soon afterward, meaning the trial would have been suspended until he recovered or a new trial ordered.

p. 178 *. . . the best prisoner they had . . .*
Works Progress Administration, Charlton interview.

11. THE CASTLE ON THE PLAINS

p. 184 *. . . more than 100 prisoners . . .*
Not all were happy to be working there. In 1901, prisoners working in the mine staged a mutiny, with two of them killed when guards crushed the uprising.

p. 184 *. . . an extremely high-profile warden . . .*
Chase also proved to be unique in a set of state officials noted for corruption. He appointed his sons and a daughter to positions in the penitentiary's administration, and another daughter became a teacher at the prison school. Chase was later accused of "indiscretions" with female prisoners and forced to resign in June 1895.

p. 187 *. . . It was June 8, 1894 . . .*
Afterward, an alternate story circulated in which Bill Dalton was shot dead from ambush after playing with his crippled daughter.

p. 187 *. . . never to return to Oklahoma . . .*
Bill Dalton was buried between two palm trees in the front yard of Jennie's parent's mansion in Livingston. When they moved in 1896, Bill's body was exhumed and buried in an unmarked grave in Turlock Cemetery.

p. 187 *. . . a reputation as a brave man . . .*
Tetterington, 145.

p. 188 *. . . killed by a posse . . .*
Dalton and Jungmeyer, 305.

p. 189 *. . . to the newspapers' credit . . .*
Kansas City Star, May 30, 1894.

p. 189 *. . . bigger and better things . . .*
Kansas Semi-Weekly Capital, December 14, 1897.

p. 191 *. . . the wild environment of . . .*
Sunday World-Herald, October 27, 1901.

p. 192 *. . . Emmett's application was denied . . .*
Kansas City Star, May 6, 1904.

p. 193 *. . . was once again refused . . .*
This was the last attempt to win a pardon involving Otto Eckstein, who died in 1904 from complications following an appendectomy.

p. 193 *. . . Bob asked him to go . . .*
Kansas City Star, August 22, 1905.

p. 195 *. . . the making of a man . . .*
Ibid., July 6, 1907.

p. 195 *. . . paying $2.50 a day . . .*
The hotel, one of the finest in the city, was near the State Capitol and was regarded as an unofficial headquarters for the Republican Party. It was destroyed by fire in 1909.

p. 195 *. . . before it was injured . . .*
Topeka State Journal, July 10, 1907.

p. 196 *. . . I guess that we all hope . . .*
Coffeyville Journal, July 19, 1907.

p. 197 *. . . I will see a battle . . .*
Los Angeles Herald, October 12, 1907.

12. OLD COWBOYS IN HOLLYWOOD

p. 201 *. . . the end of the long journey . . .*
Kansas City Star, November 3, 1907.

p. 201 *. . . he had relatives there . . .*
Ibid., November 7, 1907. There was also a rumor that Emmett had written to Deputy US Marshal Heck Thomas enquiring about a job; the response was short, sharp, and negative.

p. 204 *. . . to watch short films . . .*
Slatta, 123–128, has an excellent coverage of the topic.

p. 205 *. . . show business in his blood . . .*
No complete versions of *The Famous Dalton Raid on the Two Banks of Coffeyville* are believed to exist. Part of it can be found on YouTube, and one site also includes footage of Julia and Emmett outside their Bartlesville home.

p. 207 *. . . on first name terms . . .*
Hart would always call Western movies "horse operas."

p. 208 *. . . any of the original characters . . .*
Fitzgerald and Magers, 146.

p. 208 *. . . where it actually happened . . .*
Ibid. Lee went on to make another sixteen films, the last in 1936. She died at Englewood in 1996.

p. 209 *. . . was now shooting movies . . .*
MacDonald won a Pulitzer Prize in 1931 when, working for the *Kansas City Star*, he wrote a series of articles that helped solve a murder in Amarillo, Texas.

p. 209 *. . . two land deals in Hollywood . . .*
Abilene Daily Reporter, March 24, 1931.

p. 210 *. . . can you imagine Jesse James? . . .*
Emmett maintained a lifelong interest in the outlaws of the Old West. While living in Hollywood, he traded Dalton brothers photographs with pioneer Texas photographer Noah Rose, getting James brothers and Younger brothers photographs in return.

p. 214 *. . . he deeply regretted the tragedy . . .*
See http://www.mykindred.com/dalton/hoax/misc.php.

AFTERWORD

p. 218 *. . . the devil prodded them . . .*
Oakland Tribune, August 1, 1937.

p. 218 *. . . helped Bob and Emmett to escape . . .*
The Heritage Auctions website is http://www.historicalha.com, and the quote was taken from a letter Litt wrote, to a newspaper reporter from memory. The letter was subsequently sold at auction and its contents taken down from the website.

p. 219 *. . . their lasting valley legacy . . .*
The Historical Marker Database, http://www.hmdb.org/m.asp?m=27962.

REFERENCES

BOOKS

Dalton, Emmett, and Jack Jungmeyer. *When the Daltons Rode.* New York: Doubleday, Doran and Co., 1931.

Dary, David. *The Santa Fe Trail*. New York: A. A. Knopf, 2000.

Drago, Harry. *Road Agents and Train Robbers*. New York: Dodd, Mead and Co., 1973.

Drake, Charles C. *Who's Who? Kansas and Montgomery County*. Coffeyville, KS: Self-published, 1943.

Elliott, David S., and Ed Bartholomew. *The Dalton Gang and the Coffeyville Raid*. Fort Davis, TX: Frontier Book Co., 1968.

An Eye Witness. *The Dalton Brothers and Their Astounding Career of Crime*. Chicago: Laird & Lea, 1892; New York: Frederick Fell, 1954.

Fitzgerald, Michael, and Boyd Magers. *Ladies of the Western*. Jefferson, NC: McFarland and Co., 2002.

Gilmore, Donald. *Civil War on the Missouri-Kansas Border*. Gretna, LA: Pelican, 2006.

Hanes, Bailey. *Bill Doolin: Outlaw O.T.* Norman: University of Oklahoma Press, 1968.

Hough, Emerson. *The Story of the Cowboy.* New York: Grosset and Dunlap, 1897.

Kansas: A Cyclopedia of State History. 1912.

Kinney, John J. *Captain Jack and the Dalton Gang*. Lawrence: University Press of Kansas, 2005.

Kirkman, Paul. *Forgotten Tales of Kansas City.* Charleston, SC: The History Press, 2012.

Kutler, Stanley, ed. *Dictionary of American History*. New York: Charles Scribner's Sons, 2003.

Memorial and Biographical History of the Counties of Fresno, Tulare and Kern, California, Chicago: Lewis Publishing Co., 1892.

Miller, Nyle, and Joseph Snell. *Why the West Was Wild.* Topeka: Kansas State Historical Society, 1963.

Ohnick, Nancy. *The Dalton Gang and Their Family Ties.* Meade, KS: Ohnick Enterprises, 2005.

O'Neal, Bill. *Encyclopedia of Western Gunfighters*. Norman: University of Oklahoma Press, 1979.

Pannill, Mark. *The Day Coffeyville Bled*. Bloomington, IN: AuthorHouse, 2005.

Preece, Harold. *The Dalton Gang.* New York: Signet, 1964.

Shirley, Glen. *West of Hell's Fringe: Crime, Criminals, and the Federal Peace Officer in Oklahoma Territory, 1889–1907.* Norman: University of Oklahoma Press, 1978.

Slatta, Richard. *The Cowboy Encyclopedia*. Santa Barbara, CA: ABC-CLIO, 1994.
Smith, Robert Barr. *Daltons! The Raid on Coffeyville, Kansas*. Norman: University of Oklahoma Press, 1996.
Tetterington, Bill. *Broken Promises*. Lytham St. Anne's: Golden West Press, 1973.
Tilghman, Zoe. *Outlaw Days*. Oklahoma City: Harlow Publishing Co., 1926.

ARTICLES AND MONOGRAPHS

Benziger, Jeff. "The Daltons in Livingston and Turlock." *209 Magazine*, October 12, 2017.
Boggs, Johnny D. "On the Trail of the Dalton Gang." *True West Magazine*, October 2011.
Brackman, Barbara. "Hyer, Justin and the Origin of the Cowboy Boot." *Kansas History* 18, no.1 (1995): 34–47.
Hougen, Harvey R. "The Impact of Politics and Prison Industry on the General Management of the Kansas State Penitentiary, 1883–1909." *Kansas Historical Quarterly* 43, no. 33 (1977): 297–318.
Hunter, Kathleen. *Coffeyville, Kansas: The Town That Stopped the Dalton Gang*. Washington, DC: National Park Service, 2002.
Rife, Ronald. *Constructing Social Bandits: The Saga of Sontag and Evans, 1889–1911*. Master's thesis, California State University, 2011.
Scott, Mark C. "Insured against Train Robbers: A Kansas Christmas Tale." *Kansas History* 32, no. 4 (2009/2010): 267–273.
Works Progress Administration. Indian-Pioneer History Project for Oklahoma, James Charlton Interview, November 17, 1937. http://www.digital.libraries.ou.edu/cdm/ref/collection/indianpp/id/7013.

ONLINE ARTICLES

Angel, Myron. "A Memorial and Biographical History of the Counties of Fresno, Tulare and Kern, California." Originally published by the Lewis Publishing Company, Chicago, 1892. Hathi Trust Digital Library, http://www.catalog.hathitrust.org/record.
Bell, Bob Boze. "Adair before They Die." *True West Magazine*, March 1, 2007. https://truewestmagazine.com/article/adair-before-they-die/.
——. "Dalton Debacle." *True West Magazine*, July 17, 2014. https://truewestmagazine.com/article/dalton-debacle/.
Burton, Art. "Oklahoma's Frontier Indian Police." Originally published in the *Oklahoma State Trooper Magazine*, 1996.
Euston, Diane. "An Ode to the Darker Youngers." *Martin City Telegraph*, February 26, 2019. https://martincitytelegraph.com/2019/02/26/an-ode-to-the-darker-youngers/.

McMahan, Liz. "Dalton Train Hold-up Put Leliaetta on Map." *Coweta American*, August 31, 2020.

Raymond, S. "Kentucky Has Immortalized Herself in the Fight." Kentucky Guard, February 22, 2019. https://ky.ng.mil/News/Article/2615866/kentucky-has-immortalized-herself-in-the-fight/.

Ward, Nathan. "Confessions of the Outlaw: The Lazarus Life of Emmett Dalton." January 30, 2018. https://nathanward.medium.com/confessions-of-the-outlaw-the-lazarus-life-of-emmett-dalton-7506868e4ab5.

Western Home Journal (Lawrence, KS). August 31, 1871.

INDEX